Once the Buddha Was a Monkey

Once the Buddha Was a Monkey

Ārya Śūra's *Jātakamālā*

Translated from the Sanskrit by Peter Khoroche

With a Foreword by Wendy Doniger

The University of Chicago Press *Chicago and London*

Frontispiece: *The Mahakapi Jataka.* Sandstone. Second Century B.C. From Bharhut. Courtesy of Indian Museum, Calcutta.

The University of Chicago Press, Chicago 60637
The University of Chicago Press, Ltd., London
 Published 1989
Paperback edition 2006
Printed in the United States of America
15 14 13 12 11 10 09 08 07 06   6 5 4 3 2
ISBN: 0-226-78215-8 (paperback)

Library of Congress Cataloging-in-Publication Data

Āryaśūra.
[Jātakamālā. English]
Once the Buddha was a monkey : Ārya Śūra's Jātaka-mālā / translated from the Sanskrit by Peter Khoroche : with a foreword by Wendy Doniger.
p. cm.
Translation of: Jātakamālā.
Bibliography: p.
1. Tipiṭak. Suttapiṭak. Khuddakanikāya. Jātaka—Paraphrases, English. 2. Gautama Buddha—Pre-existence. I. Khoroche, Peter. II. Title.
BQ.1462.E5K5 1989   89-33190
294.3′823—dc20   CIP
ISBN 0-226-78003-1 (alk. paper)

⊗ The paper used in this publication meets the minimum requirements of the American National Standard for Information Sciences—Permanence of Paper for Printed Library Materials, ANSI Z39.48-1984.

Contents

Foreword

Peter Khoroche's new translation of the *Jātakamālā* will be welcomed by scholars—and, indeed, by anyone who loves stories. The text deals ostensibly with the former lives of the Bodhisattva, but these lives are actually folktales that have been absorbed into the Buddhist canon, and some of the more ambiguous and ambivalent animals are often rather awkwardly assimilated to the flawless moral character of Gautama. This tension between the worldly (and often cynical) ethics that gave birth to the ancient stories and the new Buddhist moral literature that became their foster parent is part of what makes these stories such fun to read. Starving tigresses who devour their starving whelps, fish stranded out of water, too-trusting apes—the Bodhisattva sometimes encounters, sometimes becomes such animals; and the humans whom he meets and helps and sometimes converts to Buddhism are usually more bestial than the animals.

The old Pali stories about these lives, the *Jātakas*, are numerous and rather rough-hewn. The *Jātakamālā* is a much later Sanskrit work that has selected thirty-four stories and transformed them into much more elaborate and polished works. It thus combines, as do few other works (such as the *Kathāsaritsāgara* [the *Ocean of Story*], or the *Buddhacarita* of Aśvaghoṣa), the simple joys of rough peasant fare and the more epicurean (often even gourmand) pleasures of the cuisine of Sanskrit court poetry.

This is also a work of considerable historical importance. It became a part of the Northern Buddhist school and was assimilated in interesting ways to and from Hinduism; later it was carried with Buddhism to other parts of Asia. Stories such as the tale of King Śibi's grotesque self-sacrifice became paradigmatic for both Hindus and Buddhists. The *Jātakamālā* is much cited and much used in studies of Indian storytelling, Buddhism, and world folklore.

In 1895 Max Müller published, in his *Sacred Books of the Buddhists* series, a translation of this text by J. S. Speyer, and this translation has been reprinted and remained in general use. It is not a terrible translation, but there are numerous howlers in it, and, like most of the books in that series, it is so stilted and artificial as to be virtually unreadable for pleasure; it is merely a research tool. The need for a new translation has often been remarked.

This is that new translation. Peter Khoroche is a Sanskritist of impeccable training and credentials; his remarks in the Introduction, moreover, show what care he has taken not merely to correct Speyer's errors but, in fact, to establish an entirely new Sanskrit text with many important new readings. Yet Khoroche has not sacrificed elegance for accuracy. His text has captured the charm of the original; it flows and sparkles and is altogether a delight to read. It would be a waste of the reader's valuable time to allow this foreword to postpone any longer the pleasure of reading the work itself.

Wendy Doniger
Mircea Eliade Professor of the History of Religions
The University of Chicago

Preface

This translation was initially prompted by aesthetic considerations: the pioneering effort of Speyer gave no inkling of Śūra's style and tone. However it soon became clear that any translation aiming at fidelity would have to be in some degree un-English, so great is the gulf between fourth-century India and twentieth-century England—between Sanskrit and English. The impossibility of reproducing two essential characteristics of the original—the sound of the words and the constantly varying rhythm of the verse passages, for both of which Śūra was famous—also dooms any translation of the *Jātakamālā* to being no more than a pale shadow of the original.

Every translation involves interpretation and, to a certain extent, the invention of a parallel mode. Translation is alchemy, not algebra. But I have made no attempt to mitigate strangeness or to achieve greater smoothness and sophistication by excision.[1] That would be treacherous to the author as well as patronizing to the reader. The intention has been to convey—to anyone who has an interest in the literature and civilization of ancient India and in the legend of the Buddha but who does not have a knowledge of Sanskrit—some idea of the feel of the original, as well as its content.

In the course of making this translation, it was found necessary to reexamine the manuscripts on which Kern based his edition, and this led to a separate study of the manuscript evidence for the *Jātakamālā*. Readers who turn back to the Sanskrit text should be warned that the translation, though based on Kern's edition, takes account of corrections made in the light of this fresh evidence. They should also be reassured that very few of the hundreds of corrections make any substantial difference to the way one translates. For details, and for all matters relating to the textual basis, they are referred to Khoroche (1987).

The Introduction limits itself to recording how little is known of the author, and to describing the nature and purpose of his work. Discussion of its style, language, and composition would be futile without detailed reference to the Sanskrit, and could easily fill another volume. That lies in the future, when a study has been made of the growth and development of the *campū* form (see Introduction, p. xvi)—something hardly more than adumbrated in the standard histories of Sanskrit literature, and for which the basic materials are only now beginning to be published.

It is strange how such a masterpiece as the *Jātakamālā* has received so little attention since its publication almost a century ago. Perhaps it is the victim of specialization: students of Buddhism are not necessarily concerned with the literary embellishment of material which they can find in its earlier, unadorned state in the Pali jātakas; students of Sanskrit literature have tended to neglect the work of Buddhist authors—a contribution of crucial importance historically, quite apart from its intrinsic interest.

I would like to record my gratitude to the late John Brough, who first introduced me to Śūra twenty years ago and who later suggested that Śūra's work should be made better known through translation. I am also most grateful to Margaret Cone for penetrating criticism, tactful suggestions, and sustained encouragement.

Introduction

The Author

We know next to nothing about Ārya Śūra. The *Jātakamālā* supplies no direct biographical information, and so we have to fall back on tantalizingly vague (and unverifiable) references to him in works written many centuries after his (probable) date. The sole surviving Sanskrit commentary, *Jātakamālāṭīkā,* probably to be assigned to the fourteenth century A.D., claims that Śūra was the son of a king in the Deccan, that he renounced the throne to become a Buddhist monk (hence the honorific *ārya* 'noble, reverend'),[2] and wrote the *Jātakamālā* with a stylus (*kaṇṭaka*)—or, quite literally, with a thorn—on *tamāla* leaves, while wandering from place to place. A Śūra is also claimed by the Ceylonese: the *Nikāya-sangrahava,* a history of the *saṃgha* in Ceylon, written circa 1400, gives a list of scholars who lived in Ceylon from the time of King Mahānāma (fifth century A.D.) onward. The names seem to be in chronological order, and Śūrapāda is the first in the list of laymen.[3]

Tāranātha, writing his *History of Buddhism in India* in 1608,[4] states that Mātṛceta, alias Aśvaghoṣa, alias Śūra (among others) offered his body to a starving tigress and wrote a prayer in seventy verses with his own blood before expiring—a clear case of life imitating art (see "The Tigress," the first story in this book). Tāranātha also records that Mātṛceta/Śūra had intended to write one hundred jātakas (ten to illustrate each of the supreme virtues (*pāramitā*) cultivated by the Bodhisattva, the Buddha-to-be) but lived to complete only thirty-four. This legend, also to be found in Vīryasiṃha's commentary *Jātakamālāpañjikā* (preserved in Tibetan) and in Mongolian sources, does not survive scrutiny. Whereas jātakas 1–10 can be said to illustrate the first of the supreme virtues, viz., generosity (*dāna*), jātakas 11–20 the second, viz., morality (*śīla*), and jātakas 21–30 the third, viz., forbearance (*kṣānti*), the scheme breaks down at jātakas 31–34, which cannot be taken as illustrations of the fourth *pāramitā*, viz., exertion (*vīrya*).[5] More probably the work is designed on a subtler pattern, and there is every reason to believe that it is complete as it stands. Tāranātha's legend of the intended one hundred jātakas may perhaps have arisen from the practice of dividing Buddhist works into dec-ads (*daśatī*), e.g., the *Avadānaśataka* into ten and Kumāralāta's *Kalpanāmaṇḍitikā* into nine. But even in works not di-visible exactly into tens, one finds a list of contents (*uddāna*) at the end of each decad.[6] This is the case with the *Jātakamālā* manuscripts, where a versified list of the preceding jātakas occurs at the end of the tenth, twentieth, and thirtieth. So nothing can be deduced about the intended length of the *Jātakamālā* from these divisions into ten. Equally, Tāranātha's identification of Śūra with Aśvaghoṣa cannot be taken seriously by anyone familiar with their works. Nor is there any compelling reason for identifying Śūra with Mātṛceta.[7] The linking of these names might at most suggest that the authors were thought to have lived at about the same time or in succession to each other.

Even Śūra's date remains uncertain. Kern,[8] on a subjective assessment of his style, was inclined to place him surprisingly late, somewhere between A.D. 550 and A.D. 650. Lüders (1902)[9] established that the Kṣāntivādijātaka depicted in cave 2 at Ajaṇṭā had verses (4, 15, 19, and 56) from the *Jātakamālā* inscribed below it, as did also the depiction of the Maitrībalajātaka (verse 44). He dated the script of these quotations—incidentally the earliest evidence for the *Jātakamālā*—to the sixth century A.D., thereby giving a terminus ad quem. (They belong rather to the second half of the fifth century A.D.) Another argument for the date of the *Jātakamālā* has been based on the year A.D. 434, when the *Fen-pieh-yeh-pao-lüeh-ching* (= *Karmaphalasaṃkṣiptanirdeśasūtra [A brief treatise on the fruits of action]) is supposed to have been translated into Chinese. This work is actually attributed to Ta-yung (= *Mahāśūra), not to Āryaśūra (= Sheng-yung), and is only another version of the *Fen-pieh-shan-o-so-ch'i-ching,* which is said to have been translated into Chinese by An She-kao (A.D. 148–170). Besides, the attribution by the Chinese bibliographer Seng-yeou of the *Fen-pieh-yeh-pao-lüeh-ching* to *Mahāśūra only dates from A.D. 597 and is suspect.[10]

I-Tsing, writing toward the end of the seventh century A.D. describes a work called *Chö-tö-k'ie-mo-lo* (Jātakamālā) and praises it, but without giving its author's name.[11] Since *jātakamālā* had by then become a generic term (see below, p. xvi), I-Tsing may not necessarily have been referring to Śūra's work.

Haribhaṭṭa, in the introduction to his *Jātakamālā,* refers to Ācārya Śūra's *Jātakamālā* as his model (his collection also consisted of thirty-four stories). Since there is evidence to suggest that Haribhaṭṭa flourished in the early decades of the fifth century A.D., this would place Śūra in the fourth century A.D., if not earlier.[12] It is impossible at present to be more precise.

In the Tibetan Tripiṭaka five works, apart from the *Jātakamālā,* are attributed to Śūra:[13]

1. *Bodhisattvajātakadharmagaṇḍī* (= Peking Tibetan Tripiṭaka [PTT] no. 5657)—a short poem of thirty-five verses, serving as a table of contents to the *Jātakamālā;*
2. *Supathadeśanāparikathā* (= PTT no. 5675)—a sermon;
3. *Prātimokṣasūtrapaddhati* (= PTT no. 5605)—a commentary on the *vinaya* of the Sarvāstivādins;
4. *Subhāṣitaratnakaraṇḍakakathā* (= PTT nos. 5424 and 5668—twice translated)—a composite work compiled in the tenth century A.D. (see Hahn 1982);
5. *Pāramitāsamāsa* (= PTT no. 5340)—a product of the later Mahāyāna (seventh/eighth centuries A.D.?) treating

the six *pāramitās* in 363 verses and translated into Tibetan in the late eighth century A.D. (see Meadows 1986). Numbers 1–3 are no longer extant in Sanskrit, and none of the five works shed any light on Śūra.

The Work

The *Jātakamālā* (Garland [*mālā*] of stories-about-the-(previous)-births/incarnations [*jātaka*] [of the Buddha]) has the alternative title *Bodhisattvāvadānamālā* (Garland [*mālā*] of noble deeds [*avadāna*] [performed by] the Buddha-to-be [*bodhisattva*]). It was a work that enjoyed near-canonical status among the Northern Buddhists.

Jātakas are, in many cases, adaptations of popular tales that are used to teach Buddhist morals. Elements of the animal fable can also be found in them (sometimes incongruously): the ethical and moral superiority of animals over men is a typical theme. There are over five hundred jātakas preserved in Pali, the language of the Southern Buddhists, and some, if not all, of these were already in existence in the third/second centuries B.C., on the evidence of the inscriptions accompanying the carvings that depict jātaka stories at Bhārhut and Sāñcī.[14] The prose in the Pali versions is simple and unadorned, and the verses which form the older core, though often obscure, have no pretension to artistry. By contrast, Śūra's treatment of the jātaka themes shows a conscious concern for style. As he says in his prologue, "may these edifying tales give greater enjoyment than ever before" (verse 2). One may compare Aśvaghoṣa's words at the end of *Saundarananda:* "I have treated other subjects in my poem besides salvation, because that is the way of poetry (*kāvya*)—one adds honey to bitter medicine to make it palatable" (18.63). The title of Kumāralāta's work, *Kalpanāmaṇḍitikā* (sc., *Dṛṣṭāntapaṅkti*), which translates as *A Collection of Parables Adorned with Poetic Invention,*[15] declares the same intention: to present the Buddhist ethic in attractive and easily assimilable form. The result, in the case of Śūra's work, is that, while the basic story remains simple, the treatment is quite sophisticated, both psychologically and artistically.

Both the Pali jātakas and Śūra's are in a mixture of verse and prose. But the similarity is deceptive. The verses in the Pali form the main structure of the story, which is filled out by linking passages of prose. (Only the verse portions are accepted as canonical: the prose is considered secondary, like a commentary). In Śūra's versions the use of verse and prose is dictated by artistic considerations, and both are written with the same conscious care. Somendra, in the introduction to his father's *Avadānakalpalatā* (verse 7), describes the writers of jātakamālās (i.e., Śūra and his successors) as "unfettered in their use of verse and prose" (*gadyapadyaviśṛṅkhalāḥ*). Some verses Śūra has taken over from his source, sometimes with a heightening of language and sometimes not. But otherwise one can only make general statements about what dictated his use of verse and prose. Dialogue is often, but not always, in verse. Descriptive passages are more frequently in prose than in verse: autumn (22.17+), the rainy season (22.18+), and spring (31.3+) are all described in prose. Similarly, noon (6.21+), sunset/twilight (14.32+), the festival of the autumn full moon (13.7+ and 32.6+), and six out of seven descriptions of forest scenery (6.0, 9.51+, 21.5+, 25.3+, 26.0, and 30.0; cf. the seventh, in verse, 9.33f.). On the other hand a water party (28.5f.), festivities at a royal birth (32.1–4), and the torments of sinners in hell (29.19–45) are all depicted in verse. Apothegms in verse can comment on—and interrupt—prose narrative, but about a quarter of the total number of verses actually occur in plain narrative. The switch from prose to verse can be quite sudden—sometimes in mid-sentence (e.g., 2.5, 6.33, 7.7, 9.55, and 13.5)—but is not arbitrary, and often serves to heighten a dramatic moment in the telling of the story. The Bodhisattva's sermons are in verse, as befits the lofty tone of their message. Generally, the verse (in some thirty varieties of meter, some of them very rare[16]) acts like a constant change of time signature to the rhythm of each story. There is no marked difference in language between verse and prose portions: the contrast is simply between metrical and unmetrical.

Śūra was not the inventor of this literary genre of mixed verse and prose which came to be called *campū*.[17] Fragments have survived from earlier works of the kind: Kumāralāta's *Kalpanāmaṇḍitikā Dṛṣṭāntapaṅkti,* which Lüders placed circa A.D. 150, and remnants of eight tales by Saṅghasena (fl. early third century A.D.), surviving in a fifth-century-A.D. palm-leaf manuscript found at Qizil in Chinese Turkestan.[18] Though Śūra's work appears to be a considerable refinement on Kumāralāta's, the formal similarities are unmistakable.[19] And, in the same way, the jātakamālās of Śūra's successors, Haribhaṭṭa (fl. fifth century A.D.) and Gopadatta (fl. before the eleventh century A.D.) show a development from Śūra's.[20]

It can be seen from the brief generalizations made above that what dictates Śūra's use of verse hardly corresponds to our notions of the appropriate occasion for 'breaking into poetry'. It would consequently be quite misleading to attempt to produce English verse equivalents for each of Śūra's verses. Only the apothegms lend themselves to some sort of rhyming jingle in English.

In the tenth century A.D. Ratnaśrījñāna, himself a Buddhist, holds up the *Jātakamālā* as an example of the so-called Southern style (*vaidarbhī rīti*),[21] characterized by balance and proportion, and in the eleventh-century A.D. anthology *Subhāṣitaratnakoṣa* (verse 1698) Śūra is praised for the purity of his expression (*viśuddhokti*). Rājaśekhara (fl. ca. A.D. 900), in his treatise on poetry, *Kāvyamīmāṃsā,*[22] includes Sūra (*sic*) in a list of poets—Kālidāsa and Bhāravi among them—whose work was at one time adjudged and approved (*parīkṣita*) by a committee of brahmins at the royal court of Ujjayinī. These high opinions give welcome support to what may otherwise be only our own subjective appreciation of Śūra's chaste but also rich style—for instance, his pleasing use of sound effects (*śabdālaṃkāra*), such as alliteration (*anuprāsa*) and, in particular, echo (*yamaka*). Of wordplay and other figures (*arthālaṃkāra*) he is more sparing, though simile (*upamā*), metaphor (*rūpaka*), and (the despair of the translator) double entendre (*śleṣa*) all add their piquancy. The impossibility of producing an English equivalent of Śūra's verbal artistry results in the paradox that precisely the most skillful and musical verses become the dullest and most awkward in translation (e.g., 29.50–55). (This may also be the moment to say that not all the stories are equally vivid or interesting.)

The *Jātakamālā* is written in correct classical Sanskrit with few grammatical peculiarities. Its vocabulary is rich: besides the words with a specialized Buddhist sense, there are many others rarely attested elsewhere, previously recorded only in dictionaries, or not recorded at all. Böhtlingk and Roth's great Petersburg Dictionary was completed in 1875, sixteen years before the publication of the *Jātakamālā*. But Kern lent the proofs of his edition to Böhtlingk—he even dedicated it to him—so that a fair number of the more interesting words and usages were recorded in the appendix to the Shorter Petersburg Dictionary in 1889. These Schmidt carried over and added to in his *Nachträge* of 1928, and Edgerton's *Buddhist Hybrid Sanskrit Dictionary* of 1953 also includes much of the vocabulary special to the *Jātakamālā*. Even so, there are errors and omissions in these dictionaries, and a comprehensive glossary to the *Jātakamālā* has yet to be made.

It is not possible to state precisely what sources Śūra drew on for his selection of jātakas. There are parallels to thirty of his thirty-four jātakas in the Pali collection, and the frequent identity of phrases—and, on occasion, even whole verses—in the two versions shows that for some stories Śūra had either the Pali as we know it or something close to it as his exemplar. Parallels to the stories can be found in non-Buddhist works: in the epic, in the Purāṇas, and in the eleventh-century-A.D. rehandling of popular tales, Somadeva's *Kathāsaritsāgara*. But the interest lies not so much in tracing his sources as in isolating what in treatment and emphasis is peculiar to him.

In the *Jātakamālā* there is greater emphasis than in the Pali jātakas on the Bodhisattva ideal of self-sacrifice for the good of the world (the Bodhisattva as *lokatrātṛ;* see 2.8 and 30.21/2). Of the four jātakas which have no parallel in the Pali collection, three are about the Bodhisattva sacrificing his body for others (nos. 1 ["The Tigress"], 7 [Maitrībala], and 30 ["The Elephant"]) and the different ending of the Pali version of number 6 ("The Hare") where the hare escapes being burned, is also significant. Though this may suggest a Mahāyānist tendency, it would be wrong to see any marked sectarian bias in the *Jātakamālā.* The Mahāyāna is mentioned only once (1.28), and then only by a periphrasis *yānavara* "the best way/vehicle" (see note to tale 1, no. 8).

The fourth of the jātakas without a parallel in the Pali is number 18 ("The Man without an Heir"), whose theme is the renunciation of worldly life (*gārhasthyam*) in favor of the homeless life of an ascetic (*pravrajyā*). The condemnation of worldly ties and preoccupations is another theme which receives greater emphasis in the *Jātakamālā* than in the Pali jātakas (e.g., 1.6, 7.2+, 21.1+, 28.0, and 32.43–48): it forms the subject of jātakas 18–20.

The major theme of the *Jātakamālā* is that of the virtuous ruler. The whole work reflects a courtly milieu, not only in its content but in the refinement of its style, and it addresses itself to kings and princes. Generosity (*dāna*), morality (*śīla*), and forbearance (*kṣānti*), the first three perfections, illustrated in jātakas 1–30, are preeminently the qualities of a ruler,[23] and Śūra is concerned to show how the Buddhist morality should be adopted by the ruler in preference to the realpolitik (*nīti*) advocated by the *Arthaśāstra* (see note to tale 6, no. 2). Whether it is possible to deduce any biographical information from this preoccupation with the morally sensitive ruler and the homeless ascetic by linking it with the statement in the *Jātakamālāṭīkā,* quoted earlier, that Śūra was a prince who renounced the throne to become a wandering ascetic, must remain in doubt.

Although Śūra's main purpose was to edify, he also wished to give pleasure. We can admire the moral ethos of the *Jātakamālā* but also appreciate the glimpses it gives of life in ancient India and of the landscape and townscape which are its vivid backdrop. That these stories appealed to the imagination (as Śūra hoped they would) is proved by the frescoes at Ajaṇṭā and by the reliefs on the first gallery of Borobudur in Java—the greatest surviving monument of the Buddhist world—both based specifically on Śūra's versions of the jātakas.[24]

Once the Buddha Was a Monkey

In homage to all the Buddhas and Bodhisattvas

Prologue

[1] With this handful of flowers—my poem—I will celebrate the wonders performed by the Holy One in previous incarnations. Glorious they were, and rich in good consequences because of his own fine qualities. Their fame is assured since they capture the imagination and never grow dull. [2] These praiseworthy exploits are like conspicuous signs pointing the way to perfection. As such may they soften even the hardest of hearts. And may these edifying tales give greater enjoyment than ever before.[1]

[3] Conscious that my words have power to do good in the world, I will keep scrupulously to the evidence of tradition and revelation in my account of the outstanding deeds of the All Highest. [4] The exquisite goodness he showed in his active concern for others could not be matched even by those intent on their own betterment.

To him who has no equal, whose radiant glory is truly summed up in the title *Omniscient,* to the Teaching, and to the community of monks, I bow my head in reverence.

Figures in brackets in the text refer to corresponding verse numbers in the original.

The Tigress 1

ALREADY IN HIS PREVIOUS INCARnations the Lord was wont to lavish disinterested affection on all beings, identifying himself with every living creature. And that is why one should have complete faith in the Lord Buddha.

Tradition tells of a particular exploit performed by the Lord in a previous incarnation, and the story of it was told by my own teacher, a teacher of the three-jeweled[1] Buddhist faith, a teacher respected for his own good life and fine stock of virtues.

While still a Bodhisattva, the Lord already blessed mankind with a stream of kindnesses: he gave generously, spoke lovingly, and instigated goodness. All this followed from the supreme vow[2] he had taken, and was vouched for by his wisdom.

Once he is said to have been born into a great brahmin family which had attained eminence simply by being content to perform the duties expected of it and by leading a sober life. He received the traditional series of sacraments—the various rites, from birth onwards, marking his development. His native intelligence and special tutelage, his thirst for knowledge and love of work, soon made him master of the eighteen branches of knowledge[3] and of all such skills as were not incompatible with his family position. [5] Among brahmins he was revered like the Veda itself, among the ruling class he was honoured as a king, to the common people he seemed like Śakra[4] in person, and to those in quest of knowledge like a helpful father. His good fortune and outstanding personal qualities earned him considerable respect and repute, as well as material rewards. But from these the

1 · 6 Bodhisattva could derive no pleasure, committed as he was to the path of renunciation and fully absorbed in the study of the Law[5] [6] To one whose awareness had become completely clear in the course of previous lives, worldly pleasures could only seem like so many evils. He therefore shook off worldly ties as though they were an illness and went to grace some lonely retreat. [7] There, with a detachment and serenity made perfect by wisdom, he seemed almost to reproach mankind, whose persistent wrongdoing bars it from the wise man's peace of mind. [8] His kindly presence had a calming effect on the wild beasts, who stopped preying on each other and began themselves to live like hermits. [9] Because he was so transparently good, so self-disciplined, content, and compassionate, even strangers felt affection for him, just as he felt affection for them. [10] His needs were so modest that he was innocent of turning his holy status to advantage. Indeed, he had rid himself so thoroughly of any desire for fame, fortune, or comfort that even the gods were inclined to look upon him with favor. [11] Men heard that he had renounced the world, were captivated by his fine qualities, and abandoned family and possessions to go to him for instruction, as though that in itself were final bliss. [12] He powerfully impressed upon these pupils the need to behave with integrity, to cultivate their moral sense, never to let their attention be distracted, to be detached, and to concentrate their thoughts on friendliness and the other cardinal virtues.[6]

His flock of disciples had swollen in numbers. Almost all had attained perfection. The way to enlightenment had been laid down, and mankind set on the right road to renunciation. The gateway to perdition was shut, the paths to bliss opened into broad highways.

Then it was that the Noble One went out with Ajita, his disciple at that time, to enjoy the world about him. His walk took him through the dells and thickets that are conducive to meditation. [13] There, in a mountain cave, he noticed a tigress so overcome by the pangs of giving birth that she was too weak to move. [14] Her eyes were hollow with hunger, her belly horribly thin, and she looked upon her whelps, her own offspring, as so much meat, [15] while they, trusting their mother and without a qualm, sidled up to her, thirsty for milk. But she menaced them with ferocious roars, as though they were strangers. [16] The Bodhisattva remained calm at the sight of her, but compassion for another creature in distress made him shake like Himalaya in an earthquake. [17] It is remarkable how the compassionate put a brave face on things when they themselves are in dire trouble—but tremble at others' distress, however slight. Though emotion gave emphasis to his words, the Bodhisattva spoke to his disciple in tones that by force of pity were subdued but that also showed his exceptional character.

"My dear boy, [18] look how futile it is, this round of birth and rebirth. Starvation forces this beast to break the laws of affection. Here she is, ready to devour her own offspring. [19] Oh! how fierce is the instinct for self-preservation, such that a mother can be willing to eat her own young. [20] How can one allow this scourge to continue unabated—this self-love which prompts such atrocities? Go quickly and search everywhere for something to appease her hunger, before she does harm to her young ones or to herself. In the meantime I too will try to stop her from resorting to violence." Ajita promised to do so and set out on his quest for food.

After despatching his disciple on this pretext, the Bodhisattva began to reflect: [21] "Why search for meat from some other creature when there is my entire body available right here? It is a matter of luck whether or not the boy succeeds in finding any meat, and meanwhile I may be losing an opportunity to act. Besides, [22] this body is only so much matter. It is frail, without substance, a miserable ungrateful thing, always impure. One would be a fool not to welcome the chance of its being useful to someone else. [23] There can only be two reasons for taking no notice when someone else is in difficulties: selfish concern for one's own well-being, or sheer helplessness. But I cannot be happy as long as there is someone who is unhappy. And anyway, how can I take no notice when it is in my power to help? [24] Suppose there were some criminal in abject misery and I took no notice of him even though

1 · 25 I could be of help. It would be the same as committing a crime: I would burn with remorse, like deadwood in a forest fire. [25] Now, suppose I fell down this mountainside; my lifeless corpse might serve to prevent this creature from killing her young and save the whelps from the advances of their mother. And, what is more, [26] this would be an example to those who strive for the good of the world, an encouragement to those who falter, a delight to those who are practiced in charity, a powerful attraction to noble hearts. [27] It will bring despair to the great hosts of Māra,[7] joy to those who love the fine qualities of a Buddha, and be a source of shame to those who are wrapped up in their own affairs and whose souls are ravaged by greed and selfishness. [28] It would inspire faith in those who follow the Better Way[8] and would confound those who sneer at renunciation. It would clear the broad highway to heaven and please all men of generous heart. [29] I might also thereby fulfil my dream of some day being of help to others even if it meant sacrificing my life, and so come closer to perfect enlightenment. Besides, [30] neither ambition nor desire for fame nor a longing for heaven nor the position of king nor even endless bliss for myself underlie my concern—nothing except to assure the well-being of others. [31] By doing this may I gain the power always to bring happiness to mankind and at the same time to remove its sorrow, just as the sun has power to bring light and banish darkness. [32] Whether I am seen, heard, or remembered, or am talked of as a result of personal contact, may I in every way benefit all creation and assure it unfailing happiness."

[33] On making this decision to be of use to another creature, though it cost him his life, he felt a surge of joy, then astounded even the calm minds of the gods by hurling himself down.

The sound of the Bodhisattva's body as it fell to earth aroused the curiosity and impatience of the tigress. On the point of slaughtering her young, she paused, looked around, and, catching sight of the lifeless corpse, immediately bounded over and began to devour it.

 Meanwhile his disciple had in fact found no meat, and returned, wondering where his teacher had got to. As he peered around he caught sight of the tigress eating the Bodhisattva's lifeless body. But any feeling of grief or sorrow was countered by amazement at such an extraordinary deed. Somehow he seemed to be voicing his regard for the Bodhisattva's goodness in the words that he now spoke to himself: [34] "Oh! how compassionate the Noble One has shown himself to those in distress, how indifferent to his own well-being. In him noble conduct has reached its apogee, while the renown and glory of its adversaries lies crushed. [35] Oh! what supreme love he has shown—bold, fearless, and full of goodness. Oh! how his body, which was of no mean worth, is now effectively an object of the highest regard. [36] Kind by nature, and as firm as the ground, how intolerable to him were the misfortunes of others! How his valiant deed shows up my own waywardness. [37] Certainly there is no need to pity the world now that it has such a protector in him. Well may Māra groan in troubled apprehension of defeat. Homage in the highest to this blessed Being who is a refuge to all creation, whose compassion is unbounded, whose goodness is immeasurable, who is a Bodhisattva for the good of the world."

He then informed his fellow students of what had happened. [38] Amazement showed in the faces of those disciples and of the whole hierarchy of beings,[9] when they heard of this deed. And the ground that contained the treasure of his bones was strewn with showers of garlands, fine apparel, ornaments, and sandal powder.

So, then—remembering how already in his previous incarnations the Lord was wont to lavish disinterested affection on all beings, identifying himself with every living creature, one should have complete faith in the Lord Buddha.

2 *Śibi*

SINCE THE LORD SUFFERED HUNDREDS of hardships to acquire the good Teaching for us, we should listen to it with respect.

According to tradition, when the Lord was still a Bodhisattva he was at one time king of the Śibis.[1] This was because his store of good deeds had, by dint of constant accumulation over an immense period of time, become part of him.

Already as a boy he had taken pleasure in waiting on his elders and had been attracted to a life of discipline. His subjects loved him, for he looked after them as if they were his own children. Though naturally intelligent, he broadened his mind by intensive study. He was energetic, decisive, powerful, capable, and favored by fortune. [1] He happily combined within himself the whole gamut of qualities necessary for the three pursuits of life.[2] They shone out harmoniously, their brilliant effect unspoiled by any shock of incompatibility. [2] And success, which to rude upstarts is but a mockery, which fools mistake for dire misfortune, which to the weak willed is like an intoxicant, was for him just what its name implies. [3] He was a true king as much because of his nobility and compassion as because of the wealth at his disposal. It gave him pleasure to see petitioners' faces light up with unclouded joy at getting what they wanted.

This king was so charitable that all over his capital city he had built special halls for almsgiving and had filled them with every kind of provision, with money and with grain. In keeping with his generous nature, he showered gifts, like a cloud in the Golden Age—gifts that were given graciously, that gave delight, that were welcome for being so prompt, and that fulfilled each person's desires: food for the hungry, drink for the

thirsty, lodging, clothing, meals, perfumes, garlands, silver, 2.8
gold—whatever was asked for. People were amazed and overjoyed when they heard of the king's liberality, and flocked to his country from all the known regions of the habitable world. [4] Though they ranged the whole world in imagination, the needy discovered no one else to whom they had a chance of putting their requests, and so, with joyful expressions, they gathered around him, as wild elephants around a pool. The crowds of beggars that converged from all quarters, overjoyed at the prospect of success, managed to conceal their personal charms beneath their traveler's garb. [5] But the king opened his eyes wide with delight, as though it were long-absent friends that he saw before him. He welcomed each petition as if it were good news, and granting them made him even happier than the recipients. [6] Such generosity earned him fame, whose fragrance was spread by the breath of the beggars. It crushed the pride of other kings just as the ichor of a scent elephant overpowers that of other elephants.

One day the king, on his round of the alms halls, noticed that, because the beggars' needs had been satisfied, the gathering of petitioners had dwindled. Not being able to proceed with his habitual almsgiving made him feel discontented. [7] While the beggar had only to go to him to have his wants removed, it was not so with the king himself after he had satisfied the beggar: giving had become an addiction. No beggar, however great his request, could quell the king's passion for giving. It occurred to him how very lucky those paragons of goodness were, whom beggars approached in full confidence and without reserve, even to ask them to part with their own limbs. To him beggars only made timid requests for money, as though intimidated at the thought of meeting with a harsh refusal. [8] Divining the king's truly noble idea—proof of his indifference to his own body as well as of his generous leanings—the Earth itself trembled, like a woman devoted to her husband.[3] And as the ground shook so did great Mount Sumeru,[4] glinting with the sparkle of its various precious stones, so that Śakra, lord of the gods, began to

2 · 9 wonder what this could portend. He then realized that the earth tremor was due to King Śibi's extraordinary idea. Overcome with astonishment, he wondered [9] why the king should be so carried away by his passion for giving as to come to such a idea: why should he be prepared to take this wilful generosity so far as to be set on giving away parts of his own body? He decided to find out about him.

The king was sitting in his audience chamber, surrounded by a crowd of ministers, and the usual proclamation had been made, inviting any beggar in need. Heaps of gems, gold, silver, and coins were on display under the supervision of the treasurer. Baskets crammed with all kinds of clothing were being unfastened. Brightly colored vehicles, yoked to the shoulders of various well-schooled draught animals, were being brought forward. And a crowd of beggars formed. Among them, Śakra, lord of the gods, in the guise of a blind old brahmin, caught the king's eye. The king gave him a look suffused with such compassion and benevolence, so calm, kind, and gentle, that it was as if he had come forward to embrace the brahmin. The courtiers invited him to say what it was he wanted. So he approached the king, hailed him, and said: [10] "King of kings, I, a blind old man, have come from afar to ask for your eye. For surely, my lord, one of your lotus-eyes is sufficient for observing the affairs of the world." The Bodhisattva felt elated at having his dearest wish fulfilled but was not sure whether the brahmin had really said as much or whether he had merely imagined it through having it constantly in mind. In his eagerness to hear those delightful words, framing a request for his eye, he asked the man: [11] "Who told you to come here and ask for my eye, noble brahmin? To part with one's eye is no light matter, they say. Who assumes that in my case this does not hold true?"

Reading the king's thoughts, Śakra, in his brahmin disguise, answered: [12] "Śakra. It is at the bidding of an image of Śakra that I have come here to ask you for your eye. Prove his assumption right and my hopes true by giving me that eye."

At the mention of Śakra, the king felt sure that through divine intervention he would be the means of restoring sight to the brahmin, and in his joy he cheerfully replied: [13] "Brahmin, I shall grant the wish that brought you here. You are hoping to get one eye from me, but I shall give you both. [14] Go as you please. Two wide lotus-eyes will adorn your face. And, on seeing you, people will hesitate, uncertain as to whether it really is you or not, and finally will realize to their surprise that it is."

When the king's ministers learned that he had decided to give away his eyes, they were distressed, agitated, and worried. Full of misgivings, they pleaded with him. [15] "Your majesty, this passion for giving things away has blinded you to the fact that it is unwise and can lead to no good. Please, your highness, do not do this. Do not part with your sight. [16] Do not brush us aside for the sake of this one brahmin. How can you submit your subjects to the burning agony of grief after bringing them up in happiness? [17] Give money which brings prosperity, or jewels, or cows that give milk, or chariots with well-schooled horses in harness, or elephants disporting themselves in the full pride of rut. [18] Give houses which are comfortable in every season of the year, which are brighter than clouds in autumn, which resound to the tinkle of women's anklets. But do not part with your eyesight, you who are the apple of everyone's eye. Besides, your majesty, just think: [19] how can one person's eye possibly be of use to another? And if it is a question of divine intervention, then why should it be your eye that is required? Anyway, [20] what does this poor man need an eye for? To see other people in prosperity? Give him money, your majesty, and do not act recklessly."

Politely and gently the king replied to his ministers: [21] "Whoever decides not to give, after saying he will, once again entangles himself in attachment after having let it drop away. [22] Can there be anyone more wicked than he who promises to give and then, because meanness saps his will, changes his mind? [23] To raise a beggar's hopes by promising a gift and then cruelly to break one's word is unpardonable. And as to your wondering why his eye cannot be produced solely by divine power, listen: [24] everyone knows that success depends on a variety of factors, so that even Fate, though supernatu-

2 · 25 ral, has to rely on one means or another. Therefore, kindly do not try to oppose me now that I am set on making this exceptional gift."

"Your majesty," replied the ministers, "we merely requested that you be so good as to donate money, grain, and jewels rather than your own eyesight. We are hardly inciting your majesty to evil by doing that."

[25] "One must give what people ask for," said the king. "Unwanted presents give no pleasure. What use is a drink to someone being carried off by a flood? I shall therefore give this man what he asked for."

"You will do no such thing, sir!" broke in the chief minister, who was very much in the king's confidence and forgot etiquette in a burst of affection. [26] "To attain the position of king demands no small amount of self-sacrifice and dedication. Its attainment, by means of countless hecatombs, means also the attainment of glory and heavenly bliss. You have attained it. Yet, though you rival Śakra in power, you choose to disregard it. What consideration prompts your lordship to give away your eyes? How comes it? What do you mean by it? [27] Your sacrifices have gained you a place among the gods. Your renown shines out in every direction. As kings do obeisance, your feet are tinged with the luster of their diadems. What do you hope to gain by giving away your sight?"

The king answered his minister courteously: [28] "I am striving neither for world dominion, nor for heaven, nor for final release, nor for fame. I am concerned only to save the world and that the trouble this man has been to in making his request should not prove vain."

The king then gave orders for one eye—an eye whose radiant beauty was like that of a piece of blue lotus petal—to be extracted, slowly and without causing it damage, in the medically prescribed manner.[5] With perfect love he handed it to the beggar. Whereupon Śakra, lord of the gods, by an act of magic made it seem to the king and his entourage that the king's eye was lodged in the beggar's eye socket. To see the beggar with one eye open filled the king's heart with extreme delight, and he immediately offered him his other eye as

well.[29] With its eyes removed, the king's face looked like a 2 · 36
lotus pond without lotuses. But it wore a happy expression, which was not, however, shared by the citizenry. The brahmin appeared to be able to see perfectly. [30] Everywhere, in the palace and the royal capital, tears of grief sprinkled the ground. But Śakra was full of delighted admiration at the king's unshakable resolve to attain perfect enlightenment. Overcome with amazement, he thought: [31] "What endurance! what courage! what altruism! I can hardly believe my eyes. This marvelous being should not have to suffer like this for long. I shall therefore endeavor to restore his sight and show him a means to that end."

The wounds to the king's eyes gradually healed, and, in palace, city, and countryside, people's grief abated and all but disappeared. One day the king wanted to be alone and was sitting cross-legged beside the lotus pond in his park. The place was overspread with fine trees that bowed under the weight of blossom. A cool fragrant breeze blew softly, and swarms of bees hummed in the air. Suddenly Śakra appeared before him. The king asked who he was, and he answered: [32] "I am Śakra, lord of the gods, come to pay you a visit." The king welcomed him and asked how he could be of service. Śakra returned this politeness by replying: "Saintly king, make a wish. Say what it is you want." The king was in the habit of giving; he was not used to trudging the road of poverty and beggary. But, restraining both pride and astonishment, he said to Śakra: [33] "Great is my wealth, Śakra, big and powerful my army, but blindness now makes death seem sweet to me. [34] Since I can no longer see beggars' faces brighten with boundless love and devotion when I grant their wishes, death is dear to me, Śakra." "Stop insisting on it," interrupted Śakra. "Only saints attain to such a state of mind. But let me ask you this: [35] when beggars have reduced you to your present condition, how is it that even now you still show concern for them? Just state the truth, without evasion, and you may free yourself from your present plight and start afresh.[6]" "Why do you force me to boast?" answered the king. "Even so, listen, lord of the gods: [36] if it is true that the sound of beggars' voices, earnestly asking favors, is now and always has been as pleasant to me as if they were blessings, then may an eye materialize for me."

Now, as a result of taking his stand on truth, and thanks also to his exceptional store of merit, the king had no sooner spoken than an eye appeared. It looked like the petal of a blue lotus with a splinter of sapphire set in its center. The king was overjoyed when this miraculous eye appeared, and again addressed Śakra: [37] "Just as I gladly gave both my eyes to him who only asked for one, and felt nothing but joy and love, so may I in turn receive another eye."

The moment the king said this a second eye appeared, rivaling the first. [38] The earth shook, and so did the mountains. The ocean broke its bounds and surged forward. The drums of the celestial gods rolled deep and steady—a delightful sound. [39] The whole expanse of heaven looked beautifully clear, and the sun shone with an autumn brightness. Out of the sky fell a shower of bright flowers tinged with the sandal powder that was whirling around. [40] The gods gathered there with a bevy of celestial nymphs, wide-eyed in amazement. The breeze that blew was peculiarly pleasant, and joy blossomed out in the heart of every living thing. [41] All around, lovely voices were heard, raised in a paean of praise for the king's extraordinary deed; hosts of supernatural beings were exclaiming in wonder and rapture: [42] "Oh what nobility! oh what compassion! see how pure is his heart! how little he cares for his own happiness! Glory be to you, whose courage and fortitude are so outstanding! [43] Indeed, the world is orphaned no more, now that your beautiful lotus-eyes are open once again. Nor is it futile to store up merit, since virtue is sure to triumph in the end."

Śakra then congratulated him and spoke again: [44] "We were not unaware of what you felt in the pureness of your heart, dear king. That is why we gave you back your eyes. [45] They will have power to see without obstruction for a hundred leagues around, even things that are hidden behind mountains."

With these words Śakra disappeared there and then. The

ministers who had followed behind were full of wonder and delight. They were so wide-eyed they hardly blinked at all. The townspeople stared at the Bodhisattva, and brahmins greeted him with shouts of "Hail!" and "Victory!" as he approached the palace which, with its bright banners and hoisted flags, had a festive look. He took his seat in the assembly hall amid a crowd that had gathered to do him honor. At the head were his ministers, and then came senior brahmins and people from town and country. To these he preached the Law, taking his own experience as theme: [46] "After seeing how I have obtained these eyes of supernatural power by virtue of my generosity, who on earth could be in two minds about making beggars happy by giving them money? [47] I can see any visible object anywhere—be it hidden by mountain ranges or even a hundred leagues away—as clearly as if it were close by. [48] What is more rewarding than generosity, born of modesty and compassion? See how once I parted with my mortal sight and have, already in this life, been rewarded with sight that is superhuman and divine. [49] Take note of this, my people, and make your wealth bear fruit by giving it away and spending it. This is the way to fame and happiness, in this world and the next. [50] Money is in itself a meaningless trifle; only when someone bent on being of use to the world gives it away does it come into its own. Giving money away is like laying up treasure—hoarding it spells ruin."

So, then—since the Lord suffered hundreds of hardships to acquire the good Teaching for us, we should listen to it with respect.

3 The Dumpling

NO GIFT GIVEN IN GOOD FAITH TO A worthy recipient can be called small, its effect is so great.

According to tradition, the Lord, while still a Bodhisattva, was once king of Kośala.[1] He was exceptionally well endowed with the qualities of a king: energy, decisiveness, power, ability, and the like. But these were eclipsed by the divine favor he enjoyed. [1] Crowned by the favor of the gods, his virtues shone out all the more, as do moonbeams when autumn unveils their loveliness.[2] [2] Fortune was at his side, meting out wrath and favor to other kings in such a way that she deserted his enemies, however proud, and cherished his dependents like a devoted woman. [3] He himself was too good to take a cruel delight in the discomfiture of his enemies. But his subjects displayed such devotion that the odds were against his foes.

One day the king recalled his last incarnation and felt revulsion at the memory. To monks, brahmins, poor people, and beggars he further increased his gifts which were the cause of well-being. He fulfilled his moral obligations assiduously and observed the fast days at the moon's quarters. He also wanted to direct people's thoughts toward the bliss of final release, by proclaiming the power of virtue. To this end he was constantly reciting two verses with great fervor and earnestness, both in the public assembly and in his private quarters: [4] "Even the smallest service to a follower of the Buddha is rich in reward. Hitherto this has been merely hearsay. Now see how magnificent is the reward for one dry, unsalted, sour, brownish dumpling. [5] This powerful army of mine, glinting with chariots and horses, dark with noble elephants in rut; the whole wide world; great riches; Fortune's favor; a noble wife—behold this dazzling array of rewards for a mere dumpling."

Neither his ministers nor the senior brahmins nor the leading citizens, though all in a whirl with curiosity, dared question the king about what he meant when he constantly recited this pair of verses. But the chief queen, because she was the king's favorite, felt less constrained about asking. When the opportunity arose to discuss it, she asked him in open assembly: [6] "My lord, you are always reciting these verses as though you were giving expression to heartfelt gladness. But what you say fills me with curiosity. [7] If I may be permitted to hear, my lord, kindly explain what it is that you recite. Were it a secret, you would never proclaim it as you do, and that is why I am asking you about it in public."

The king gave the queen a look of tender devotion. His face broadened into a smile, and he said: [8] "You are not the only one to have had his curiosity aroused by hearing this dictum of mine without understanding the reason behind it. [9] This whole circle of ministers is in a restless whirl of surmise about it, and so is the city and the royal household. So hear why I recite these verses. [10] I remember my last incarnation just as if I had woken from a dream. In it I was a workman living here in this very town. I led a sober life but scraped a living by honest work for people whose only distinction was their wealth. [11] One day I was about to begin on some hired work—that rich source of insult, exhaustion, and misery. Self-preservation was my only motive: I was afraid of no longer being able to keep body and soul together. Suddenly I caught sight of four monks begging alms. They were self-possessed and, it seemed, surrounded by the holy aura of monkhood. [12] My heart melted with devotion. I bowed to them and in my house devoutly offered them a simple dumpling. The little seedling I planted then has grown so that now the diadems of kings shed their rays on the dust of my feet. [13] It is with this in mind that I recite these verses, my queen, and take pleasure in doing good and seeing holy men."

The queen was wide-eyed with delight and astonishment. She gazed at the king respectfully and said: "Such exceptional good fortune is a fitting reward for good deeds. After all, your majesty bears witness to the result of virtue, by taking pains to practice it. That is why you shun all evildoing and concentrate instead on caring properly for your subjects, as a father for his children. You are set on amassing both merit and virtue. [14] You hold firm sway over the heads of rival kings, in a blaze of glory that is all the greater for your generosity. Long may you rule with wisdom and justice over the earth whose ocean-mantle is creased by the wind."

"Indeed, my queen, why not?" said the king. [15] "I shall endeavor to keep once more to the path that leads to perfect bliss, whose lovely signposts are conspicuous. Once people are aware of the rewards of charity, they are eager to give. How could I fail to be generous after observing my own case?"

The king then gave the queen an affectionate look and noticed as he did so that she was as radiantly lovely as a goddess. Wondering what could be the reason for this beauty, he spoke again: [16] "You shine out among women as the crescent moon among the stars. Have you done something, my dear, that would account for this lovely effect?" "Yes, I have, my lord," replied the queen. "I too clearly remember something that happened in a previous incarnation." And since the king eagerly insisted that she tell it straightaway, she told her story: [17] "Like some childhood experience, I clearly remember being a servant and respectfully offering a portion of food to a dispassionate monk. It is just as if I had fallen asleep there and woken up here. [18] I remember this good deed, my lord, because thanks to it I gained you as a husband whom I share with the Earth.[3] And the monk said exactly what you said: 'no service rendered to holy men is negligible.' "

The king noticed how completely astonished the assembly was and how this example of the fruits of virtue had won it over and aroused a respect for goodness. And so he earnestly addressed the gathering in some such terms as these: [19] "After seeing how far-reaching and splendid are the consequences of a good deed, however modest, can anyone be less than eager to do good by practicing generosity? If a man is very rich and yet fails to get a name for being generous, because he is so benighted by meanness, then he ought not to show himself. [20] One day you will inevitably have to part with your money, and it will be of no use then. If one stands to gain some merit by parting with it now, in a suitable manner, is one likely in such circumstances to adopt a selfish attitude, knowing full well about the pleasure of doing good, about the other qualities, such as kindness, inherent in generosity and about the good repute that attends all these? [21] Indeed, Charity is a great and lasting treasure, immune to theft and to everything else. Charity cleanses the heart of the sins of selfishness and greed. Charity is a pleasant vehicle which banishes the weariness of traveling from one birth to the next. Charity is the constant and perfect friend, ready with whatever is needed for endless happiness. [22] Whether one wants to amass a fortune or gain unlimited power, live with the gods in heaven or look beautiful, Charity will provide it all. On considering the matter, who could fail to be generous? [23] Giving, they say, is getting the best out of wealth. Giving, they say, is the root cause of power. Giving is the noble expression of the benevolence of the mighty. Even dust, given in childish innocence, is a good gift."[4]

The assembly was impressed by the king's convincing words and was all ready to give things away and to do good generally.

So, then—no gift that is given in good faith to a worthy recipient can be called small; its effect is so great.

4 *The Merchant*

GOOD MEN DISCOUNT PERSONAL RISK in their readiness to give. How can anyone in comfortable circumstances refuse to do so?

According to tradition, the Lord, while still a Bodhisattva, was once a merchant. Through great good luck and successful enterprise he amassed a large fortune and also earned people's respect for being scrupulous in his dealings. He was well-born and had enlarged his mind by studying many branches of learning in the arts and sciences. His virtuous and noble nature gained him a place of honor with the king, while his habitual generosity meant that in effect he shared his fortune with others. [1] His petitioners were well-contented and praised him far and wide, so that the name he earned for his largesse spread to every corner of the earth. [2] In his case no suppliant needed to worry whether he would give or not: a whole crowd of suppliants could, with perfect confidence, make their requests to him whose noble deeds were renowned. [3] He did not hoard his wealth for his own pleasure, or in competition with others, or in contempt of the world. It was simply that he could not bear the suffering of the needy and consequently denied them nothing.

Now one day at mealtime, when the Great Being had bathed and anointed himself, a variety of food was served. It had been prepared by a skilled and excellent cook, and the color, taste, texture, and aroma of both food and sauces were of the finest quality. At that moment a monk approached to beg alms and stationed himself at the gateway to the house. It was a Pratyekabuddha,[1] who, with the fire of wisdom, had entirely burned up the fuel of depravity and now wanted to add to the merchant's store of merit. [4] There he stood, calm and confident, gentle but firm, looking at the ground a couple of yards in front of him.[2] With sweet serenity he clasped his alms bowl in his lotus-like fingers. 4·7

Now Māra, the evil one, could not bear the Bodhisattva giving alms and, to stop him, conjured up a bottomless hell between the doorstep and the venerable monk. It measured the length of many men and looked fearsome. Flames flickered in its gaping center, and the noise of it was terrifying. Hundreds of writhing bodies were piled up inside.

On seeing the Pratyekabuddha who had come to beg alms, the Bodhisattva called to his wife: "My dear, go yourself and give the holy man a generous helping of food." She said she would, and set off with some delicious food and drink. But, on catching sight of the hell, she hastily turned away from the gateway, with fear and bewilderment in her flickering eyes. Her husband asked her what was the matter, but she was so panic-stricken that her throat constricted and she could hardly tell him. The Bodhisattva was then so worried that the holy man might leave his house without receiving any alms that he paid no attention to what his wife was telling him and instead took the delicious food and drink himself, such was his eagerness to bestow alms on the noble monk.

As he came to the gateway he saw the terrifying hell between, and, while he was wondering what it could possibly be, Māra, the evil one, sprang from the wall of the house and, assuming by miraculous means the guise of a god, hovered in the air. Then, as though concerned for the Bodhisattva's well-being, he said: "Master merchant, this is the great hell called Mahāraurava.[3] [5] It is the home of those who, in their perverted generosity, are seduced by the flattery of beggars and gladly give up their possessions. They spend many thousands of years here, and escape is not easy. [6] Material wealth is the prerequisite for pursuing the three objects of life.[4] Do away with wealth and how can you avoid doing away with virtue too? And if by squandering wealth you preclude virtue, hell is surely where you belong. [7] Your passion for giving has led you into sin: you have squandered your wealth and thereby struck at the root of virtue. As a result, this hell, like the jaws

4 · 8 of Death, with its tongue of flame, has sprung up to devour you. [8] So please put a stop to this generosity. That way you will avoid falling down this instant and sharing the fate of these almsgivers who writhe and groan piteously. [9] On the other hand, people who receive alms renounce the vicious habit of giving and are on the way to becoming gods. So stop obstructing the path to heaven with your zeal for giving, and practice some restraint instead."

The Bodhisattva realized that this was obviously an attempt on the part of the Evil One to thwart him in his almsgiving. He was too courageous to flinch, nor did he waver in politeness or charm, but spoke firmly to Māra: [10] "In your concern for my good you have considerately shown me the proper path to take. How very fitting that deities should express their compassion for others by taking appropriate action. [11] But while it is right to try and cure an illness before it declares itself, or immediately it does so, once a disease has made progress, owing to a wrong regimen, it is futile to apply remedies. [12] This generosity I suffer from has, I fear, gone beyond the reach of medicine. For, despite your concern for my good, my heart will never shrink from charity. [13] And, as for what you said about wickedness being the outcome of generosity and about wealth being the prerequisite of virtue, my weak human intellect cannot grasp how wealth without generosity can be called the path to virtue. [14] Does wealth produce virtue when it is hoarded away, or when thieves lay violent hands on it, or when it sinks to the bottom of the sea, or when it serves as fuel for a fire? [15] And what you said about the donor going to hell and the recipient going to heaven, so far from restraining me, has made me more eager to give. [16] May your words come true and may my petitioners reach heaven. For I enjoy giving because of the good it does others, not as a means toward bringing about my own happiness."

Again Māra, the evil one, persisted in addressing the Bodhisattva, as though for his own good: [17] "Decide for yourself whether what I have said is sound advice or nonsense. Then take whichever course you like. In happiness or in remorse you will have reason to remember me with respect."

"My dear friend," replied the Bodhisattva, "you must excuse me. [18] I would rather fall into this raging hellfire and have the flames lick my lolling head than ignominiously reject the opportunity of doing favors for those petitioners whose requests are an act of friendship."

With these words the Bodhisattva, knowing the strength of his luck and certain that generosity was no sin, shook off his family and retainers, who were intent on restraining him. His desire to give alms was greater than ever as he proceeded imperturbably through the hell. [19] Then, by the power of his merit, a lotus sprang up before him. It was not rooted in mud like other lotuses and, with its bright row of petals, seemed to be baring its teeth in a contemptuous grin at Māra.[5] This lotus, which had been produced as a result of the Bodhisattva's exceptional merit, served him as a stepping-stone to reach the Pratyekabuddha. Gladness and joy filled the Bodhisattva's heart as he gave the Pratyekabuddha alms. [20] And to show his pleasure, the monk flew up into the sky, where he shone with the splendor of a cloud, blazing and coruscating with the glitter of lightning. [21] Māra's brightness, however, grew dim with despair, as his hopes lay shattered. He could not bear to look the Bodhisattva in the face and disappeared forthwith, together with the hell.

What, then, has this exemplified? That good men discount personal risk in their readiness to give. How can anyone in comfortable circumstances refuse to do so?

5 *Aviṣahya the Merchant*

GOOD PEOPLE DO NOT CURTAIL THEIR generosity either when they notice their money dwindling or in the hope of building up a fortune.

According to tradition, the Lord, while still a Bodhisattva, was once a merchant who had a host of good qualities: generosity, decency, good breeding, self-discipline, religious learning, wisdom, humility, and so on. He was like Kubera,[1] so rich was he, and his hospitality to all comers resulted in a ceaseless flow of gifts and alms. He was a model of generosity, devoting himself entirely to the good of others. And, as neither selfishness nor any other vice could corrupt him, he was known to all as Aviṣahya, the Incorruptible. [1] The moment he and his petitioners set eyes on each other both parties were overjoyed, since mutual satisfaction was a certainty. [2] He could not say no to the earnest demands on his generosity: great compassion had ousted from his heart all attachment to material things. [3] When beggars emptied his house of its valuables he was absolutely delighted, for he well knew that possessions, being such a formidable and massive liability, can cause a sudden, inexplicable feeling of aversion. [4] Riches make most people greedy, and so are like caravans lurching down the road to perdition. But his were riches in the true sense, since they brought happiness to others as well as to himself.

The Great Being gladdened the beggarfolk for miles around, not merely because he bestowed wealth without stint and always according to need but because he did so with such good grace.

Reports of his bounty reached Śakra, lord of the gods, and filled him with amazement. He wanted to test the Bodhisattva's strength of purpose, and so every day he saw to it that whatever money, grain, jewels, and clothing had been collected should disappear, thinking that the merchant might perhaps be alarmed to see his property drain away, and that this would induce him to think a selfish thought. Yet the Great Being remained as devoted as ever to giving things away. [5] As his goods vanished, like drops of water under the sun's assault, so, in his munificence, did he bring more from his house, just as though it were on fire. Śakra's amazement grew when he realized that the merchant was quite set on giving things away even while the best part of his fortune was disappearing.

One night he made Aviṣahya's entire stock of belongings disappear, except for a coil of rope and a sickle. When the Bodhisattva woke as usual, at dawn, he saw neither money nor grain, neither clothing nor even attendants—not one of his belongings. The house stood empty, in desolate silence. It might have been ransacked by demons, it looked so bleak. Wondering what this could mean, he made a round of the house; but all he could find was the coil of rope and the sickle. It occurred to him that someone unused to begging, who lived by his daring, had perhaps favored his home with a visit. If so, his wealth had found a good use. On the other hand, it would be a pity if someone resentful of his great prosperity had pointlessly hidden away his fortune. [6] He already knew that wealth is a fickle friend, but that the needy should suffer on that account was torture to him. [7] How would they feel when they came to his house and found it empty—they who had long been used to being treated with gifts and hospitality? They would be like thirsty men coming to a pool that had dried up. Even so, relying on his own strength of character, the Bodhisattva did not taste the bitterness of despair. Nor could he bring himself, even in his present plight, to appeal to others for help—not even to people he knew—for the role of beggar was alien to him. Indeed, realizing now just how hard it is to beg, he felt all the more sorry for those who were forced to do so. He was anxious still to welcome and be of help to the beggarfolk, and so, taking

5 · 8 the coil of rope and sickle, the Great One went out every day and cut grass. And with the tiny sums he earned by selling it, he attended to the needs of beggars.

When Śakra, lord of the gods, saw how resilient the Great One was and how, even in extreme poverty, his thoughts were only of giving, he felt respect as well as amazement. Nevertheless, he revealed himself in his celestial, supernatural form, hovering in the air, and addressed these words to the Great Being, to dissuade him from being so generous: "Master merchant, [8] neither kings nor thieves nor fire nor water[2] have deprived you of your fortune: it is your own excessive generosity that has reduced you to this state which is a cause for anxiety to your friends. [9] Therefore it is with your own good in view that I tell you to curb this disastrous passion for giving. Even in your present state you could still regain your former opulence were you to stop giving. [10] Constant expenditure, however modest, eventually exhausts one's earnings, just as constant heaping builds up anthills—from which you may conclude that if one wants to get rich the only way is to practice restraint."

In replying to Śakra, the Bodhisattva showed the magnanimity inherent in his habitual generosity: [11] "God of the thousand eyes, any decent person finds it extremely difficult to do something base, even when in dire straits. I would rather have no money, if I have to be a miser to get it. [12] When poor men fall back on something as soul destroying as beggary to escape their woes, can anyone with pretensions to nobility dash their hopes with a refusal, like a bolt from the blue? [13] How could someone like myself possibly accept a jewel, or money, or even the rulership of heaven and not use it to gladden beggars' faces that are pale with the strain of begging? [14] Any possession that increases the sin of selfishness or does nothing to confirm one's wish to renounce what one has is nothing but a drawback in disguise and is itself to be renounced by such as myself. [15] Riches are as fickle as the flicker of forked lightning. They are a prey to all comers and cause endless tribulation, while gifts are a source of happiness. How, then, can any decent person choose to be selfish? [16] I am touched by the concern you show for me in giving this advice, Śakra, but, after getting such constant delight from giving things away, how could I be happy if I altered my ways? [17] But my lord, do not let this incline you to anger: the hostile citadel presented by my natural disposition needs a not inconsiderable force to scale it!"

"Master merchant," answered Śakra, "you behave as though you were a man of means whose treasury and granary are piled high, whose various important affairs are making successful progress, whose future is assured, and who has imposed his authority on others. But that is not the case with you. Now look: [18] you ought to choose an honest trade. Either follow your own bent or take up some respectable employment in the family tradition. This way you will make a fortune and, like the sun, surpass all rivals in brilliance. [19] Make a point of displaying humility toward people, bring joy to your friends and relations; then, when you have won respect from the king himself and when Fortune seems to embrace you like a loving woman, [20] any impulse you may have to give things away or to enjoy yourself will cause no comment. But a ruined man wanting to be generous is rather like a nestling wanting to soar into the sky. [21] So, then, acquire a fortune by exercising self-control and modesty—and, in the meantime, enough of this urge to give. Besides, how can your failure to give be termed meanness when you have nothing to give?"

"My lord, you insist too much," said the Bodhisattva. [22] "Even someone who finds his own affairs more important than other people's ought to give, without regard to his means. For, however great his wealth, the pleasure he gets from it cannot compare with the satisfaction of overcoming his own miserliness by giving things away. [23] Mere wealth will not get you to heaven, while generosity will at least earn you a reputation for goodness. Since money prevents one from overcoming selfishness and other such faults, who can refuse to be generous? [24] But he who is compelled by pity to dedicate himself to looking after all creatures, even those in the grip of old age and death, he who knows not the savor of happiness because of other people's unhappiness—what could he possibly want even with your divine splendor? Moreover, [25] the enjoyment of wealth is as uncertain as the duration of life. Therefore, when one receives a beggar one should not give a thought to one's means. [26] If one carriage makes a track on the ground, the next one travels along it that much more surely, and so does the one after. Consequently I have no desire to abandon the good road I have set out on and to take to a bad one instead. [27] And should I ever recoup my fortune, I will certainly use it to bring joy to the hearts of beggars. But, even as things stand now, I shall give as much as I can, and, my lord Śakra, may I never neglect my vow of charity."

The lord of the gods was completely won over by what the Great One said; he applauded him and, with a look of respect and affection, said: [28] "There is no cruelty, no baseness to which people will not stoop in pursuit of gain, even though it harm their good name. They are so concerned for their own well-being that they are heedless of danger and are led astray by their silly ideas. [29] You, however, are quite oblivious to your lost fortune and blighted happiness as well as to my own inveiglements. By concentrating on the furtherance of other people's affairs you have shown how great your own attainments are. [30] Your heart radiates an exceptional nobility. Oh how free it is of all taint of selfishness, such that, even when your riches have vanished, it does not alter and become less generous in the hopes of retrieving them. [31] Yet it is not surprising that you, who suffer at the suffering of others, you, who by force of pity seek to better the world, should no more be shaken in your bounty by me than a snow-white mountain be shaken by the wind. [32] I have hidden your possessions so as to bring you even greater glory by putting you to the test. It is just the same with a gem, which, however beautiful it may be, only becomes famous as a jewel of great value by means of assay. [33] And so, shower gifts on beggars like a huge cloud filling up ponds. By my favor your riches will never fail. And please forgive the way I have behaved."

With these words of approval, Śakra restored the Great

One's large fortune to him, begged his pardon, and disappeared there and then. 5 · 33

So, then—good people do not curtail their generosity either when they notice their money dwindling or in the hope of building up a fortune.

6 *The Hare*

EVEN WHEN BORN AS ANIMALS THE noble-hearted show a bent for generosity, as far as they are able. What excuse, then, can a human being have for not being generous?

There was a certain wild region where hermits used to live. Trees, shrubs, and grasses grew there in lovely profusion with masses of fruit and flowers, and at the forest edge flowed a beautiful river with clear water of an aquamarine blue. The ground was covered with soft turf, pleasant underfoot and a delight to the eye. Here, according to tradition, the Bodhisattva was once born as a hare. [1] Because he was courageous, handsome, extremely strong, and full of energy, the dangerous animals did not give him a thought and he lived there without fear, like the king of beasts. [2] With his own pelt serving as the hermit's goatskin shawl and with his fur doing duty for the loincloth of bark, he was like a hermit himself, content to live off tufts of grass. [3] His every thought, word, and deed was so transparently kind that animals who were openly vicious generally behaved as gently as disciples.

He had three companions—an otter, a jackal, and a monkey—who were specially devoted to him and full of love and respect for his exceptional qualities. They lived together on terms of intimacy, like relatives bound by mutual affection, like friends whose friendship has grown by respecting one another's needs. Contrary to animal nature, they showed pity to living things. They had mastered greed, and so never thought of stealing. They lived a blameless life, in harmony with nature, and, being keenly intelligent, behaved with the punctilious courtesy and the moderation expected of respectable people. All this was a source of wonder even to the gods. [4] To opt for the side of good when faced with a choice between pleasant-but-wrong and unpleasant-but-right earns even a man some distinction, not to speak of a being in animal form. [5] Of the three, the one in the form of a hare was their teacher. He was accomplished and also showed great compassion for others. His fine character was so richly endowed with a whole gamut of virtues that their fame reached even as far as heaven.

One evening the friends came to hear the Teaching and were respectfully sitting at the feet of the Great One. The moon had risen and was almost full. Because of its distance from the sun it shone brightly, like a silver mirror without a handle. And since part of the rim was slightly eclipsed, the Bodhisattva realized it must be the fourteenth night of the bright half of the month, and said to his companions: [6] "Look! the moon is waxing full and seems to wear a smile on its shining face, as it announces the holy fast day[1] to all good men. Tomorrow must be the fifteenth. So be sure you carry out the fast-day rule of not seeing to your own sustenance without first presenting choice food, obtained in the prescribed manner, to any guest who chances to arrive. For you realize: [7] all attachments end in parting, high attainments in rude downfall. Life hangs by a thread and is as transient as a flicker of lightning. Therefore you should constantly be on the alert [8] and at the same time make every effort to increase your store of merit by being generous and crowning your generosity with a good character. For merit is the main prop for creatures struggling on their hard journey from one birth to another. [9] That the moon in its loveliness outshines the host of stars, that the sun in its splendor eclipses all the lights of heaven, is due to the intensity of their good qualities. [10] It is by force of merit that monarchs make their haughty ministers and vassal kings submit to the yoke of their authority like docile horses, all pride abated and almost with gladness. [11] Ill fortune dogs those who are without merit, despite their worldly wise[2] maneuvering, for, finding it intolerable to be rebuffed by those who are rich in merit, she courts those who are set against it. [12] So shun the path of demerit with its inherent misery and inevitable disgrace and concentrate instead on opportunities for acquiring merit: they are a splendid way of procuring happiness."

The others readily accepted his advice, saluted him with respect, walked round him in reverence, and went off each to his own home.

Before his companions had gone far it occurred to the Great One: [13] suppose a guest were to arrive; the others could somehow receive him with due honor, but he himself was in a lamentable position—[14] he could not possibly offer his guest blades of grass which he had nibbled off with his own teeth; besides they tasted terribly bitter. How utterly helpless he was! [15] Such pathetic inadequacy made life seem pointless to him. A guest, who should be a source of joy, would only cause him anguish. How, then, might he be of use to someone by ridding himself of this puny body which, in its inability to attend to the needs of a guest, was of no use?

At this point in his deliberations the Great One collected his wits. Of course, [16] he had the very thing with which to regale a guest adequately. It was ready to hand, there was nothing the matter with it, and it certainly was his, namely, his own body. Why then despair? [17] He had found something suitable to offer a guest and so could banish wretched despair from his heart. With this paltry body of his he would satisfy the needs of any guest as they arose.

On reaching this conclusion the Great Being felt supremely happy, as though he had made a great gain. And he remained where he was.

[18] The marvelous idea that had blossomed in his heart revealed to the celestial beings both his kindness and his strength. [19] The earth and the mountains shook with delight, so it seemed, and earth's garment, the ocean, grew restless. The sound of heavenly drums pervaded the air, and the sky gloried in a pellucid brightness. [20] All around, dazzling clouds, wreathed with lightning, rumbled continuously but softly, smothering him with a thick shower of flowers whose pollen was shaken out as they collided. [21] The wind blew

steadily and lifted the fragrant pollen off the various flowering trees in such a way that it seemed to be joyfully honoring him with veils of muslin, whose patterns became distorted as they billowed out. On all sides the deities were talking of the Great One's wonderful idea in delighted amazement, and when Śakra, their lord, came to hear of it, surprise and curiosity got the better of him, and he wanted to find out what sort of a being this was. 6 · 25

Next day, at noon—when the sun reaches its apogee and the heat of its rays is at its fiercest, when the sky is swathed in a web of shimmering light and the glaring heat acts as a veil to prevent one seeing it, when shadows in the forest shrink and the lisp of cicadas sounds louder, when birds cease to flit about and wayfarers become weary and enervated in the heat—then Śakra, lord of the gods, in the guise of a brahmin, pretended he had lost his way and burst out with a loud lament in the pathetic tones of one who was overcome with hunger, thirst, exhaustion, and despair. He uttered these cries not very far from where the four animals lived: [22] "I have lost touch with my traveling companions and am alone and astray in this deep forest. Will some kind person please rescue me. I am weak with hunger and exhaustion. [23] I cannot tell the right path from the wrong, have lost all sense of direction, and am walking at random, alone in this wilderness. Will anyone comfort me with some reassuring words?—I who am faint with heat and thirst."

The sound of this pitiable call for help shook those Great Beings to the core. Anxiously they made for the spot as fast as they could, and, catching sight of someone with the woebegone look of a traveler who had lost his way, they went up, gave him a polite welcome, and consoled him, saying: [24] "Do not fret any more about being lost in the wilderness; in our company you will feel just as though you were among your own group of disciples. [25] Today at least, dear sir, do us the favor of accepting our hospitality. Tomorrow you may go as you please."

Taking his silence to imply that he accepted the invitation,

6 · 26 the otter hurried off in a flurry of excitement and returned with seven carp. He explained as he offered them: [26] "I found these seven fish on dry land, looking as though they had fallen asleep in sheer exhaustion. Either some fishermen carelessly left them there or they leapt out of the water in fright. Eat them and spend the night here."

Then the jackal too fetched such food as lay ready to hand, made the traveler a bow, and respectfully said: [27] "Here, I have got a lizard and a bowl of sour milk which someone has left behind. Take them to please me, and make this forest your home, you who are a home for good qualities." So saying, he handed the food to the traveler and felt extremely pleased.

Next, the monkey brought some mangoes. Their perfect ripeness could be judged by their soft texture, by their deep orange color (as though they had been dyed in realgar), by the base of their stalks being deep red, and by their roundness. Putting his hands together in salutation, the monkey said: [28] "Ripe mangoes, delicious water, and shade as refreshing as the pleasure of good company—these I have to offer, most worthy brahmin. Enjoy them and spend the night here."

Finally the hare came forward, greeted the traveler politely, and, looking at him with respect, invited him to accept his own body: [29][3] "A hare who has grown up in the forest has no beans, no sesamum, no rice to offer. But cook this body of mine and eat it. Then stay overnight in this hermitage. [30] On the happy occasion when a guest arrives and is in need, everyone provides something from his store to satisfy the guest's wants. I possess nothing but my body. So please accept this my entire belongings." To this Śakra replied: [31] "How could I, a brahmin, possibly kill another creature, let alone someone like you, who has shown me such friendliness?" "That, coming from a brahmin imbued with compassion, is as it should be," said the hare. "But at least, sir, do me the favor of staying here while I find some way of doing myself a favor as well."

Śakra, lord of the gods, guessed what was in his mind and conjured up a heap of live coals the color of refined gold.

Tongues of flame darted out, a mass of sparks scattered wide, and there was no smoke. The hare, who was looking around everywhere, caught sight of this fiery mass and delightedly said to Śakra: "Here is how I can do myself a favor. Please fulfil my hopes of doing so by consuming my body. For you must realize, great brahmin, [32] giving is a duty, and my heart is set on it. A guest such as you is worthy of such a thing, and an opportunity like this is not easily come by. I count on you. So do not disappoint me." With this entreaty the Great One pressed his hospitality upon Śakra, so anxious was he to do him honor. [33] Then he looked at the blazing fire as eagerly as a beggar would stare at a pile of treasure, and suddenly threw himself onto it in an ecstasy, like a solitary goose alighting on a lake of bright lotuses. The sight filled Śakra with utter astonishment. He resumed his own shape and expressed his admiration for the Great One first with a shower of flowers from heaven, then with words that delighted both heart and hearing. Then he took him in his hands, lovely as pink lotuses and adorned with beautiful rings, and showed him to the gods. "Behold, you gods who dwell in heaven, and rejoice at the remarkable exploit of this Great Being. [34] See how he has just now unselfishly sacrificed his body out of kindness to a guest, while irresolute people cannot even throw away a faded garland without dithering over it. [35] How incongruous with his animal state is this noble self-sacrifice and keen intelligence! It is an open reproof to all those who show little enthusiasm for acquiring merit, be they gods or men. [36] Oh how his mind must be steeped in the habit of virtue, how devoted to goodness he shows himself to be in acting so nobly."

Śakra then wished to proclaim this extraordinary deed, with a view to the good of all creatures, and so, both at Vaijayanta, his royal palace, and at Sudharmā, the gods' assembly hall, he adorned the finials over the upper apartments with the image of a hare. And he had it painted on the moon too. [37] To this day the hare's image shines in the sky when the moon is full, like a reflection in a silver mirror. [38] Ever since then the moon, which opens the white lilies and is the mark

6 · 38 on the forehead of Night, has been popularly known as "hare marked."[4]

And the otter, the jackal, and the monkey—they left this world and reached heaven, thanks to their good friend.

So, then—even when born as animals, the noble hearted show a bent for generosity, as far as they are able. What excuse, then, can a human being have for not being generous?

Agastya

7

GENEROSITY ON A HEROIC SCALE IS a fine thing even in an ascetic, let alone in a layman.

According to tradition, the Lord, while still a Bodhisattva, traveling the round of birth and rebirth for the good of the world, at one time graced a certain eminent brahmin family who, in their outstanding integrity, were like an auspicious mark on the face of the earth. He was like the full moon in autumn, rising clear in the sky. First he underwent the series of purificatory rites prescribed by scripture and tradition, beginning with the birth ceremony. Then he studied the Vedas and the ancillary works, including all the texts on ritual. His reputation for learning spread throughout the world, and, with the wealth he received by approaching charitable people who were lovers of virtue, he came into a vast fortune. [1] Like a huge cloud showering rain over the land, he used his wealth to bring happiness to any of his friends, relatives, or dependents who were in distress, as well as to his guests and teachers whose position demanded it. [2] This munificence brought an added luster to his fame for learning, just as the moon is even more beautiful when it shines with full luminosity in the clear nights of autumn.

But the Great One found that there was little to relish in worldly life and that it leaves one dissatisfied. It brings one into close contact with all kinds of vile practices, and that does great harm. It makes one uncaring, and the preoccupation with getting and keeping money is troublesome. It is the target of hundreds of arrows, each one of them a misfortune that precludes peace of mind. And it wears one out, since it involves one in endless activity.

On the other hand, he could see that renunciation brought

about a happiness that was quite free from these evils and favored the pursuit of things spiritual and that it was the basis for undertaking that discipline which leads to final release. So he rid himself of his fortune, great as it was, which he had acquired without trouble and which gave him the pleasure of other people's respect, just as though it were a wisp of straw. And he became absorbed in the discipline and restraint demanded by the life of an ascetic and mendicant. Yet, even when the Great Being had renounced the world, people seeking spiritual bliss would still come to him, partly because of his wide repute, partly because they cherished the memory of previous intimacy, partly because they admired his virtues, and also because of his remarkable composure. Such was the attraction of his multiple virtues. But he did not value the company of these worldly people: it ruined the peace of solitude and prevented him from ridding himself of attachments. Because he cherished solitude he retired to the island of Kārā, which lies in the middle of the Southern Ocean. Its shores are lapped by shimmering surf, the waves, tossed by a strong wind, being deep blue in color like slivers of sapphire. The ground there is strewn with white sand, all kinds of trees adorn it with their branches decked with fruits and flowers and buds, and inshore lies a clear lake. By settling there he added a hermitage to the island's charms.

[3] His austerities there made him thin, but he radiated such energy that he did not look it—like the crescent moon in the sky, slender yet, by reason of its loveliness, perfect. [4] There he lived in the forest, his sole delight being to keep his vows. His gentle manner and subdued senses were a sign of his inner calm. Even the birds and beasts, with their limited mental powers, realized he was a holy man and followed his ways.

The Noble One was so used to being generous that even living as a hermit he would receive any chance guest with such fruit and edible roots as he had to hand, with fresh water, a heartfelt welcome, and the usual blessings of an ascetic. Whatever was left of the forest fare after the guests had eaten, he ate himself, but only enough to keep alive on.

As a result of his extreme austerity his fame spread abroad, 7 · 7
and even Śakra, lord of the gods, was fascinated and wanted to test the Great Being's perseverance. So he gradually eliminated from that wild spot every single edible root and fruit that could serve as food for an ascetic. But the Bodhisattva was absorbed in meditation and in the habit of feeling content. He was free from attachments and indifferent about food and his body, and so he did not trouble about why the fruit and edible roots should have disappeared. He boiled some fresh leaves, and these served as a meal. He felt no pangs, no longing for better food, but continued as happy as ever: [5] those whose needs are modest never have difficulty in finding sustenance: there are always leaves, grass, and a pond somewhere.

The Bodhisattva's staying power amazed Śakra even more and confirmed the high opinion he had formed of his virtues. But to test him still further he stripped the trees, shrubs, and grasses in the jungle of every single leaf, as does a scorching wind in summer—whereupon the Bodhisattva gathered the freshest of the fallen leaves, boiled them, and lived off them without complaint. Wrapped in the bliss of meditation, he lived there as though he feasted on ambrosia: [6] modesty in the learned, contentment in the hermit, unselfishness in the rich—these are the crowning virtues of each.

At the Bodhisattva's amazing, imperturbable contentment Śakra grew more astonished still. In indignation almost, he appeared before him in the guise of a brahmin, pretending to be a guest. This was just when the Great Being, at the time prescribed by his vow, had poured a libation on the fire, completed his prayers, and was scanning the horizon in the hope of seeing a guest. The Bodhisattva, in delight, went up to him, gave him a friendly greeting, informed him that it was time for a meal, and invited him to partake. Concluding from the brahmin's silence that he accepted the invitation, the Noble One's [7] face lit up, and his eyes opened wide with delight at the thought of giving. He welcomed the brahmin with affectionate words that pleased both heart and hearing, and he gave him all the boiled leaves that he had gathered so pains-

7 · 8 takingly, while he himself was satisfied simply with the pleasure this caused him. Just as always, he went into the hut where he meditated, and he passed that day and night in joy and gladness.

On the following day, and again on the third, Śakra appeared before him in the same way, at the moment when the Noble One observed his vow of hospitality. And the Bodhisattva in turn received him with the same respect and with even greater joy: [8] the habit of compassion makes a good man increasingly generous; he does not retract meanly even when in desperate difficulties.

By now Śakra was overwhelmed with utter amazement. He realized that the Bodhisattva's extraordinary asceticism was such that the sovereignty of heaven was his for the asking. This made Śakra fearful and uneasy. So, reassuming his divine shape of marvelous beauty, he questioned the Bodhisattva about his motive for doing penance: [9] "What have you pinned your hopes on, that you have forsaken your dear family who weep for you, your household and your possessions which were a source of happiness, and now dedicate yourself to a life of hardship and austerity? [10] After all, no man in his senses would reject pleasures that can be had without effort, desert his grief-stricken relatives, and retire to a forest hermitage which precludes all comforts, without some serious reason. [11] If you feel you can tell me, then please satisfy my curiosity. What is it that could so bewitch even your mind with the call of virtue?"

"Sir, let me tell you the reason behind my efforts," replied the Bodhisattva. [12] "Endless rebirth is a great affliction, and so are old age, death, and the various forms of illness. Thoughts of mortality disturb the mind. So I have resolved to save the world from these things."

Śakra felt relieved that this man had no designs on his sovereignty, and his fine words inclined him to feel well disposed. "Quite right," he said, with approval, then asked what favor he could bestow on the Bodhisattva: [13] "Holy anchorite, these words of yours are fine and fitting. I grant you a wish. So choose what you like."

The pleasures of life meant nothing to the Bodhisattva. Even having to ask for something seemed to him irksome, as he was naturally content. [14] "If you want to do me the kindness of granting me a wish," he said to Śakra, "then this is the favor I beg from the foremost of the gods: [15] the fire of greed—which can leave the overheated imagination still unsatisfied even when one has got a wife after one's own heart, children, power, and riches vaster than one had dreamed of—may it never enter my heart."

The Bodhisattva's predisposition to contentment, evinced by his fine words, pleased Śakra all the more. Again he commended him highly and urged him to make another wish. [16] "Holy man, since what you have just said is again fine and fitting, I gladly offer you another favor, as a gift in return."

Then, to show how difficult it is to rid oneself entirely of defects, the Bodhisattva again taught him the Law, though ostensibly asking a favor: [17] "If you are going to grant me a wish, Śakra—you in whom all good qualities reside—then I beg this second favor, and it is no mean one. O lord of the gods: [18] the fire of hatred—which overwhelms people like an enemy, so that they suffer loss of money, purity of caste, and the happiness of a good name—may it keep far away from me."

On hearing this, Śakra was overcome with admiration. "Excellent! excellent!" he said, respectfully congratulating him. [19] "How right that Fame, like a loving woman, should attend those who have renounced the world. So accept a favor from me for yet another fine saying."

In the guise of accepting his offer the Bodhisattva expressed his aversion to human defects by condemning any contact with people who suffered from them. [20] "May I never have to hear, see, or speak to a fool or endure the misery and oppression of having to stay with one. This is the favor I beg of you."

[21] "Surely anyone in distress is especially deserving of a good man's sympathy," said Śakra. "Now, because it is the root of all evil, stupidity is regarded as the worst affliction, [22] and it is the fool who has a particular claim on your sympa-

thy. How is it that someone as compassionate as you does not even want to set eyes on such a one?"

"Because there is no help for him," replied the Bodhisattva. "Look sir, [23] if a fool could somehow be cured, how could anyone like me fail to make every effort on his behalf? But you must understand that such a case will not benefit from treatment. [24] He does the wrong thing as though it were the right, and he wants to coerce his neighbor into it too. Politeness and decency are alien to him. So he gets angry even when someone speaks to him for his own good. [25] In the all-consuming illusion of his self-conceit he is truculent and ill-tempered even with well-wishers. He is lax about exercising self-control and behaves impetuously. Tell me, how can one help such a person? [26] Since not even the compassionate have power to help a worthless fool, O best among the gods, I have no wish even to set eyes on one."

"Excellent! excellent!" said Śakra, applauding what he heard. Well pleased with these wise words, he continued: [27] "Pearls of wisdom have no price, I know. But, like a token offering of flowers, I gladly grant you a wish in return for them."

The Bodhisattva, to show how good people are a delight in all circumstances, said to Śakra: [28] "I would like to see a wise man, listen to him, stay with him, talk with him. Grant me this wish, O greatest among the gods."

"You certainly seem to be a great partisan of the wise," said Śakra. "So tell me now, [29] what have the wise done for you, holy sage? Say why it is that you show this slightly absurd eagerness to see a wise man."

To demonstrate the nobility of good men, the Bodhisattva said: "Sir, hear why I have conceived this desire to see a wise man. It is because [30] he follows the path of virtue himself and also guides others that way. He is not impatient of good advice, unpleasant though it may be. [31] Being so conspicuously sincere and modest, he is always open to good advice. That is why my heart, which inclines toward virtue, goes out to him who does likewise."

"Excellent! That is absolutely right," said Śakra with ap-

proval, and, feeling more kindly disposed than ever, he invited the Bodhisattva to make another wish. [32] "Since you are the quintessence of contentment, everything must be perfect for you. But consider it as a kindness to me, and please make a wish: [33] a favor that is offered in the hopes that it will be of help, that is tendered with devotion, and that stretches one's resources to the utmost, causes great unhappiness if not accepted."

The Bodhisattva saw how much Śakra wished to be of service, and so, with the intention of pleasing and edifying him simultaneously, he displayed the full force of his own desire to give. [34] "Your ambrosial food, which is faultless and never failing, your tender heart, which delights in being generous, your beggars who are patently genuine—may all these be mine. That is the wish I would like fulfilled."

"You really are a fount of eloquence," said Śakra. [35] "Not only will everything be just as you ask, but I shall give you yet another wish in return for these fine words."

[36] "Greatest of all the gods," said the Bodhisattva, "if you are going to grant me a wish that will be of assistance to me, then do not come near me again blazing like this. Such is the wish I beg from the destroyer of the demons."

At this Śakra was completely taken aback and replied in apparent indignation: "Do not say that! [37] People here on earth say prayers, make vows and offerings, and endure austerities just to get a glimpse of me. Now why should you have no such desire? I am here only because I want to grant you a wish."

"Please, no more of this show of anger," replied the Bodhisattva. "I humbly entreat your lordship: what I said was not meant to be rude or to show disrespect or to imply lack of devotion to your highness. But [38] when I set eyes on your extraordinary, superhuman form, serenely beautiful yet blazing with fiery energy, I am afraid the sight of you, however mild and gentle, might distract me from my austerities."

Then Śakra bowed, walked around him with reverence, and disappeared then and there. At daybreak the Bodhisattva espied a great quantity of food and drink, brought from

7 · 39 heaven by Śakra, and many hundreds of Pratyekabuddhas[1] who had been summoned at Śakra's behest, as well as a host of godlings, tightly girded and ready to serve. [39] The holy man was sublimely happy to be able to entertain those great sages to a meal with the food and drink provided, while he himself was content with the subsistence proper to an ascetic and, likewise, with the restraint necessary to achieve the successive stages of meditative trance and the four cardinal virtues.[2]

So, then—generosity on a heroic scale is a fine thing even in an ascetic, let alone in a layman.

8 *Maitrībala*

THE TRULY COMPASSIONATE ARE SO upset by the hardships of others that they give no thought to their own well-being.

According to tradition, the Bodhisattva, in the nobility of his soul, was steeped in compassion and so determined to save mankind that he was forever surpassing himself in generosity, self-control, restraint, gentleness, and all the other superior qualities needed to achieve good in the world. It was then that he is said to have been a king, called Maitrībala, who was kindhearted toward all creatures. [1] In sorrow or in joy the king was at one with his subjects, and from this came his skill at governing both by political means and by the sword. [2] His sword, however, was merely decorative, since even kings received his commands with bowed heads, while his political acumen was apparent in the prudent measures he took for promoting the welfare of his subjects. [3] He dealt out rewards and punishments impartially, and in his benevolence and political skill he was to his subjects like an attentive father.

While ruling his people with such fairness, he promoted the welfare of others through being truthful, generous, calm, and wise. Every day he added to those sublime deeds that are the essential prerequisite for attaining enlightenment.

One day five ogres visited his realm. Kubera[1] their master had banished them from his kingdom for some offence. These ogres sapped people of their vital strength and were expert murderers as well. They soon saw that the country was free from any sort of trouble and was extremely prosperous and that, in consequence, its people were happy, contented, and thriving, always with some festival or other in progress.

This only spurred them on to drain the population of its vigor. [4] Yet, though they exerted themselves to the utmost in their task, they failed to weaken the people who lived in the king's realm. [5] His power was so extraordinary that the mere thought that one possessed it oneself was the best possible protection. And so it was that the ogres were unable to sap the people's vigor.

When, even after one last effort, they quite failed to debilitate a single inhabitant of that country, they looked at one another and said: "Friends, what can this possibly mean? [6] It is not as if they had some special knowledge or spiritual reserves that give them supernatural power capable of counteracting our might. Yet here we all are, no longer able to live up to our name."

Thereupon the ogres turned themselves into brahmins, and as they walked along together they caught sight of a cowherd who lived in the forest. He was sitting on the grass under a shady tree and was wearing sandals and a garland woven of sprigs and blossoms from the trees of the forest. He was by himself and had laid his crook and hatchet down on his right. As he pored over a rope he was twisting, he sang with noisy abandon.

The ogres went up to him as he sat there, and said: "Cowherd! hey there! How comes it you're not afraid, roaming this forest all by yourself, meeting no one, cut off from the world?" He looked up at them and said: "What's there to be afraid of?" The ogres replied: "Have you never heard before of the frightful habits of ogres, goblins, and imps? [7] Even if he had others for company and was fortified with spells, spiritual powers, and charms, a man would find it hard to escape those goblins who feed on human flesh and fat. Bravery and contempt for fear would not be enough. [8] So how is it that you aren't afraid of them, all by yourself in these deep woods, remote and eery?"

The cowherd burst out laughing at what they said, and answered: [9] "The people of this country are protected by a powerful talisman. Even the chief of the gods can do nothing to them, let alone cannibals. [10] And so I roam this forest, day

and night alike, as though I were in my own home, all alone, yet as secure as if I were somewhere crowded with people."

The ogres were full of curiosity and tried to draw him out by speaking in deferential tones: "Sir, do please tell us what sort of special talisman this is of yours."

Again the cowherd laughed, and said: "Well, just listen to what sort of a marvel this special talisman of ours is. [11] His breast is as broad as a crag on Mount Meru.[2] His face is as lovely as the clear moon in autumn. His arms are long and brawny and look like bars of gold. He moves and looks just like a bull. Such is our king. And such is our special talisman." Then, looking at the ogres with surprise, he indignantly added: "But how extraordinary—[12] when our king's prowess is so far-famed, how comes it that news of it hasn't reached your ears? Or perhaps you have heard about it but discounted it as too extraordinary, and so it has left no impression. [13] I expect the people in your country are averse to the pursuit of virtue or simply do not care about it. Or else the king's renown will have escaped them because the stock of good fortune has run out where you have come from. But you must still have some good luck left, seeing that you have left such a savage land and come here."

"Gentle sir," replied the ogres, "tell us what kind of power this king has, such that demons can do no harm to the people who live in his realm."

"Our king's power comes to him as a result of his noble nature," answered the cowherd. "You see, my worthy brahmins, [14] his power rests on kindness: his army with its motley pennants is a mere matter of form. Anger is unknown to him. He cannot utter a harsh word. He rules his country properly. The Law he follows is good policy, not deceitful statecraft. His wealth is at the service of all good men. And, paragon that he is, he neither appropriates bad people's money nor succumbs to pride: such are the countless qualities with which our lord is endowed. That is why nothing untoward can affect the people who live in his realm. But I can tell you only a little. If you want to hear about the king's merits you'd best go to the capital itself. There you will see people content

with their lot and so keeping within the bounds of propriety; happy and prosperous in the assurance of continued security and abundant provisions; beautifully but not showily dressed; and extremely kind to visitors and guests. They are so captivated by the king's goodness that they take delight in rehearsing hymns that redound to his glory, as though chanting some magic formula or charm. The sight of these people will give you some idea of the scale of the king's goodness. The great regard for his merits will be so much in evidence that you will want to see him and witness his goodness yourselves."

The ogres, who could not bear the way the king resisted their power, were by no means softened by this eulogy, well-deserved though it was, and spoken with affection:

[15] A fool's fuming anger is fanned to a blaze
When the object of his fury wins any praise.

Aware of the king's generous leanings and bent on his undoing, the ogres approached him at the time he gave audience, and begged a meal. The king was delighted, and ordered his stewards to be quick and give the brahmins a sumptuous meal. The meal was brought. It was fit for a king. But the ogres refused it, as tigers would refuse green grass. "This isn't the sort of food we eat," they said. At this the king went up to them and asked: "Then what sort of food would you like, so that it can be fetched?" To which the ogres replied: [16] "Human flesh, dripping blood, warm and fresh. That is what ogres have for meat and drink, O lotus-eyed monarch who would never go back on his word." Thereupon they resumed their own distorted, terrifying features—mouths with gaping fangs, bloodshot eyes asquint and blazing fiercely, noses flat and misshapen with flared nostrils, red hair and beards flaming like tongues of fire, complexions dark as storm clouds.

At the sight of them the king realized the truth: they were demons, not men, and that was why they did not like the food and drink he had offered them. [17] In the pureness of his heart,

the king, who was compassionate by nature, felt even greater compassion for them. He felt nothing but pity as he bewailed the plight of the ogres. And, inexorably, he reasoned as follows: [18] "For a sensitive person to procure such food and drink would be no light matter, and he would have to go in search of it day after day. Think of the utter misery it would cause him. [19] A hard-hearted person may fail in his attempt to get it and so merely feel frustrated. But suppose he did succeed; what would be more pernicious than habitually committing such a crime? [20] These evil-hearted ogres, devoid of pity, craving for this kind of food, and destroying their own best interests both in this world and the next—will they ever reach the end of their misery? How, then, could I procure them the right food, if only for a day, and so obviate their need to injure others? [21] I do not remember ever having disappointed any of those who have come to me with a request—and so to have banished the gleam of hope from their faces, making them look as woebegone as lotuses withered by the winter wind. But wait! I have it! [22] From my own body I shall give them some thick, solid lumps of flesh, dripping with blood. What else could I do that would answer the needs of those who have come to me for help? [23] For the flesh of those who have died a natural death is bloodless and no longer warm and certainly won't please these ogres, whose ravenous hunger shows in their physical suffering. In the first place, how can I take flesh from another living being? And, second, how can these creatures who have come to me, hollow eyed and sunken cheeked with hunger and thirst, go away like this, feeling even more frustrated because the hopes they had formed have proved barren? So this is the moment to act. [24] Like a malignant ulcer, this body is a constant nuisance and source of pain. I shall now put it to extraordinary use and make some return in kind that will give me ample satisfaction."

His eyes and face brightened in an access of joy at having come to this decision, and, pointing to his body, the king said to the ogres: [25] "If this flesh and blood, which I maintain

purely for the good of the world, were now to be of use in giving hospitality, it would be a positive gain to me, and I would consider myself most fortunate."

The ogres realized what the king had in mind, but found it so extraordinary that they were incredulous. Even so, they replied: [26] "Once the petitioner has betrayed his own wretched state by sinking to beggary, then it is up to the donor to judge the fitting response."

The king took this to mean that they accepted his offer, and he was overjoyed. He summoned his doctors to carry out the bloodletting. But when his ministers learned of his decision to donate his own flesh and blood, they were puzzled, indignant, and alarmed. Affection demanded that they speak out clearly, somewhat as follows: "Your highness, you should not let your passion for generosity make you heedless of the consequences for good or evil to your devoted subjects. Nor can your honor be unaware of the fact that [27] demons take pleasure in whatever causes harm to your subjects. They batten upon other people's discomfiture with glee. Such is the way of their kind, O monarch without fault. [28] Your majesty bears the onus of kingship with no thought for your own pleasure, purely for the benefit of your people, but your decision to give away your own flesh deviates from this main purpose. So abandon it. [29] There is no doubt that these ogres can do nothing to your people as long as they are under your powerful protection. Now that their capacity to do harm has been brought to naught, they are plotting ill for your subjects by underhand means. [30] Offerings of fat, marrow, and suchlike, poured onto the fire at sacrifices, are perfectly acceptable to the gods. Yet, the refined delicacies carefully prepared for your majesty are apparently not to the taste of these ogres. Though your highness has ideas that cannot be conceived by the likes of us, nevertheless, concern for our own affairs compels us in this case to depart from our usual polite acquiescence. Can it really be in the line of duty for your majesty to plunge the whole country into chaos for the sake of these five? Besides, how can you have so little faith in us as to offer your own flesh and blood when our own, though hitherto

kept in reserve, are at the service of your highness, and still intact?"

The king then replied to his ministers: [31] "If someone plainly asks for something, how can anyone such as I say 'I haven't got it' when I have—or shamefully reply 'I will not give it'? [32] As your leader in matters of duty and morality, suppose I were to take the wrong course: what would become of my subjects, who would follow my example? [33] So it is precisely with my subjects in view that I am about to extract some good out of my body. If I were fainthearted and allowed selfish considerations to sway me, would I still have the power to do good to my people? And as to your asking how I could have so little faith in you as to be ready to give my own flesh and blood when yours are still intact—words instinct with love and respect for me and full of personal feeling—let me try and convince you on this point: nothing has happened to stem my feeling of affection toward you. It is not that I am no longer sure of you and so am fencing myself off behind a barrier of mistrust. But [34] while it would be right to make one's needs known among friends if one's wealth had gradually dwindled or, by the will of fate, vanished altogether, it would not do for a prosperous man to apply to the needy. [35] My body is big and bulky and well fed. It exists entirely for the sake of the needy. To appeal to you would be monstrous. [36] I cannot bear it even when strangers suffer, so imagine how I would feel if you did. Therefore I wish to give my own flesh. Besides, it is me they are asking, not you. So enough of this bold attempt to prevent me doing my duty, though I know it springs from deep devotion. Your attitude toward my petitioners is quite wrong. Just consider: [37] is it or is it not proper to restrain someone who wants to give food or whatever for his own good—and especially in a case such as this? Please do not insist any further. Think the matter over sensibly, and that should put a stop to wild thoughts and make them more consonant with your office as counselors. Indeed, a few words of approval from your lordships would be more in place than these anxious looks. 'Why?' you ask, [38] 'don't people come every day begging money for this or that?' Yes, but how often will you come across someone with a request like this even if you are in the gods' favor? [39] Here they are. This is what they want. And since my body is perishable anyway and a source of misery, the slightest hesitation in the matter would be base. To suffer from selfishness is to live in the depths of delusion. So, gentlemen, please do not obstruct me."

With this speech the king convinced the assembled courtiers. He then summoned his doctors and had five veins in his body opened, saying to the ogres: [40] "Gentlemen, please do me the greatest favor and assist in this act of piety by accepting this gift." They agreed and, cupping their hands, began to drink the king's dark blood, which was as red as sandal water. [41] As those night fiends lapped the king's blood, his body shone like gold—like Mount Meru swathed in louring rain clouds, tinged with twilight. [42] The king was so overjoyed, so courageous, so resilient, that his body did not succumb and he did not lose consciousness. Nor did the flow of blood diminish.

When they had quenched their thirst and refreshed themselves, the ogres told the king: "That's enough." [43] And now that his body, that ever ungrateful object which harbored endless ills, had served to show proper regard for the needy, the king felt nothing but joy at their having made use of it. With mounting delight his eyes and face brightened. He then took a sharp sword whose blade was blue and speckless as a lotus petal and whose lovely hilt glittered with bright jewels. With it he sliced off one piece of flesh after another and offered them to the ogres. [44] The joy of giving constantly distracted his mind from dwelling on the pain of the sword cuts. [45] The agony brought on by each stroke of the sharp sword was each time suppressed by his joy and so was slow to register in his mind, as though exhausted by the effort of doing so. [46] As he fed the pieces of his own flesh to those night fiends, he felt pure joy, and it was noticeable how, as a result, even the ogres' cruel hearts softened. [47] He who, through love of virtue or by force of pity, is moved to sacrifice his own dear body for the sake of others can resuscitate an answering tenderness in hearts that have been seared by the fire of hatred.

When the ogres saw the king intent on cutting off his own flesh, not flinching at the pain and even preserving a look of untroubled serenity, they were deeply moved and full of wonder. [48] "How extraordinary! What a marvel! Can it really be true?" they wondered, with mixed feelings of delight and surmise. Then, stifling all hostility toward the king and proclaiming their mood of devotion by singing his praises and bowing before him, they said: "That is enough, your majesty. Stop torturing your body with such zeal. We are fully satisfied with your marvelous response, which is enough to delight any beggar." Hurriedly prostrating themselves, they restrained the king, and, gazing up at him with respect, their faces wet with tears of tender devotion, they continued: [49] "How right that out of love people should grow loquacious in your praise. How right that Fortune should disdain her bed of lotuses[3] and proudly associate herself with you. Indeed, were heaven to look down upon this land, safeguarded by your might, and not grow envious, despite Śakra's protectorship, alas, it would certainly be deceiving itself. Need we say more? Mankind is fortunate indeed to have such a one as its guardian, while we are disconsolate at being party to your torments. Still, in the hope that we may put an end to our evil practices and that, by resorting to someone like you, we may, even in our condition, succeed in saving our souls, we ask you, [50] In taking this course, without regard for your royal rank that was so easily come by and so much enjoyed, what extraordinary position do you hope to attain? [51] Is it to be king of the universe that you submit to this harsh penance, or do you want to become a Kubera[4] or Indra[5] or to be absorbed into Brahma and achieve final release? [52] With your determination, no wish is beyond fulfilment. If we are permitted to hear, please tell us, sir."

"Listen to the reason for my efforts," answered the king. [53] "High rank depends on circumstances. It can only be achieved with effort and is effortlessly lost. It is not conducive to contentment or happiness, even less to peace of mind. So I have no desire for royal rank even in heaven, let alone elsewhere. [54] Nor can I find satisfaction in merely ridding myself of life's ills. I am concerned for those helpless creatures who are sick of nagging cares and bitter woes. [55] Through this good deed may I reach enlightenment, may I vanquish the host of evils, and so deliver all living creatures from the ocean of existence with its billowing waves of old age, sickness, and death."

The ogres thrilled with intense emotion as they prostrated themselves and said to the king: "What you have just done is entirely in keeping with your extraordinary resolution. So we venture to predict with some certainty that whatever a person of your caliber might wish will soon come about. [56] Of course all your efforts are directed toward the good of the world at large. But when the time comes, have a special care for our well-being: please, do not forget us. [57] And forgive us for having thus, in our ignorance, caused your lordship torment—blind even to our own interests. [58] Meanwhile, could you please, as a mark of favor, give us some command, but without reserve, as you would to your ministers."

The king realized that their hearts had melted with devotion, and said to them: "On the contrary, you did me a service: it was no torment. So no more of this misplaced anxiety about it. Besides, [59] the path of virtue being what it is, how could I forget, when I attain enlightenment, those who helped me along it? You will be the first to whom I impart the teaching on liberation, the first to get a share of that ambrosia. [60] And if you wish to please me, then you will avoid, like poison: harming life, coveting your neighbor's wife or possessions, wicked talk, and the evils of drunkenness." [6]

The ogres promised to do so, bowed, respectfully circled around him, and disappeared then and there. But at the very same moment that the Great Being had resolved to give his flesh and blood, [61] the earth shook repeatedly and made Mount Meru sway. The tremor made the drums upon it resound, and the trees shed their flowers. [62] These the wind tossed up into the sky so that at first they looked like a cloud, then like a squadron of birds, from one angle like a vast canopy and from another, as they spread out, like a woven garland. Then, all together, they scattered around the king. [63] The ocean heaved and swirled as though it were trying to ward off the monarch of the earth. It looked majestic in its onrush, its waters making more stir and noise than usual.

[64] Perplexed at first as to what this could mean, Śakra then discovered the reason and rushed to the palace in dread that the king might have died. There everyone was overwhelmed with grief and foreboding—[65] except for the king, who, despite the state he was in, looked serene. In utter astonishment Śakra went up to him and, with joy and deep feeling, praised his action in pleasing tones: [66] "This is the very acme of noble bearing, the highest ideal of virtue in practice. How tenderhearted you are in your kindness to others. Entrusted to you, the earth is certainly in good keeping."

After commending him in this way, Śakra, lord of the gods, put an end to the king's suffering and restored his body to its former state by applying special herbs, some known to men, others supernatural, which had the power to heal wounds immediately. The king then courteously returned the compliment, showing due deference and polite attention. Then Śakra returned to his abode.

So, then—the truly compassionate are so upset by the hardships of others that they give no thought to their own well-being.

9 *Viśvaṃtara*

THOSE WHO ARE MEAN OF HEART scarcely even approve of the way a Bodhisattva acts, let alone follow his example.

According to tradition there was once a king of the Śibis[1] who was called Saṃjaya. Controlling his senses had become second nature to him, so that his vigorous enterprise, tempered by discretion and modesty, met with triumphant success. By paying strict attention to the elders, he had gained a thorough mastery of the Vedas and of logic, and his just rule showed in the way his devoted subjects were each content with his own lot and were used to a carefree and happy life: under him the various trades and professions flourished.[2] [1] Like a virtuous woman, Royal Fortune kept faith with him because of his great qualities, while to other kings she remained as unimaginable as a lion's guarded den is to other beasts. [2] Those who devoted their efforts to a life of austerity or to the arts and sciences would visit his court, and they had only to show their worth to be sure of earning his particular esteem and respect.

The king had a son called Viśvaṃtara who was heir apparent and next to him in rank, though his equal in the number of good qualities he displayed. [3] Though young still, the prince had the pleasing serenity of the old; though spirited, he was naturally forbearing; though learned, he was innocent of intellectual pride; though living in state, there was no trace of arrogance in him. [4] His fame spread far and wide in every direction until it pervaded all three spheres. There was no room for other people's trifling claims to fame: they hardly dared to put themselves forward.

[5] Viśvaṃtara could not bear that distress should hold

proud sway over his people, and he engaged it, in all the fury of battle, with a shower of arrows in the form of gifts from his broad bow of compassion. Every day he delighted the gathering of petitioners by giving them more even than they asked for, stinting nothing and adding to their pleasure by talking kindly and showing them attention. At the end of each week, exemplary in observing both the duties and the calm of the holy day, he would wash and perfume his head, put on a fresh linen garment, and mount the royal elephant, a superb tusker, famous as a must-elephant and remarkable for its speed and energy, its docility, and the auspicious marks on its body, which, in size and color, was like a peak in the Himalaya. When in rut, streams of ichor patterned its face.[3] 9 · 8

Viśvaṃtara would ride this elephant to inspect his alms halls which were situated all over the city and had become places of refuge for the needy. This gave him immense pleasure, since [6] money that lies idle at home gives far less satisfaction to a generous person than does that which is consigned to the needy.

One day a neighboring king heard about Viśvaṃtara's passion for charity from successful petitioners, who in their joy were spreading the news far and wide. He concluded that, by playing upon this addiction of Viśvaṃtara's, it would be possible to outwit him. Accordingly, he dispatched some brahmins to carry off that prize elephant.

Viśvaṃtara was inspecting his alms halls, the pleasure of it showing in his visibly brightening features, when these brahmins came and stood before him, right hands raised and outstretched, loudly hailing him with cries of "Victory!" He reined in his elephant, exchanged polite formalities, and then enquired what might be the purpose of their visit, adding that he was theirs to command. To this the brahmins answered: [7] "The qualities of this elephant, which moves with such grace and dignity, together with your own munificence, have transformed us into beggars: [8] present us with this elephant, which resembles the peak of Kailāsa,[4] and, in so doing, completely astound the universe."

The Bodhisattva's heart filled with joy at what they said,

9 · 9 and he thought: "At long last I have some petitioners who are prepared to make a serious demand. And yet, what can these brahmins want with a lordly elephant such as this? Obviously this is some miserable ploy concocted by a king who is eaten up with greed and envy. [9] Very well, then, since he seems bent on doing me good, regardless of his own reputation and moral duty, let him not suffer disappointment."

On reaching this decision the Noble One promptly dismounted and, standing before them with a golden pitcher raised aloft,[5] begged them to accept the elephant. [10] Though he knew that for reasons of state one had to stray from the path of goodness in pursuit of one's own advantage, he nonetheless gave away that magnificent elephant, so attached was he to doing good. Base considerations of expediency could not sway him. [11] The prince felt utterly happy about giving away that noble elephant, adorned with its bright trappings of gold which looked like forked lightning against an autumn cloud mass. The city, however, preferred the path of prudence and was upset.

In fact, the Śibis were furious when they heard that their best elephant had been given away. The brahmin elders, the ministers, military leaders, and prominent citizens created a terrible fuss and went to see King Saṃjaya. So incensed were they and so indignant, that they threw politeness and tact to the winds, saying: "Your highness, you are not going to turn a blind eye to this seizure of the Royal Mascot? Your highness must surely realize that in so doing you would increase the chances of disaster overtaking the realm?"

When the king, in alarm, asked them what they were talking about, they answered: "What, your highness does not know? [12] That elephant whose face is aswarm with humming bees and whom the breeze, fragrant with its ichor, is wont to caress, easily and effortlessly freeing itself from all traces of the ichor of other proud elephants, [13] that elephant whose vigor cows the valor of enemy armies, casting a spell of sleep upon their pride,—that elephant, our mascot, has been presented to our neighbors by Viśvaṃtara and is at this moment being led away. [14] Cows, gold, food, and clothing are suitable presents for brahmins, your majesty, but to give away this superb elephant who assures us of victory—that really is taking generosity too far. [15] How can Royal Fortune be expected to attend someone so aloof from practical considerations? This is not a matter your majesty can overlook: before long he will be giving your enemies cause for joy."

The king loved his son, and hearing this made him feel less than friendly toward these spokesmen. But out of duty he feigned alarm and said: "Yes, yes of course." Then he tried to appease the Śibis: "I know Viśvaṃtara is passionately addicted to giving things away, regardless of considerations of state, and, for someone entrusted with the responsibility of ruling, this is not how to behave. But now that he has disposed of his own elephant as though it were his vomit, who is going to reclaim it? Anyway, I myself will see to it that in future Viśvaṃtara recognizes some limit to what he can give away. So please stop being angry." "Your highness," replied the Śibis, "you certainly won't convince Viśvaṃtara on this matter simply by administering a reprimand." "Well, what else can I do?" asked Saṃjaya. [16] "He will have nothing to do with anything evil. His sole vice is his addiction to doing good. Would I be making amends for this elephant by putting my own son in prison, by executing him? So, calm yourselves. I shall restrain Viśvaṃtara."

But the Śibis had been roused to anger, and they said to the king: [17] "Sire, nobody is asking for your son to be executed or to suffer imprisonment. But, being so religious, so tenderhearted, and so compassionate, he will not bear the strain of having to rule. [18] The throne is for those who have earned a name for themselves by showing enterprise and who are able to cultivate all three of the objects of life—goodness, happiness, and prosperity.[6] Viśvaṃtara's exclusive devotion to goodness makes him heedless of practical good sense. He ought to go and live in a hermitage. [19] When kings mishandle affairs, it is their subjects who suffer the consequences. The subjects, as you know, manage to survive—but not so the kings, whose authority is then undermined. [20] But why all this talk? We Śibis cannot connive at your ruin, and have

9 · 21 decided that the prince had best cultivate his spiritual leaning by going to Mount Vaṅka, a favorite resort of holy adepts."

The people could foresee the disastrous consequences of Viśvaṃtara's indiscretion, and it was purely out of affection and a feeling of intimacy, as well as concern for the king's own good, that they spoke to him in such brutal terms. But the king was embarrassed by his subjects' angry reaction, and bowed his head. The thought of being parted from his son overwhelmed him and, heaving a sigh of distress, he said to the Śibis: "If you insist on it, gentlemen, then at least allow him twenty-four hours' grace. Tomorrow at daybreak Viśvaṃtara will comply with your wish." The Śibis agreed to this humble request, and the king asked his chamberlain to inform Viśvaṃtara of what had taken place.

With tears of grief streaming down his face, the chamberlain obediently went to Viśvaṃtara, who was in his palace, and fell at his feet, weeping loudly under the stress of emotion and grief. "Is everything alright at court?" asked Viśvaṃtara anxiously. The chamberlain broke down and indistinctly blurted out: "Yes, all is well at court." "Then why are you in such a state?" asked Viśvaṃtara. The chamberlain was choking with tears, but between sobs and heavy sighs he managed slowly, syllable by syllable, to gasp out the following: [21] "The Śibis have rudely disregarded the king's wishes, though couched in the mildest terms, and in their anger have had you banished from the realm, my lord." "Me . . . the Śibis . . . have banished . . . in their anger. What does this mean?" asked Viśvaṃtara. [22] "I have never taken pleasure in flouting morality, and I loathe any sort of laxity. What crime have I committed unawares to make the Śibis angry with me?" "You have been overgenerous," replied the chamberlain. [23] "Your pleasure was unclouded by selfish thoughts, but the delight those beggars felt was thoroughly selfish. When you gave that noble elephant away, your honor, the Śibis lost their temper, [24] and, breaking all bounds, have vented their anger on you. Now you will have to follow the path of exile."

Then the Bodhisattva showed both his tender love toward beggars, which sprang from deep-rooted compassion, and his extraordinary composure, by saying: "The Śibis are, of course, fickle by nature, and, it would appear, ignorant of my true character. [25] Quite apart from outward possessions, I would give away my own eyes, my head—it is purely for the good of the world that I keep my body alive. As to clothes or beasts of burden, that goes without saying. [26] If a beggar demands it, I am ready to offer him my whole body. And they imagine that by intimidating me they can stop me giving. That shows how foolish and superficial they must be. [27] Let the entire nation come and banish me or put me to death; I shall never stop giving. Still, to the hermitage I will go."

Then the Bodhisattva said to his wife, who looked distraught at the unpleasant things she heard: "My lady, you have heard what the Śibis have decided?" "I have, my lord," replied Madrī. Viśvaṃtara continued: [28] "Then, my flawless beauty, put away your money—whatever you may have got from me, as well as your own patrimony." "But, my lord, where am I to put it?" asked Madrī. [29] "I mean, always give generously to people of integrity," answered Viśvaṃtara, "and do so with good grace. Money so given is a lasting treasure and cannot be taken from you. [30] Be kind to your mother- and father-in-law and look after our children. Behave properly, take care, and do not grieve at my absence."

Though in her heart she felt anguish at what she heard, she did not want to make her husband falter. So, regardless of her grief and misery, she said: [31] "It is not right, your majesty, that you should go to the forest alone. Wherever you go, my lord, I shall follow. [32] I would happily die, so long as I can remain at your side. To live without you would be a fate worse than death. Nor does life in the forest seem to me such a hardship, my lord. For [33] there are no nasty people there. The rivers and trees are untouched. The air echoes with all sorts of birdsong. There are deer everywhere and lovely grass, as green as a pavement of beryl. In fact forest retreats are more delightful than our own pleasure gardens. Besides, my lord, [34] when you see our two children decked out and crowned with garlands, playing in the wild thickets, you will forget about being king. [35] The forest's ever-changing beauty, carefully contrived by each successive season, and its watery river brakes will delight you. [36] The varied music of the birds' mating cries, the peacocks' dances, whose steps are taught them by that learned dancing master Passion, [37] and the hum of bees whose charm never grows stale—this woodland concert will delight your heart. [38] The rock faces at night, veiled with gauzy moonlight, the caressing forest breeze, scented by flowering trees, [39] the soft murmur of river water tumbling over loose pebbles like the clash of women's jewelery—all this will gladden your heart in the forest."

His wife's entreaty made him eager to set out for the forest. But he did not forget the needy, and first made ready to bestow great largesse.

Meanwhile, as news of Viśvaṃtara's banishment reached the royal palace, a confused sound of wailing arose, and the beggar folk were so overcome with grief and sorrow that they almost fell into a swoon or else acted as if they were raving mad, pouring out laments such as: [40] "Mother Earth must have lost her senses to let the hatchets fell this shady tree that gives sweet fruit, and yet feel no shame. [41] If there is no one to prevent those who want to destroy that well of cool, pure, sweet water, then the Guardians of the World are misnamed, or absent abroad, or nothing but hearsay. [42] Injustice is surely awake and Justice asleep or perhaps dead when Prince Viśvaṃtara is thrown out of his kingdom. [43] Who has such a sharp appetite for wrong that he can be so savagely intent on liquidating us who innocently scrape a pittance by begging?"

Thereupon the Bodhisattva presented his entire fortune to the beggars, giving to each according to his deserts—first, the contents of his treasury, which was packed with gold, silver, and precious gems amounting to many hundreds of thousands, then money and grain of various kinds which were piled up in the vaults and granaries, then menservants and women servants, carriages, draft animals, clothes, personal belongings, and so on. After that he prostrated himself at the feet of his parents, whose composure had given way to overpowering grief and sorrow. Then, with his wife and children, he mounted his royal carriage. From the huge crowd came the sound of lamentation, like a sad farewell, as he left the capital. He had difficulty in turning back the crowd, who followed him out of affection, their faces streaming with tears of grief. Taking hold of the reins himself, he set out along the road to Mount Vaṅka. Calmly he passed the outskirts of the city, encircled by beautiful parkland, and in due course came to open country where shady trees were few and far between and the population sparse. The horizon was clear all round, herds of deer were roaming at large, and the chirping of crickets filled the air. Then, out of the blue, appeared some brahmins who begged him for the horses that were drawing his carriage. [44] Delighted at being able to give something away and regardless of the consequences, he gave his four horses to the brahmins, even though he was on a journey of many miles, without companions and with a wife to look after.

Then, just as the Bodhisattva was tying his belt tighter, with the intention of himself taking the place of the carriage horses, four young sprites in the guise of red deer came up to the carriage and of their own accord put their shoulders to the yoke, just like well-schooled, docile horses. On seeing them, the Bodhisattva said to Madrī, who was wide-eyed with astonishment and delight: [45] "See what a powerful atmosphere there is in this forest, thanks to the hermits who grace it with their presence. Kindness to strangers has taken root even in these marvelous antelopes." [46] "I suspect this is due to your own superhuman powers," replied Madrī. "Goodness, however deep-rooted it may be, does not manifest itself alike in all circumstances. [47] When the beauty of stars reflected in water is outshone by luminous night lilies, the cause lies in the moon emitting its rays, as if in curiosity."

And so they talked affectionately to one another, in mutual harmony, as they traveled along the road. Then another brahmin approached, and begged the Bodhisattva for the royal carriage. [48] And since he was indifferent to his own comfort but a dear friend to any beggar, the Bodhisattva fulfilled the brahmin's wish. Gladly he helped his family out of the carriage, presented it to the brahmin, and, taking the boy Jālin on his hip, set off on foot, while Madrī, in no way down-hearted, took the girl Kṛṣṇājinā on her hip and followed behind.

[49] The trees seemed to invite him to feast on their delicious fruit by bending down the tips of their branches and, like humble disciples, bowed low at the sight of him because of his great merit. [50] Wherever he wanted a drink, ponds appeared, covered with orange pollen and filaments from lotuses shaken by the wings of geese. [51] Clouds provided a lovely canopy, soft and sweet blew the wind, and magic spirits shortened the road, finding it intolerable that he should suffer fatigue.

And so the Bodhisattva, with his wife and children, enjoyed the walk as much as a stroll in the royal park, without any of the weariness of tramping the road, and, on arriving there, he caught sight of Mount Vaṅka. A forester showed him the way, and he entered the sacred wood situated on that mountain. Here all sorts of beautiful trees grew in profusion, with a fine show of flowers, fruit, and sprays of foliage. The air echoed with the various cries of birds joyfully courting each other. A flock of peacocks added beauty to the scene by performing their dances, and numbers of deer roamed at large. The gentle wind was flecked red with pollen, and, around all this, like a girdle, flowed a river of pure, blue water. Here he settled in a solitary leaf hut constructed by Viśvakarman[7] himself on Śakra's orders. It looked delightful and was pleasant in all seasons. [52] For over half a year, attended by his dear wife, listening to the sweet, artless chatter of his children, and forgetting the cares of kingship, as though he were in the royal park, he practiced austerity in that forest.

One day, the princess had gone to gather fruit and edible roots and the prince was staying in the hermitage to keep an eye on the children, when a brahmin arrived. His feet and ankles were dirty with the dust of the road, his eyes were sunken, and his face was drawn with weariness. He carried a wooden stick over his shoulder, and from it hung a gourd. His wife had given him strict orders to find some servants. At the sight of a beggar approaching after such a long time, the

Bodhisattva felt so glad that his eyes and face grew bright. He went out to meet him, greeted him warmly, invited him into the hermitage, offered hospitality, and then asked the purpose of his visit. The brahmin was so devoted to his wife that he had banished all reserve or feeling of shame and was set solely on getting what he wanted. So he spoke bluntly, to this effect: [53] "People travel where the road is smooth and the visibility good, not by the dark and difficult path. But that and no other is the path my request must take, this world being for the most part wrapped in the dark of selfishness. [54] Your reputation for generosity on a heroic scale has spread, as it must do, everywhere. That is why I have taken upon myself this irksome task of begging. Please give me your children as servants."

The Bodhisattva, that Great Being, [55] for whom the pleasure of giving had become a habit and who had never learned how to refuse, gladly agreed to this request. "I shall even give you my two beloved children." "Bless you!" cried the brahmin. "Well then, what are you waiting for?"

At the mention of their being given away, the children grew desperate and their eyes swam with tears. The Bodhisattva felt a surge of affection in his heart and said: [56] "These two are yours—I have given them to you—but their mother is away in the forest gathering fruit and edible roots. She will be back this evening. [57] Let her see them once more decked out with garlands on their heads, and let her kiss them goodbye, while you rest here overnight. Then tomorrow you can go off with my children." "My good man, please don't insist on it," replied the brahmin. [58] " 'Perverse' is a common epithet for womankind, and she herself might object to this gift. So I have no wish to delay." "Don't worry about her possibly objecting to their being given away," said the Bodhisattva. "She is a true wife and helps me to fulfil my duties. However, do as you please, dear sir. Another thing though, your holiness, is that [59] these two are still at a tender age—mere children—with no experience of doing chores. Are they really going to give you any sort of satisfaction as servants? [60] Now if the king of Śibi, their grandfather, were to see them reduced to such cir-

9 · 61 cumstances, he would certainly ransom them at whatever price you name. [61] So do, please, take them to his realm. You will be doing a good deed as well as making a handsome fortune." "No," said the brahmin, "I cannot go to the king with such a hateful offer. It would be as dangerous as approaching a venomous snake. [62] He might snatch these two away from me or inflict some punishment on me. So I shall take them as servants for my brahmin wife." "In that case, so be it," replied the Bodhisattva, without saying any more. Gently he told the children how to behave as servants. Then he tipped the water pot over the brahmin's hand, stretched out to receive the gift.[8] [63] By an effort of his will, water fell from the water pot. Effortlessly it fell from his eyes, dark red as lotus petals.

The brahmin was so overjoyed at his success that he became quite distracted and, in his haste to carry off the Bodhisattva's children, gave only a cursory blessing. Then, ordering them in a harsh tone to get out, he began to drive the children out of the hermitage. But their hearts quailed in utter dismay at being separated, and they fell at their father's feet. With tears streaming from their eyes, they implored him: [64] "Daddy, you are ready to give us away while Mummy is out, but please don't until we have seen her once more."

Thinking that their mother would be back shortly or else that affection for his children would make their father repent, the brahmin tied their hands, like a bunch of lotuses, with a creeper. Threatening them as they struggled and turned around to look at their father, he dragged those sensitive children away.

Then Kṛṣṇājinā, the girl, broke into loud sobs at this her first experience of unhappiness and said to her father: [65] "Daddy, this cruel brahmin is hurting me with a creeper. Obviously he isn't a brahmin. Brahmins are supposed to be good. [66] It is an ogre disguised as a brahmin. I'm sure he's carrying us off to eat us. Daddy, how can you take no notice when we're being carried off by a goblin?"

Then Jālin, the boy, bewailing his mother, said: [67] "It isn't the brahmin hurting me that makes me unhappy but that I

haven't seen Mummy today. That really breaks my heart. [68] 9 · 77
Mummy is bound to cry for hours when she finds the hermitage empty. She will be miserable without her children, like a thrush when her chicks have been killed. [69] What will Mummy do when, after gathering lots of fruit and roots for us, she returns from the forest to find the hermitage empty? [70] Here, Daddy, are our toy horses and elephants and chariots. Give half of them to Mummy. They will stop her being sad. [71] Say goodbye to her for us and, at all events, keep her from feeling sad, even though we're hardly likely to see either of you ever again. [72] Come on, Kṛṣṇā, we may as well die. What's the point in our going on living now that Father has given us to a greedy brahmin?" With these words they departed.

Though shaken by his children's pathetic lament, the Bodhisattva asked himself how anyone could feel remorse after making a gift in such circumstances. But his heart was consumed by a burning grief that was not to be assuaged. He felt so greatly disturbed, it was as though he were being drugged by some powerful poison, and he sank down on the spot. The cool wind fanned him, and he regained consciousness. But when he noticed how still the hermitage was without the children, he said to himself, choking with sobs and tears: [73] "Oh, that shameless brahmin! How is it that he did not hesitate to strike quite openly at my heart, that is, my children? [74] How will they last out the journey, walking barefoot and, at their tender age, quite without stamina, now that they have become that man's servants? [75] Wayworn and weary, who will now give them rest? Whom can they go and appeal to, when overcome with hunger and thirst? [76] If I, who cultivate fortitude, am made to suffer like this, what sort of state can my two children be in, who were brought up in comfort? [77] Oh! it sears my heart to be deprived of my children, Yet, could anyone who knows where a good man's duty lies feel regret?"

Meanwhile, Madrī was growing nervous because of certain evil omens that seemed to forebode something unpleasant. Gathering up her fruit and roots, she wanted to return home as quickly as possible. But wild beasts barred her path, so it took her longer to reach the hermitage. When she didn't see her children either at the spot where they usually came out to meet her or in the places where they played, she grew even more anxious. [78] Sensing something amiss, she glanced around nervously for her children, and, when no answer came to her repeated calls, she felt so distraught that she began to wail aloud: [79] "The forest, echoing with the children's chatter, has always seemed such a lively place. But, now that they have vanished, it has turned into a forbidding wilderness. Could those two little ones possibly [80] have tired themselves out playing, felt drowsy, and fallen asleep? Or might they have got lost in the depths of the forest? Or are they hiding somewhere in childish pique at my being back so late? [81] But why aren't even the birds singing? Perhaps they have seen them come to grief and are too upset? Or could the strong current of the river have carried them off in the unbridled fury of its splashing waves? Oh, but may my suspicions prove vain and empty even so, and may all be well with the prince and the children. Or at least let these forebodings of evil take effect on my own person. But, then, why should I feel drained of joy for no apparent reason: why is my heart engulfed in dark distress and ready to split in twain? My legs seem to be giving way. I am losing my bearings, and the forest has grown dim and seems to be spinning around."

She then entered the hermitage, put away her fruit and roots, went up to her husband and, after greeting him respectfully, asked where the children were.

The Bodhisattva knew the tender affection in a mother's heart and found it hard to tell her the unpleasant news. So he could make no reply. [82] For, if one is sensitive, it is extremely hard to inflict pain on someone by telling him something unpleasant when he comes deserving to hear something pleasant.

From her husband's silence, which betrayed deep sorrow, Madrī realized that all was clearly not well with her children. Like one distracted, she scanned every corner of the hermitage, and, not seeing her children, she spoke again, her voice quavering with tears: [83] "I cannot see the children, and you do not say a word to me. I feel wretched and miserable: silence usually means bad news."

Delivering these words that came from a heart seared with sorrow, she collapsed like a creeper severed at the root. But the Bodhisattva caught her as she fell, carried her to a bed of grass, sprinkled cold water over her, and, when she recovered her senses, comforted her, saying: [84] "Madrī, I did not tell you the bad news immediately because one cannot expect endurance in a heart that is tender with affection. [85] A brahmin came to me. He was suffering from old age and poverty. I gave him both our children. Be brave! Do not lose heart. [86] Look to me, Madrī, not to the children. Do not lament, my lady. Do not strike at my heart, which is already pierced with grief for our children. [87] Were I asked to give my life, could I withhold it? So, my dear, try and accept my having made a gift of the children."

When Madrī, whose deepest fear had been that the children were dead, heard that they were still alive, her anguish abated. Not wanting her husband to falter, she dried her eyes and, looking up at him with wonder, said: "Astonishing! What else can I say? [88] Surely even the gods above must be amazed to see how selfishness has no sway over your heart— [89] which is why, in their eagerness to spread your fame, they have filled the heavens with a continuous but distinct flow of words, while, all around, the roll of celestial drums reverberates in every direction. [90] The Earth heaves her breasts, the great mountains, as though shivering in ecstasy. Flowers of gold fall from the heavens so that the sky seems ablaze with lightning. [91] So do not give way to sorrow. Be glad that you have made a gift. Be a refuge for all creation—and give yet again!"

When the earth shook, Meru, lord of mountains, radiant with the gleam of many different gems, itself felt a tremor, and Śakra, lord of the gods, wondered what this could mean. When he discovered from the World Protectors, who were wide-eyed in wonder, that the earthquake was caused by Viśvaṃtara's gift of his children, he felt giddy with wonder and

9 · 92 delight and, disguised as a brahmin with a favor to ask, went to Viśvaṃtara at daybreak. The Bodhisattva received him hospitably and then enquired what it was he wanted. Śakra then begged him for his wife. [92] "A good man's duty to give no more dries up than does water in a big lake. So I beg you for your wife who looks like a goddess: please give her to me."

The Bodhisattva, without at all losing his composure, agreed to do so. [93] Taking Madrī with his left hand and a water pot with his right,[8] he poured water over the brahmin's fingers but scorching fire on Māra's[9] soul. [94] Yet, Madrī was not angry, neither did she weep. For she knew his character. Suffering under this fresh burden of misery, she just stood, motionless as a picture, looking at him.

At the sight of this, Śakra was overcome with utter amazement and praised the Great Being, saying: [95] "Oh! what a gulf lies between the good and the bad in the way they behave. The spiritually ignorant could not even believe such an act possible. [96] Still to feel love, and yet to give away one's own dear wife and children like this, unselfishly—what true nobility! [97] When your fame spreads to every quarter, thanks to the reports of those who admire your virtue, it will certainly eclipse the renown of other men, however brilliant, as the blaze of the sun outshines all other lights. [98] Already this superhuman act of yours is being applauded by the whole hierarchy of heaven, including myself."

So saying, Śakra resumed his own brilliant appearance and, revealing his identity, said to the Bodhisattva: [99] "To you I now restore Madrī, your wife. For moonlight cannot exist without the moon. [100] Do not be anxious about being parted from your children, nor fret for your lost kingdom. Your father will arrive with them and will provide for the kingdom by providing it with you!"

With these words Śakra disappeared there and then. Thanks to him the brahmin brought the Bodhisattva's children to that very same kingdom of Śibi, and, when the Śibis and their king Saṃjaya heard about the Bodhisattva's extremely compassionate, immensely difficult deed, their hearts melted. They ransomed the children back from the brahmin, and, after making amends to Viśvaṃtara and recalling him from exile, they instated him as king. 9 · 100

So, then—the doings of a Bodhisattva are miraculous. Consequently one must neither despise nor hinder such exceptional beings as strive to attain that state.

10 *The Sacrifice*

THE PURE IN HEART CANNOT SUCCUMB to the enticements of evil. Try, therefore, to make your hearts pure.

According to tradition, the Bodhisattva was once the ruler of a country which came to him by hereditary succession. Ultimately this was due to his great store of merit. All his vassals were obedient, and, after quelling ills both in his immediate sphere and beyond, he ruled supreme, without foe or rival. [1] This ruler had also subdued those other enemies, his senses, and was not given to pleasures whose enjoyment grows stale. His whole being was pledged to the good of his people; his single purpose was to do right: he was like a holy man. [2] For he knew that people naturally aspire to imitate their superiors, and, as his devout wish was that his subjects should attain supreme bliss, he took special care to hold to his own moral duty. [3] He gave alms, preserved his integrity, cultivated forbearance, and strove for the good of the world. His kind manner showed how dedicated he was to his subjects' well-being—so much so that he seemed the embodiment of virtue.

And yet, despite the protection of his mighty arm, it happened that some parts of the realm were at one time afflicted with drought. This was due partly to the negligence of the rain spirits and partly to the bad karma of the population. The king was convinced that the calamity was caused either by himself[1] or by his subjects having failed in their proper duties. So deep-rooted was his desire for the good of his people that he could not endure their distress. For advice on how to remedy the situation, he therefore asked senior brahmins headed by his own household priest, all of them highly regarded for their profound knowledge of correct procedure. He also consulted his advisers.

They were of the opinion that a sacrifice, as prescribed in the Veda, would bring a good rainfall. Though the mass slaughter involved made it repugnant, this was what they recommended. But when the king heard that this sacrifice required the taking of life, his compassionate soul did not wholeheartedly welcome their advice. Out of politeness, though, he did not brusquely reject it but let the matter drop by changing the subject. But his council, unaware of the hidden depths of the king's character, seized the opportunity offered by this discussion about correct procedure, and advised him to go ahead with the sacrifice. [4] "You never lose an opportunity to fulfil the duties laid down for kings in the business of acquiring and safeguarding territory, nor do you neglect ethical considerations in fulfilling them. [5] How comes it, then, that you who are adept in the three pursuits of life[2] and are ready to take up arms in defense of your people seem to feel no enthusiasm for performing a sacrifice that some have called 'the bridge to heaven'? [6] Kings respect your wishes as do servants, seeing that they will certainly be fulfilled. You who seal the fate of your enemies, now is the time for you to add further to your illustrious reputation by making a sacrifice, [7] though it must be admitted that your generous propensities and scrupulous self-discipline keep you in a constant state of preparedness for making one. Even so, it would be fitting for you to discharge your debt to the gods by actually performing the sacrificial rites celebrated in the Vedas. [8] A good sacrifice pleases the gods, and they reciprocate by sending rain to all living things. So be pleased to perform a sacrifice that will benefit your people and bring you fame."

To the king these people seemed pathetically weak-minded and gullible, unquestioning in their faith and blindly devoted to tradition. He knew for a fact that [9] it is the very people who are considered pillars of society who instigate bloodshed in the name of religion. He pitied the man who followed the evil ways they suggested: that man would find

10 · 10 himself struggling in the grip of disaster. [10] What, he wondered, could animal slaughter have to do with religion? or with going to heaven? or with propitiating the gods? [11] The animal slaughtered to the accompaniment of magic incantations supposedly goes to heaven. That is the justification for killing it. People even maintain that it becomes holy as a result—but they are mistaken, since why should anyone be rewarded in the next world for what others have done? [12] Why should an animal who had neither curbed its tendency to do wrong nor resolved to do right go to heaven simply because it had been slaughtered at a sacrifice, without reference to its own actions? [13] And if, when slaughtered at a sacrifice, it did go to heaven, then surely the brahmins ought logically to offer themselves as sacrificial victims? But, as no one had ever witnessed such a proceeding, how could one possibly accept this advice of theirs? [14] Were the gods really going to give up their delicious nectar served by heavenly nymphs, with its incomparable flavour and aroma, as well as its magical invigorating properties, and take pleasure instead in some poor beast's slaughter so that they could taste its offal? No. The right course was clear to him now. The king then pretended he was eager to proceed with the sacrifice, and agreed to their proposal, saying: "How well you look after me, gentlemen. I am obliged to you for being so concerned for my well-being. Very well, I would like to have a human sacrifice performed, with a thousand victims. Each of my ministers, in his own department, must be instructed so that everything requisite for the occasion is assembled. A suitable site must be found for erecting the hall of sacrifice, and a moment chosen when everything—date, time of day, hour, and conjunction of moon and asterism—is favorable.

The household priest then advised him: "To succeed in your purpose, your highness should undergo the concluding purification already at the end of the first sacrifice. Then one can gradually proceed with the others. For, if all thousand of these victims were seized at once, it would certainly cause alarm among your subjects." The brahmins agreed, but the king replied: "Gentlemen, do not worry about my subjects getting upset. I shall arrange matters so as not to cause them alarm." The king then called a meeting of people from town and country and addressed them: "I have decided to make a sacrifice with one thousand victims. But I cannot coerce anyone who is innocent into becoming a victim against his will. So be it understood that from now on I shall be watching you through my spies, who are sharp-eyed, tireless, and alert. And whomever I catch breaking the bounds of morality in defiance of my royal command, I shall arrest as both a disgrace to his family and a public nuisance and designate as one of the scapegoats for this sacrifice."

Then the leading members of the audience stretched out their cupped hands in humility and said: [15] "Your majesty, everything you do tends to the good of your subjects. So what reason could we have to object? Brahmā himself would be bound to approve of what you are doing. Your highness, you are a model of goodness: you are our ideal. [16] Whatever pleases your majesty pleases us too, for you are pleased with nothing unless it gives us pleasure and profit as well."

Such was the reaction to the king's announcement from town and country alike. And so, with a great deal of noisy publicity, he despatched trusty agents to the towns and villages to arrest any miscreants, while every day he had this proclamation made throughout the land: [17] "The king has it in his power to grant safety and will do so to all people who continue to live an honest life. But those who are bent on mischief he intends to sacrifice, offering them as a hecatomb for the good of his people. [18] So from now on anyone who in wanton pride vaunts his disregard for the king's command, which even neighboring kings respect, will by his own actions necessarily become a victim for the sacrifice. His body will be tied to the stake, and he will languish in misery for all to see."

The inhabitants of the realm soon became aware of his diligent search for delinquents whom he could use for his sacrifice: every day they heard his terrifying proclamation, everywhere they saw the king's agents swooping down, intent on arresting malefactors. The result was that all inclination to misbehave left them, and instead they were all eager to vow themselves to a life of virtue. In their readiness to love and respect one another, they turned their backs on petty feuds. Quarrels and disputes ceased, and they abided by their elders' decisions. Sharing became commonplace, and hospitality too. They took pride in behaving with politeness and modest reserve. It was as though they were living in the Golden Age. [19] Fear of death made them take thought for the afterlife; family pride demanded that they guard their good name; an absolutely clear conscience gave them an increased sense of shame, and, as a result, their unsullied virtue was plain to see. [20] The more intent they became on doing right, the more closely did the king's watchmen search for anyone who might misbehave. The consequence was that no one lapsed at all.

[21] When the king heard what the situation was in his country, he was visibly delighted and, in return for the good news, rewarded his spies generously. Then he informed his ministers: [22] "My main aim is to look after my subjects. They now deserve to be rewarded for their virtue, and the money set aside for the sacrifice will be spent as I originally intended when suggesting it. [23] Let everyone receive at my hands as much money as he may want to kindle a sense of well-being. In this way we shall banish the poverty that now oppresses our realm. [24] If I think of my firm resolve to look after my subjects and of the powerful means for doing so that I possess in you my helpers, then anger stirs within me at my people's suffering and smoulders constantly in my heart."

The ministers eagerly took up the king's command and set up alms halls in every village, town, and market and at every rest house. Then, every day, they answered the needs of the poor by bestowing gifts, just as the king had instructed. [25] Poverty gradually disappeared as the people received wealth from the king. In their rich and colorful attire they looked as striking as though some festival were in progress. [26] Contented petitioners praised the king and swelled his fame so that it reached every corner of the earth, just as ripples on a lake spread lotus pollen wider and wider. [27] So it was that, thanks to the king adopting such wise measures, the entire population was bent on leading a good life. Mounting prosperity counteracted the dearth until it lost its hold and vanished altogether. [28] The seasons were delightfully regular, like new kings anxious to abide by the law. The earth bore all kinds of crops, and the lakes were full of clear, blue water covered with lotuses. [29] No virulent epidemics afflicted the people, and the virtues of medicinal herbs increased in strength. The wind always blew in due season, and the planets, circling in their orbits, were benign. [30] There was nothing to fear either from abroad or from each other or from natural causes. It was as though, under that king, the Golden Age had dawned for those gentle people, intent on virtue and restraint.

By performing the sacrifice without bloodshed, the king put an end to the miseries of the needy as well as to the drought. The country was full of contented people and had a pleasant look of prosperity. People never wearied of showering blessings on the king, and his fame spread everywhere.

One of the king's senior ministers, overcome with joy, said to him: "How true is the saying [31] 'Constant concern with all spheres of activity—high, low, and middling—makes a king's intelligence far superior to others.' For, by performing the sacrifice in harmony with the Law, without incurring the blame attached to animal slaughter, your highness has assured his subjects' welfare in this world and the next, has brought an end to the drought, and has put a stop to the miseries of poverty. In short, your subjects are supremely fortunate. [32] You do not have a black antelope skin draped over your body,[3] like a mark on the moon. Nor has your naturally graceful demeanor slackened under the restraints imposed by a state of ritual preparedness. The elegant arrangement of the hair on your head, which is shaped like a parasol,[4] has likewise lost nothing of its beauty.[5] And, by being so generous, you have stolen the pride (and the fame on which it depends) of Śakra himself—lord of the hecatomb. [33] Generally, when people make a sacrifice in hopes of being rewarded, it is a miserable affair involving harm to life. But you in your wisdom have made a sacrifice that is noteworthy and

10 · 34 all of a piece with your character, which is blameless and captivating. [34] Happy the subjects who have you to protect them! Certainly no father would take as good care of his own children."

Another said: [35] "When people have plenty of money, they are generous, in the hopes of getting some return. Likewise, they behave well with an eye to popular acclaim, or because they want to go to heaven. But to practice both virtues as you have, out of consideration for other people's needs, is something one only sees in those who are lacking neither in wisdom nor magnanimity."

So, then—the pure in heart cannot succumb to the enticements of evil. Try, therefore, to make your hearts pure.

Śakra

11

WHATEVER THE CIRCUMSTANCES—regal splendor or grave adversity—nothing can weaken the feeling of universal compassion in a noble heart.

According to tradition, when the Bodhisattva had for some time been assiduously practicing virtue and had made a habit of generosity, self-control, restraint, and pity—when he was devoting his remarkable energies to the good of others—he was at one time born as Śakra, lord of the gods. [1] Around him the aura of celestial majesty shone with greater luster and intensity, like moonlight shedding its rays on a palace freshly coated with stucco. [2] That majesty, for the sake of which the Daitya demons breasted the furious onslaught of the world elephants,[1] whose tusks are like clubs, allowed him to enjoy great good fortune but did not tarnish his heart with pride.

His just rule of heaven and earth earned him fame that spread throughout the universe. This and his extraordinary charisma were too much for the hosts of the Daityas, and they advanced with a huge army to do battle with him. Elephants, chariots, cavalry, and infantry were all the more terrifying in that they formed one proud array. The din they made was as fearsome as a raging sea, and the glare of their bright weaponry and armor made it hard to look at them. [3] Despite his scruples, everything inclined the Bodhisattva to engage in the frenzy of battle: the enemies' presumption; the fear people felt, which put an unpleasant curb on their amusements; his own dignity; and the course of action that prudence dictated. So the Great Being mounted his royal chariot of gold, which was harnessed to a thousand fine steeds. The bright flag hoisted above had a robed monk as its emblem, and the body of the chariot itself had a dazzling appearance—glinting with all kinds of jewels and precious gems and on either side gleaming with various weapons, bright and sharp, each separately laid out ready for use. It was lined with a blanket of white wool.

Surrounded by the various divisions of his huge heavenly host—elephants, cavalry, chariots, and infantry—Śakra went out to meet the demon army at the verge of the ocean. [4] There then took place a battle that shattered the nerve of the cowardly and in which armor splintered at the clash of weapon on weapon.

[5] "Stand your ground!" "Not that way!" "Here!" "Watch out!" "Now how are you going to escape me?" "Attack!" "That's the end of you!"—such were the cries as the combatants killed one another. [6] As the battle raged and as arms clashed in tumult, the air was rent with yells and the pounding of drums. [7] The elephants were roused to fury by the scent of ichor, and, as they attacked each other, they looked as terrifying as mountains stirred by the hurricane that blows at the end of an eon. [8] Everywhere chariots swept forward with a loud rumble as of portentous clouds, and their fluttering pennants were like streaks of lightning. [9] The warriors of both armies—gods and demons—showered each other with sharp arrows which hit banners, parasols, weapons, armor, and heads. [10] Finally Śakra's army took to flight in sheer terror, tormented by the demons' swords and arrows. Śakra alone stood his ground and held back the enemy army with his chariot. Mātali, Śakra's charioteer, saw the exultant demon army gleefully swarm forward with piercing screams and yells and battle cries, and he realized that his own army was intent only on escape. As it seemed the moment to retreat, he turned Śakra's chariot around.

As they flew up, Śakra noticed, in a silk-cotton tree, some garuḍa[2] nests that were in direct line with the tip of the chariot pole and thus in imminent danger. At the sight of them his heart was seized with pity, and he said to Mātali, his charioteer: [11] "There are some birds' nests, full of unfledged nestlings, in that silk-cotton tree. Steer the chariot so that they aren't crushed by the shafts and knocked down." "But sir, the demon hosts are upon us," replied Mātali. "What of it?" said Śakra. "Make sure you avoid those garuḍa nests." "Lotus-eyed master," said Mātali, [12] "I can only save the birds by turning the chariot around, and the enemy are at last pressing their advantage and overrunning the gods." Śakra was deeply moved by pity and displayed his exceptional goodness and extreme determination by saying: [13] "Very well, turn the chariot around. I would rather that the demon chiefs battered me to death with their terrible clubs than that I live on with my reputation ruined, under the reproach of having slaughtered these creatures who are distraught with terror." Mātali agreed to do so and turned the chariot with its thousand horses in harness.

[14] Now the enemy had witnessed Śakra's prowess in battle, and, when they saw his chariot turn round, they quickly broke ranks in terror and disappeared like black clouds driven away by the wind. [15] When his own forces are shattered, it takes one man to turn around and bar the path of the enemy army for their overweening pride to shrivel at such unimaginable bravery. [16] Seeing the demon host in rout, Śakra's army immediately rallied, while the enemies of the gods, fleeing in terror, had no wish to return to the fray.

[17] The gods paid honor to Śakra with mixed feelings of delight and shame. His handsome figure was radiant with the glow of victory as he quietly left the battlefield and returned to his city and his harem which eagerly awaited him.

This was how victory was won in that battle. Hence the saying: [18] "A worthless man does wrong because he is insensitive. The man of average awareness, even though sensitive, does wrong when cornered. The good man, even if his life is at stake, is as incapable of swerving from his normal practice as the sea is of breaking its bounds."

So, then—long ago the Lord, to protect living things, imperiled not only his rule in heaven but his own life. Granted that no intelligent person ought to feel animosity toward earth's creatures, let alone do them any harm, all decent men should cultivate sympathy for living things.

12 *The Brahmin*

SELF-RESPECT IS WHAT KEEPS GOOD people from overstepping the bounds of propriety.

According to tradition, the Bodhisattva was at one time born into a great brahmin family whose pedigree and reputation were equally without reproach: it was noted for its piety, admired for its sober decorum. After receiving the various sacraments that mark each stage from birth to adolescence, he went to study the Veda with a teacher whose good birth and fine example were matched by great learning.

[1] The boy's quick grasp and retentive memory, the quiet and devout manner for which his family was noted, and the seriousness that showed in his calm bearing even at that early age—all earned him the affection and approval of his teacher. [2] For constant, uninterrupted goodness casts a bewitching spell even on people who are eaten up with burning hatred, let alone on those with a healthy outlook.

The teacher decided to put his pupils' moral sense to the test. And so, in the breaks between lessons, he would constantly harp on the miseries he suffered through poverty [3]—poverty, which even one's own kin will do nothing to revoke, which even on festive occasions dampens high spirits, which makes one loath to ask for charity and reduces every wish to an empty dream. [4] To be destitute is a dreadful fate, and, like any disaster, its ill effects are lasting: people are patronizing, life is a struggle, one is deprived of all comforts and feels utterly listless.

To this his pupils reacted like thoroughbreds to the touch of a whip. Such was their affection for their teacher that they felt conscience stricken and began to collect bigger and better helpings of alms food for him. But he told them: "Don't waste your efforts, my friends. Collecting alms food isn't going to put an end to the rigors of poverty for anyone. If you cannot bear to see me suffer these miseries, you would do better to direct your efforts toward getting some money. Why? [5] Because, though food cures hunger, though water cures thirst, and though charms and medicine cure disease, it is money and the respect it gains that cures the ills of poverty."

"What can we do?" asked his pupils. "Unfortunately, for us the possibilities are limited. Now [6] if one could get money as one gets alms, we would not leave you to suffer in poverty like this, dear master. [7] Usually brahmins receive gifts and, in that way, acquire a modicum of wealth. But the people here are not generous, and we are at our wits' end." "The law books do prescribe alternative methods for brahmins to get money," replied the teacher, "but I am getting old and no longer have the energy to put any of them into practice." "But master," said the pupils, "we are still young and energetic. If you think we can carry out what the law books prescribe, then say so. It would be a way of repaying you for the trouble of teaching us." "Young people easily lose heart, and even you might find it hard to succeed, using such methods as these for getting money. However," continued the teacher, "if you insist, then listen while I tell you one extremely good way of getting money. [8] As an emergency measure, stealing is considered a brahmin's prerogative. And surely poverty is an extreme form of emergency in this life. So it is no sin for a brahmin to appropriate other people's possessions. Especially as they are all his by right anyway. [9] Of course, you could seize money by open force. But that is not the way. One has one's reputation to think of. So always choose a lonely spot to make your attempt."

At this his pupils felt greatly relieved. Although what he said was quite wrong, they greeted it with approval, as though it were quite right. All except the Bodhisattva. [10] His innate goodness made it impossible for him to acquiesce. On the contrary, he felt strongly opposed to what the others had accepted as their duty. He bowed his head in shame, sighed gently, and kept silent.

12 · 11 The teacher had a high regard for the Great Being's inherent goodness, and, when he noticed that he neither welcomed nor rejected his proposal, he began to wonder why he should disapprove of theft. Was it because he lacked the necessary determination? Or because he had come to dislike his teacher? Or was it because he knew it was a crime? To make him reveal his feelings, the brahmin said to the Bodhisattva: "Noble brahmin, [11] these brahmins can no longer bear my plight and so are ready, like real men, to take action. But you seem unmoved and apathetic. Is it that my distress does not touch you? [12] I have spoken about it in the clearest terms, without sparing details. So how can you stand there, calm and stolid, as though all were well?"

The Bodhisattva inclined respectfully toward his teacher and said, with some embarrassment: "Heaven forbid that it should appear that I am indifferent to my master's sufferings through lack of affection or hardness of heart! Rather attribute my attitude to the fact that it is quite impossible to follow the course he has prescribed. For there is nowhere one can commit a crime and hope to escape detection. You ask why? Because one is never alone. [13] The man who does a wicked deed has nowhere in the world where he can be alone. Are there not invisible beings who keep watch over men, [14] and are there not holy men of great spiritual power whose supernatural vision is ever awake? The fool does not see them, thinks he is alone, and sets about his evil business. [15] And yet I do not know of a single deserted spot anywhere. Just because I cannot see anyone else there, a place is not empty: I am there. [16] An evil act may be witnessed by someone else or by oneself. But it is far more noticeable to oneself. [17] One person may notice what another person does, or else, if he is engrossed in his own business, he may not. But being passionately involved in the matter, one inevitably knows when it is oneself who is doing something wrong. That is the reason for my present attitude." And noticing that his teacher was quite won over, the Bodhisattva continued: [18] "Nor can I believe that your Holiness would deceive us like this for the sake of gain. Could anyone who understands the difference between virtue and vice amass a fortune at the expense of virtue? Now let me give you my own opinion: [19] I would rather go with a monk's drab robe and begging bowl to my enemy's house and see him living in luxury than shamelessly contemplate some moral outrage, even if I stood to become lord of heaven."

At this his teacher was overwhelmed with delight and admiration. He rose from his seat, embraced the Bodhisattva, and said: "How right, my noble brahmin, and how worthy of you whose wisdom shows in your calm demeanor. [20] Fools stray from the path of duty at the slightest excuse, but good people never go wrong, even when living in utter penury. Austerity, learning, and wisdom are their wealth. [21] You adorn your own spotless family as the moon does the sky when it rises in autumn. By behaving so remarkably well you have given proof of your learning, and my own efforts are rewarded by this happy outcome."

So, then,—since it is self-respect that keeps good people from overstepping the bounds of propriety, a decent person should be filled with a powerful sense of shame.

13 *Unmādayantī*

Even when suffering torment, good people are loath to do anything mean. They rely instead on their own resilience.

According to tradition, the Bodhisattva was at one time king of the Śibis and dedicated himself to the good of the world by practicing truthfulness, generosity, calm, wisdom, and other excellent virtues. He seemed to be Justice and Discipline personified, and he cared for his subjects as a father would for his children. [1] The king curbed their evil tendencies and inculcated the finer virtues, as father to son, and, as a result, his people rejoiced in this world and the next. [2] He administered justice in strict accordance with the Law and applied it with as much rigor to his own relatives as to everyone else. This barred people from the path of wrongdoing and served as a flight of steps leading to heaven. [3] Seeing that the good of the world was intimately bound up with the Law, the king made that his sole preoccupation. He gave himself up body and soul to following the Law and would suffer no one else to infringe it.

Now, a prominent citizen in the king's capital had a daughter who was the embodiment of beauty, love personified. She was like one of the heavenly nymphs, with her great loveliness and ravishing looks, and was generally considered a jewel among women. [4] She was so attractive that no one with an ounce of feeling could take his eyes off her, once he was in thrall to her beauty. And in consequence her family called her Unmādayantī, Bewitching.

Her father brought her to the king's notice, saying: "My lord, a jewel of a woman has appeared in your realm. It is for your highness to decide whether or not you wish to take her as your wife." Straightaway the king summoned brahmins who were expert in female physiognomy, and he directed them to find out whether she would be suitable for him or not.[1] Her father duly invited the brahmins to his house and asked Unmādayantī to attend to his guests. She said she would and promptly set about serving them refreshments. But, [5] at the sight of her face, their eyes fixed in a stare. Love robbed those brahmins of all composure. Like men in a drunken stupor, they were no longer in control of their eyes or their feelings. And since they were quite incapable of staying calm enough to make a sober assessment, let alone of having something to eat, the burgher removed his daughter from their sight and entertained the brahmins himself before letting them go.

The brahmins admitted that the girl's beauty was entrancing. Indeed, she had something of the sorceress about her. And for that reason they thought the king ought not even to set eyes on her. There was no question of making her his wife: her beauty would inevitably bewitch his heart, and he would attend less enthusiastically to spiritual and practical matters. By stinting the time required for his duties as king, he would prejudice his people's chance of welfare and happiness, and that would lead to disaster. [6] The sight of her would be enough to jeopardize the sanctity of a saint, let alone a susceptible young prince with a roving eye and living in comfort.

So, after deciding what was the proper thing to do in the circumstances, the brahmins approached the king at the earliest opportunity and reported as follows: "Your highness, we have seen the girl. Beauty she has but nothing else, and her looks are marred by signs of ill omen. So your highness should not set eyes on her, let alone take her as wife. [7] For a woman with ill-omened looks casts a shadow over the fame and fortune of two families, just as a cloudy, moonless night obscures the beauty and distinctness of earth and sky."

Hearing how matters stood, the king accepted that, if the girl had ill-omened looks, she was not suited to become a member of his family, and so he lost interest in her. The burgher learned that the king did not want his daughter, and

13 · 8 he forthwith gave her in marriage to Abhipāraga, one of the king's ministers.

One day, when the season of the Kaumudī festival[2] had come round, the king was eager to see the decorations with which his capital had been festooned. So he toured the city in his royal carriage. The streets and marketplaces had been swept clean and sprinkled with water. Flags and banners of all colors were hoisted. Heaps of flower offerings made patches of dazzling color at every turn. Music and dance, singing, miming, and merrymaking were in full swing. Flowers, incense, sandalwood, perfumes, garlands, and liquor mingled their various scents with those from the powders and ointments used at the bathing places and pervaded the air. All sorts of beautiful objects were exhibited for sale, and the spacious main street was thronged with prosperous, happy, and brightly dressed people, from town and country.

On his round of the city, the king passed near the house of his minister Abhipāraga. Now Unmādayantī was indignant at having been rejected by the king because she was supposed to have ill-omened looks. So, pretending she was anxious to get a glimpse of him, she stationed herself on the roof of her mansion, illuminating it as lightning does the top of a cloud, with her beautiful figure in full view. "Now let's see whether he can face a woman with ill-omened looks and remain calm and unruffled," she thought to herself.

Meanwhile the king was eagerly taking in the splendid sights of the capital, when suddenly his gaze fell upon her standing there before him. Now, [8] although he was fully accustomed to observing the physical charms of the palace beauties, yet, because of his devotion to the path of virtue and because of his persistence in subduing his senses, he had never been aroused. [9] Though he had great powers of self-control, though he was bashful—not knowing where to look when the young wives of other men eyed him—yet, despite himself, he gazed at this woman with a long, steady stare, overcome with passionate wonder. [10] Could this be Kaumudī in person? or the guardian spirit of the house? or a heavenly nymph? or a demoness? For this was no human beauty. As he puzzled over who she could be, the king could not see enough of her. But his carriage moved on, contrary to what he would have wished, past that spot and back to the palace. Like one distracted, thinking of nothing but her, now that love had shattered his will-power, he questioned his coachman, Sunanda, in private. [11] "Do you know who owns that house with white walls? And who was that woman who shone there like a streak of lightning on a white cloud?" The coachman replied: "Your majesty's chief minister, Abhipāraga—the house belongs to him, and that is his wife, the daughter of Kirīṭavatsa. She is called Unmādayantī."

When the king heard that she was already married, a shadow crossed his heart. With a fixed stare he gave himself up to sad thoughts and breathed a long and heavy sigh. Wholly preoccupied with her, he softly muttered to himself: [12] "Those soft, sweet syllables—Unmādayantī—ah! how rightly named she is, since she has indeed bewitched me with that radiant smile. [13] I would forget her, but that I have her image in my mind. For either my thoughts go out to her, or else she is a powerful presence within them. [14] And that this folly of mine should be on account of another man's wife. . . . I must be mad, since shame as well as sleep seem now to have deserted me. [15] One moment I am blissfully absorbed in thinking about the way she moves, her smile, her glance; then suddenly the gong strikes the hour, and its shattering sound reminds me that my brief respite from the cares of state is over and makes me resentful."

So it was that the king's composure was destroyed by force of passion. Though he tried to take a hold on himself, his pale, wasted features, his preoccupied manner, the way he sighed and stretched his limbs, were clear signs that he was in love. [16] However much the king determined to conceal his emotion, it showed in his fixed expression, a sign of troubled thoughts, and in his thinness.

Now Abhipāraga, the minister, was a sensitive interpreter of outward behavior and facial expression. He realized the state the king was in, as well as the reason for it, and feared it might prove fatal. For he was fond of the king and knew how overwhelming was the power of love. So, he went to him, made sure he was alone, and, by his leave, made the following declaration: [17] "My lord, just now, while I was at my devotions, a spirit appeared and said to me: 'How comes it that you are unaware that the king has lost his heart to Unmādayantī?' [18] Then the spirit immediately disappeared, without another word. I have come to you because I don't know what to make of it. If this is true, my lord, why show such lack of trust in me by keeping it quiet? Please do me the favor of taking her for yourself."

At this remonstrance the king bowed his head in embarrassment. Though hopelessly in love, he was deeply imbued with a sense of what was right. And so it was without faltering that he refused in the plainest terms: "That cannot be. And why? [19] Because such merit as I may have attained so far would immediately be canceled out—and I am not immortal,[3] because my subjects also would get to know about this sin of mine, because to be parted from her would be like fire searing your heart and then shriveling you up like deadwood. [20] Doing such a thing would have evil consequences both in this life and the next—which is why the unwise would do it, and precisely why the wise would not." "My lord, there is no need to suppose that you would be doing wrong," answered Abhipāraga. [21] "By helping me in an act of generosity, you would in fact be doing a good deed, whereas by not accepting her from me you would be preventing an act of generosity and so be doing wrong. Nor can I see how this can lay you open to public disgrace, [22] since it is a matter purely between us two. Who else need know of it? So do not worry over what other people might say against you. Besides, you will be doing me a favor, not an injury. How so? [23] Well, can a heart that is full of pleasure at serving its master's interests be troubled? So, my lord, give free rein to your heart's desire—there is no need to worry about hurting me." "Heaven forbid!" said the king. [24] "This intense devotion to me has apparently blinded you to the fact that counseling generosity does not in every instance lead to good. [25] Anyone so devoted that he will sacrifice his own life for our sake is a friend more dear than any relative, and that man's wife is surely a friend too. So it is wrong of you to lead me astray. And your claim that no one else need know does not alter the fact that it would be a sin. [26] Even if undetected, how can a wrongdoer hope to flourish, any more than someone who takes poison? The gods with their clear sight and the ascetics with their superhuman powers cannot fail to notice him. Furthermore, [27] who would seriously believe that you do not love her or that you would not feel greatly distressed the moment you forsook her?" [28] "I am your slave," replied Abhipāraga, "I and my wife and children. You are my master, my idol. So, my lord, how would you be behaving wrongly toward her, since she is your slave? And as to your claim that I love her, what of it? [29] Of course I love her. That is why I want to give her to you, your majesty. For he who gives away something that is precious to him receives in his next life precious things that give him even greater pleasure. So, my lord, deign to accept her." "Certainly not," said the king. "It would be quite wrong. [30] I would throw myself on to a sharp sword or into the flickering flames of a fire rather than strike a blow at Virtue, to which I owe my present good fortune." To this, Abhipāraga replied: "If your majesty is unwilling to accept her because she is my wife, I shall order her to become a prostitute whom anyone can have for the asking. Then, perhaps, your majesty might take her." "Are you out of your mind?" exclaimed the king. [31] "Were you to desert an innocent wife, you would not only be punished by me but would smart under the reproaches of others, in this life and the next. So stop inciting me to do wrong, and apply yourself instead to doing what is right." But Abhipāraga persisted: [32] "If what I suggest is in any way improper and if people criticize me or if I suffer for it, I will face the consequences, whatever they may be, happy in the knowledge that you are happy. [33] I know of no one in the world worthier of receiving an offering than you, great king. Through Unmādayantī I can increase my store of merit. You have only to act the priest and accept her as my fee." "Of course," said the king, "it is your extreme devotion to us that makes you so eager to be of service, without regard to whether the consequences to yourself are good or bad. That is why I am especially concerned for you. One cannot afford to be indifferent to public disapproval. Look, [34] if you behave as you please and pay no attention to what people say or to what the consequences may be, people will distrust you and success will certainly elude you—which is why I implore you [35] not to imagine there is anything, not even the saving of life, that justifies a violation of morals. The harm is great and certain; uncertain and meager the gain. Furthermore [36] no decent person pursues his own happiness if it means subjecting others to scorn and similar unpleasantness. And so, without causing pain to others and abiding by what is right, I shall face my problems alone." "But," Abhipāraga continued, "what wrong can there be either in my devotedly acting in my master's interests or in your majesty's accepting her as a gift? All the Śibis—townsmen and countrymen alike—would agree that there is nothing wrong in this. So may your highness deign to accept her." The king replied: "You really have set your heart on being of service to me. But just think a moment: which of us knows best what is right, the Śibis in town and country, you, or me?" In some confusion, Abhipāraga answered the king: [37] "My lord, thanks to your tireless attendance on the elders, your authoritative learning, your intellectual acuity, and also your surpassing knowledge of the three objects of life,[4] the truth lies within you as in Bṛhaspati."[5] "So you shouldn't try to mislead me in this matter," continued the king. "For [38] the fortunes of the world depend on the behavior of its rulers. And for that reason, bearing in mind how devoted my subjects are, I shall keep to the path of virtue, which befits my reputation. [39] Just as cows follow in a bull's tracks, be they straight or crooked, so people imitate their ruler, free of cares and without being goaded on to do so. Besides, just think: [40] if I haven't the strength even to keep myself under control, what on earth will happen to my people, who look to me as their guardian? [41] Therefore, with a view to the good of my subjects, to my own duty, and to my untarnished reputation, I will not give way to my passion. For I am the leader of my people, the bull of the herd."

Abhipāraga, the minister, was finally won over by the king's determination. Bowing and stretching out his cupped hands, he said: [42] "How extremely fortunate your subjects are to have you as their protector. One rarely finds such devotion to goodness, without regard to personal well-being, even among saintly hermits. [43] Great king . . . in your case the word 'great' rings true. Such titles, when bestowed on worthless individuals, are apt to sound unpleasantly like sarcasm. [44] But why should I feel so amazed, so excited at how you have behaved?—You are as full of virtues as the ocean is of jewels."

So, then—even when suffering torment, good people are loath to do anything mean. They rely instead on their resilience and well-developed sense of what is right.

14 *Supāraga*

To claim with truth that one's actions have been grounded in the moral Law is enough to avert disaster, quite apart from the reward of such actions. So follow the edicts of the moral Law.

According to tradition, the Great Being, when still a Bodhisattva, was once a supremely able ship's captain. (It is in the nature of a Bodhisattva, thanks to his inborn intelligence, to excel even the experts in whatever branch of art or science he chooses to master.) Knowing as he did the movements of the heavenly bodies, the Great One never lost his sense of direction. He recognized all the telltale signs around him—the usual, the unusual, and the dangerous—so that he could forecast how long good or bad conditions would last. From such clues as the fish, the color of the water, the type of terrain, the birds, and the rocks, he could easily plot his position at sea. He also had presence of mind and could fight off drowsiness and fatigue. Ever alert and tenacious, he put up with heat and cold and with the exhausting onslaught of the elements. Thanks to his skill in getting under way and making a good landfall,[1] merchants could be sure of reaching their destination. His voyages proved so extremely successful that he came to be called Supāraga.[2] And the seaport where he lived was also called Supāraga (nowadays known as Śūrpāraka). His reputation as a bringer of good luck was such that overseas merchants who wanted to be sure of a safe passage would come to him, even in his old age, and beg him as a favor to take charge of their ships.

Now, one day some merchants who had set sail from Bharukaccha[3] put in at the port of Supāraga. They were bound for Suvarṇabhūmi[4] and, wanting to be sure of a good

run, begged the Great One to come abroad. He asked them [1] 14 · 6
what help he could possibly be to them now that, by old age's stern decree, his sight was failing and bouts of lassitude made him less alert than he had been. He simply had not the energy for anything physically demanding. The merchants assured him that they were well aware of his condition and that they realized he could not endure any strain. They had no intention of assigning him any laborious duties. [2] All he had to do was to favor their ship with the touch of his lotus-like feet, and the dust would act as a talisman. Even if some great danger arose at sea, the ship would sail on in safety. That was why they had come to him.

The Noble One felt sympathy for them. And so, despite his decrepitude, he went aboard their vessel. At this the merchants were one and all delighted. They were certain now that their voyage would meet with complete success.

In due course they took to the open sea where fish of all sorts swarm in shoals, where strong gales lash the waves in wild delight and the waters roar in fury. Above, the foaming crests are like wreathes of white blossom—while below, the ocean floor, encrusted with many kinds of gems, is forever changing. But in those unfathomable depths also lie the forbidding underworld haunts of snake spirits and demons. [3] The coastline vanished as they ventured out into mid-ocean. All around them stretched the fathomless waters, deep sapphire blue. It was as though the sky had melted under the scorching rays of the sun.

Evening drew on, and the sun's ball of fire burned less fiercely. They were far out at sea when, suddenly, a vast and terrifying cataclysm burst upon them. [4] From one moment to the next the sea grew wild: the whole mass of water became turbulent and groaned horribly at the buffeting of the violent wind. Shattered waves hurled sheets of spray. [5] Whole tracts of water were tossed in the air by this hurricane and whirled about with frightening swiftness. The ocean took on a savage aspect, as does the earth at doomsday, when the mountains tremble. [6] Dark clouds, with bright streaks of lightning like the flickering tongues of many-headed snakes, obscured the sun's path, and continual thunderclaps echoed menacingly. [7] The sun gradually dipped toward the horizon, its fine mesh of rays blotted out by dense cloud, and darkness, unleashed by close of day, became palpable, enveloping all. [8] As the stinging showers of rain lashed the encircling waves, the ocean heaved in rage, and the ship, as though in fear, shuddered horribly, filling the mariners' hearts with dismay. [9] Each of them reacted according to temperament: some were panic-stricken and stood speechless and despairing, others kept calm and busily took countermeasures, while others were absorbed in praying to their guardian spirits.

The ship was at the mercy of strong currents now that the sea had been whipped up by the gale, and the seafaring merchants were adrift. Day followed day without their catching sight of any land or even of the expected seamarks. Those they did see were strange to them and only made them feel even more desperate. Fear and despondency overwhelmed them until Supāraga, the Bodhisattva, rallied them: "If you venture out into the middle of the ocean, you must not be surprised at having to face a cataclysmic storm. So, gentlemen, do not give way to despair. [10] Despair is no remedy for misfortune. So dismiss all negative thoughts. If one perseveres and is ready to take prompt action, one can overcome difficulties without difficulty. [11] Shake off this miserable apathy and meet the challenge with positive action. A person of sense displays energy and determination, and success is within his grasp, no matter what the circumstances."

The voyagers were reassured by what the Great One said, and, as they scanned the ocean in the hopes of sighting land, they noticed some creatures in human form, apparently coated in silver mail, diving and surfacing among the waves. After carefully observing their shape and peculiarities, the voyagers reported in amazement to Supāraga: "This certainly is a phenomenon never seen before in all the wide ocean. [12] They look just like demon warriors, coated in silver mail. Their eyes are frightening, and their deformed noses look like razors. Whoever they are, they seem to be enjoying some sort of game, to judge by the way they plunge into the ocean waves and surface again, all sparkling." "These are neither men nor monsters," said Supāraga, "but only fish.[5] So there is no need to be afraid of them. Nevertheless, [13] we have been driven far off from both ports.[6] This is the Kṣuramālī[7] Ocean. So try and turn back."

But the ship was being swept along by a following wind which only bore them farther out. And this, together with the violent pull of the current in the sea swell, made it impossible for them to turn back. As they drifted farther and farther out, they espied yet another ocean whose waters shone silvery bright, while a mass of foam overlaid it with white. In astonishment the travelers asked Supāraga [14] what ocean this was, clothed in white satin, to judge by the way its waters were submerged by foam. Dazzling whiteness streamed in every direction, as though the sea were made of liquid moonbeams. "Good heavens!" exclaimed Supāraga. "We really are far out: [15] this is the milky ocean called Dadhimālī.[8] It would be rash to go any farther, if there is any chance of our turning back." "We can't even slow the ship down," answered the merchants, "let alone turn her about. The contrary wind and the ship's own powerful momentum make it impossible."

After crossing this ocean as well, they saw yet another. Its rolling breakers were tinged a glowing gold, its waters shone like reddish flames. Once again, in amazement and curiosity, the merchants questioned Supāraga: [16] "It looks as if these bright swelling waters have been tinted with the radiance of the rising sun. This ocean is like a huge, blazing fire. What is it called and why?" [17] "This is the ocean called Agnimālī.[9] It is notorious, and it would be a very good thing if we could turn back from it." Through foresight the Great One disclosed only the name of this ocean, not the reason why the water had changed color.

The merchants crossed this ocean too, whereupon they sighted another, whose waters glinted with the brilliance of topazes and sapphires and that, in color, resembled the blades of kuśa grass when fully grown. Full of curiosity, they questioned Supāraga: [18] "Now which of the oceans is this,

14 · 19 with its water the color of fully grown kuśa blades? The flecks of foam on its wind-tossed waves look like flowers." "Honorable merchants," replied Supāraga, "make every effort to turn back. It would be most inadvisable to go beyond this point. [19] This is the Kuśamālī[10] Ocean, which is like an unmanageable elephant. The sheer force of its irresistible waves will carry off not only us but all chance of happiness." The merchants then made a supreme effort to turn the ship back, but they failed.

And so they sailed over that ocean also, until they caught sight of yet another. This one had greenish water, like a mixture of emeralds and beryls. [20] "Which of the oceans are we looking at now?" asked the merchants. "With its emerald-green waters, it looks like a lush meadow, while its pretty crests of foam are like white water lilies." The Great One was bitterly distressed at their impending doom. He heaved a long, deep sigh and then quietly said: [21] "We have gone too far. To return from here is scarcely possible. For this is the Nalamālī[11] Ocean, almost at the world's end." At this the merchants were overwhelmed with despair. All energy seemed to drain from their limbs. They collapsed on the spot and did nothing but heave sighs.

So they crossed that ocean as well. Then, in the evening, as the sun dipped its faint rays as though intent on slipping into the watery depths, they heard a frightful noise coming from the sea. It was as though the whole ocean were swelling up, lightning flashes were colliding, and whole forests of bamboo were ablaze and crackling. The ear-splitting sound pierced them to the heart and left them in the grip of fear. With quivering nerves they leaped up and scanned the ocean on all sides. And they beheld the whole mass of water cascading over what looked like a precipice into a huge chasm. At the sight of this they quailed. In terror they turned to Supāraga and said: [22] "The raging sea is making such a frightful din that our ears are splitting and our brains are in a whirl. One can hear it even at this distance, and ahead the whole mass of water is pouring down into a terrifying chasm. What sea is this? And do you think there is anything more we can do now?" "Alas and alack!" cried the Great One, anxiously surveying the sea. [23] "You have reached the point of no return—sailed right into the jaws of death—arrived at that fatal spot, the Mare's Mouth."[12] On hearing this and realizing they had indeed arrived at the Mare's Mouth, the merchants despaired of their lives. Fear of death overwhelmed them. [24] Some wept and wailed or cried aloud. Others were so dazed with terror that they did nothing at all. [25] Others, stunned by this calamity, turned to the gods—to Indra especially but also to the Ādityas, the Rudras, the Maruts, and the Vasus.[13] Some entreated the Ocean itself. [26] Some muttered various spells, while others duly abased themselves before Devī.[14] Others again approached Supāraga, and each in his own way made bitter lament. [27] "You never fail in compassion, and in the face of disaster you allay fear. Now is the moment for you to display your extraordinary powers. [28] Apply yourself, in your wisdom, to rescuing us who, helpless, turn to you in our hour of need, for the sea in its fury is intent on swallowing us up in the Mare's Mouth. [29] It would be wrong of you to let this company perish at sea. The ocean dare not disregard your command. So put a stop to its violence."

The Noble One, in his great compassion, shared in their affliction and spoke these words of comfort to the merchants: "Even now, it occurs to me, there is a remedy at hand. I shall try it at once. For the moment, though, you must take heart, gentlemen." The chance of a reprieve roused their flagging spirits, and the merchants watched him in hushed expectancy. Putting his upper robe over one shoulder and bending his right knee to the deck, Supāraga the Bodhisattva, concentrating his whole being, did obeisance to the Buddhas. Then he addressed the seafarers: "Honorable merchants and you special deities who inhabit sea and sky, mark what I say. [30] Ever since I have been aware of myself, ever since I have been able to discriminate, I do not recall ever having intentionally harmed a living thing. [31] On the strength of this truth and my own store of merit, let the ship turn back safe, before reaching the Mare's Mouth."

The effect of the Great One taking his stand on truth[15]

worked together with the power of his merit to make both wind and current alter, so that the ship turned back. The merchants were utterly amazed to see the ship alter course. Full of excitement, they went to Supāraga, bowed respectfully, and repeatedly informed him of it. The Great One told the merchants to keep calm and to hoist the sails quickly. Those whose duty it was did as he commanded. Joy had put new strength into them. [32] To the sound of laughter from her happy crew, the ship sped across the ocean. Her white sails outspread like beautiful wings, she looked like a snow goose in a cloudless sky. A following wind and a calm sea allowed the ship to return with the ease of a magic conveyance: it sailed on of its own accord.

Stars like jewels dotted the spreading canopy of night, but the glow of twilight had not entirely given way to darkness: there was still a glimmer on the horizon where the sun had set. As night began her sway, Supāraga addressed the merchants: "Gentlemen, as we recross the oceans familiar to us, starting with the Nalamālī, haul abroad as much sand and as many pebbles as you can. In this way, if a violent hurricane hits the ship, she will not split her sides. And if you consider the sand and pebbles as talismans, they are sure to bring you some profit." So the traders dredged up what they took to be sand and pebbles from places suggested to them by spirits who were full of love and admiration for Supāraga. But it was beryls and other precious stones that they hauled on board.

In the course of that single night the ship reached Bharukaccha. [33] By daybreak they had reached their native shores, and their ship was loaded with silver and gold, sapphires and beryls. In an outburst of joy they affectionately sang the praises of Supāraga.

So, then—to claim with truth that one's actions have been grounded in the moral Law is enough to avert disaster, quite apart from the reward of such actions. So follow the edicts of the moral Law.

The Lord of the Fish 15

WHATEVER THEIR AIMS, MEN OF INtegrity succeed and prosper already in this life, not to speak of the next. So one should make every effort to be pure in heart.

According to tradition, the Bodhisattva was once lord of the fish in quite a small lake, whose pleasant waters were adorned with lilies and lotuses, red, white, and blue. Geese, ducks, and pairs of sheldrakes further enhanced it, and the trees that grew by its shore showered blossoms upon it.

In the course of many previous incarnations the Bodhisattva had made a habit of altruism, so that even in his present circumstances he was bent on procuring the welfare and happiness of the other fish. [1] Good or bad behavior, by force of habit, becomes part of a man's nature, to such a degree that he will go on practicing one or the other even in another incarnation, quite unconsciously, as though in a dream. The Great Being felt as tenderly toward those fish, as if they were his own beloved offspring, and in various ways he showed them great kindness: he gave them presents, spoke kindly to them, and helped them to behave worthily.[1] [2] Any desire they might have to do each other harm he restrained, and instead he fostered mutual affection. Thanks to these efforts and to his own ingenuity, he managed to make them forget the cruel habits of fish. [3] Under his careful surveillance the shoal flourished, like a town freed from troubles by a king devoted to justice.

Now, at one time, partly because the creatures' store of good fortune had run out, partly because the rain spirits were negligent, there was not enough rain from heaven. As a result of this scanty rainfall, the lake did not fill up, as it had previously, with fresh water tinged yellow by full-blown *kadamba* blossom. As summer drew on, the rays of the sun blazed with ever greater intensity and, as though faint with exhaustion, drank thirstily at the lake, day after day. So did the sun-scorched earth, and the wind also, who, feeling it was pursued by tongues of flame, longed for refreshment. As a result, the lake shrank to a pool. [4] In summer the sun blazes out, the harsh wind darts flames, and the earth, as though fever stricken, is nowhere cool. You might think it was in anger that these three dry up the waters. The shoal of fish were reduced to despair. Flocks of crows were already marking them as prey, not to mention all the birds that lived at the water's edge. As he watched them helplessly wriggling, the Bodhisattva was filled with pity and started thinking: "Oh what a miserable fate has befallen my poor fish! [5] Each day the water grows less, as though to emulate life itself, and it is still a long time before any clouds can be expected. [6] There is no means of escape, and, besides, who is there to lead us somewhere else? Scenting our plight, our enemies are gathering round. [7] As soon as the rest of the water disappears, these twitching fish will provide a meal for their foes, before my very eyes. Now what would be the right thing to do in the circumstances?" On reflection, the Great One saw that the sole remedy for their distress was to take his stand on truth.[2] Out of compassion he shared in their sufferings, and so, heaving a long, deep sigh, he looked up to the sky and said: [8] "As surely as I do not recall ever having intentionally killed a living creature, even in the most desperate situation, so, by the power of this truth, may the lord of gods send rain and fill the lakes with water."

Now thanks to the Great One's store of merit and by reason of his taking his stand on truth—also because the whole hierarchy of heaven was favorably disposed toward him—dark clouds appeared on every side, even though it was not the season for them. Their rounded forms hung low, heavy with rain. From them came a gentle rumble of thunder, and streaks of lightning sported about their massive, dark summits. They seemed to expand and embrace each other, slowly stretching forward their outer edges, like arms. [9] Like mountains reflected in the mirror of the sky, those black clouds seemed to blot out the horizon and, with their lofty summits, to spread darkness all around. [10] The peacocks greeted those masses of cloud with complicated dances and prolonged shrieks of delight. The long, low rumbling of the thunder seemed like loud laughter. [11] Then the rain was unleashed and showered down like pearls released from their shells. The dust subsided, and from the earth there rose a strong smell which was wafted by the gusty wind. [12] Though the heat of the sun's rays was at its most intense, it being summer, all at once it vanished. Torrents of water flowed down the mountain slopes, covering them with flecks of froth, [13] and a slender streak of lightning, inspired by the drumming of the clouds, performed a voluptuous dance, lighting up the ends of the earth again and again with flashes of yellow and gold.

From all sides pale streams of water flowed into the lake and were filling it up. The crows and the other birds had flown off the moment the downpour had started. With renewed hopes of survival, the fish were overjoyed. But despite a general feeling of gladness, the Bodhisattva was anxious in case the rain should stop. And so he urged on Parjanya[3] repeatedly, saying: [14] "Give a deep, loud bellow, Parjanya, and upset those gloating crows. Shower down water glinting like a mass of jewels with continuous flashes of lightning."

On hearing of this, Śakra, lord of the gods, in utter astonishment appeared and congratulated him, saying: [15] "Lord of the fish, it must be due to the great power generated by your extraordinary act of truth that the clouds rumble pleasantly and pour down water like tilted water pots. [16] But it is extremely remiss of me not to join in the efforts of those, like you, who are concerned for the good of the world. [17] So from now on you need not worry: I undertake to support good people in their enterprises. Never again will this land be subjected to such an affliction, thanks to your goodness."

With these kind words he commended the Bodhisattva

15 · 17 and thereupon disappeared. The lake was filled to abundance.

So, then—whatever their aims, men of integrity succeed and prosper already in this life, not to speak of the next. One should therefore make every effort to be pure in heart.

The Young Quail 16

EVEN FIRE IS POWERLESS AGAINST words redolent of truth. One should therefore make a practice of speaking truth.

According to tradition, the Bodhisattva was once born as a young quail in the jungle. Some nights after hatching, his tender wings had still to develop, and he was so puny that all the separate parts of his body were clearly discernible. His parents had taken pains to build a nest in a bush well hidden by deep grass. Here he lived together with his numerous siblings. But even in this state he had not lost his sense of what is right, and he was unwilling to eat the living creatures that his parents offered him. Instead he kept himself alive on millet, banyan figs, and other such food as they brought. As a result of this coarse and inadequate diet, his body did not fill out and his wings did not develop properly, while the other little quails, who ate whatever they were given, grew strong and fully fledged. For it is a fact that [1] he who eats anything, without worrying about right or wrong, is happy and prospers, while he who wants to live in harmony with nature and is therefore careful about what he eats has a hard time in this world. (Moreover, the Lord said: [2] "For the shameless crow who is aggressive, bold, and not fastidious, life is easy, though tainted. [3] But for the man who has a sense of shame, who desires only what is pure, who is retiring, diffident, and honest, life on earth is beset with difficulties.[1])

While they were living like this, a huge forest fire broke out not very far away. The noise it made was terrifying and incessant; smoke spread in thick clouds, and the advancing line of flames showered sparks. It caused havoc in the depths of the forest and terrified the animals who lived there. [4] Tossed by the wind, its flames outspread like arms, leaping and roaring, with smoky hair wildly disheveled, it seemed to be performing some intricate dance. The animals panicked, [5] and the grass, swaying under the impact of the violent wind, seemed to be fleeing in terror. But the fire pounced on it in fury and scorched it with a shower of glittering sparks. [6] Whole flocks of birds took alarm and flew away in terror. Wild beasts ran around in circles, stricken with panic. Thick smoke enveloped everything, and with the hoarse crackle of flames the forest seemed to be roaring aloud in pain.

Goaded on by the sharp wind, the fire gradually penetrated the jungle and reached close to the nest. Immediately the young quails, with shrill, discordant shrieks of terror, flew up, without a thought for each other. But the Bodhisattva made no attempt to follow them: his body was too frail, and he was not fully fledged. Yet the Great Being, sure of his own powers, remained unruffled. As the fire approached impetuously, he politely addressed it as follows: [7] "My feet hardly deserve the name of feet, and my wings have not grown. Also, my parents, in awe of you, have taken flight. I have nothing suitable to offer you as a guest. So, Fire, it would be best if you turned back from this spot." This, the plainest truth, was what the Great Being said.[2] [8] And the fire, though fanned by the wind and raging amid deadwood and thickets of parched grass, immediately died down: faced with these words of his, it was as though it had come to a swollen river. [9] To this day, a forest fire, however much its blaze is stirred up by the wind, shrinks back—like a many-headed snake charmed by a spell—smothers its darting flames, and dies down altogether when it reaches that famous spot in the Himalaya.

What, then, does this story illustrate? The saying goes that [10] just as the billowy ocean, with its waves like the hoods of serpents, cannot break its bounds, just as the seeker of the spirit cannot disregard the discipline prescribed by a great
 sage—so even fire cannot neglect the command of those for

whom truth lies at the core of existence. Therefore one 16 · 10
should never desert truth.

So, then—even fire is powerless against words redolent of truth. One should therefore make a practice of speaking truth.

17 *The Jar Full of Spirits*

DRINKING SPIRITS IS A HARMFUL AND pernicious habit, which is why decent people not only abstain from it themselves but also discourage others.

According to tradition, the Bodhisattva was once born as Śakra, lord of the gods. His mind was imbued with intense compassion, and he was bent on procuring happiness and well-being for others. This worthy inclination expressed itself in generosity, self-control, restraint, and other such qualities. Though free to enjoy all the exquisite sensual pleasures of heaven, he was so dominated by this feeling of compassion that he did not for one moment relax his efforts to be of service to the world. [1] Usually when people are drunk with happiness they can no longer be bothered to consider even their own interests. Yet, even the felicity of being lord in heaven did not turn the Bodhisattva's head, and he remained as attentive as ever to the affairs of others. [2] For those who suffered all manner of harsh misfortunes he felt the same loving care as he did for his own family. Being resolute and aware of the obligations of his position, he never missed a chance of being helpful to others.

One day when the Great One, with his powerful gaze full of compassion and tender affection, was surveying the world of men, he noticed a certain king, called Sarvamitra, who, by keeping bad company, had become addicted to drink and was dragging the whole country down with him. Knowing what a great sin it is to drink spirits and that the king was not aware of this, the Noble One felt great pity in his tormented heart and thought to himself: "Alas! what a calamity has befallen these people. [3] For drink, though pleasant enough at first, is like an enticing path to perdition: it debars from heaven those who are loath to see any sin in it. Now, what is the right thing to do in the circumstances? Ah yes, I know: [4] people are generally influenced by the way their superiors behave. Consequently, the king is the only one who needs to be cured, as he is the source of whatever is good or bad among his people."

On reaching this conclusion, the Great Being transformed himself into a brahmin. His complexion glowed like refined gold, but with his shock of matted hair which was rather coarse and unkempt and with his garments of bark and deerskin, he looked formidable. A small jar full of spirits hung at his left side.

In this guise he appeared, hovering in the air, before King Sarvamitra, who was sitting in his audience hall taking part in a conversation about the different kinds of intoxicating drink. In awed respect the company rose and humbly greeted the brahmin, one by one. Then, like a raincloud deeply rumbling, the brahmin spoke out loudly: [5] "Who would like to buy this jar, filled up to its neck, its neck which is ringed with bright flowers? No ordinary jar this, with its lovely garland. [6] Encircled by a broad wreath of flowers fluttering in the breeze, this jar is gorgeously decked with tender sprays. Which of you will pay to have it?"

The king gazed up in awe, his curiosity stifled by sheer wonder. Then, holding his hands together in respect, he said: [7] "You have the brilliance of the morning sun, the beauty of the moon, and the outward form of one of the Sages. Do please tell us by what name you are known among men: your varied attributes leave us still full of surmise as to who you are." [8] "You will discover who I am soon enough," replied Śakra. "For the moment, though, concentrate on buying this jar—that is, if you are not afraid of suffering in the next life or of dire misfortune already in this one." "Your holiness certainly has an unusual approach to selling goods," said the king. [9] "The normal practice when selling one's wares to people is to cry up their good points and to keep quiet about their defects, [10] though I suppose your method suits people such as yourself, who have a horror of falsehood. After all,

17 · 11 good people will not swerve from the truth, even in a desperate situation. [11] So tell us, blessed father, what this jar is filled with and what someone in your position can possibly expect to get from us in exchange." "Listen, your highness," answered Śakra. [12] "This jar is filled neither with rainwater nor with holy water, nor with fragrant honey culled from the heart of flowers, nor with the finest ghee, nor with milk the color of clear moonbeams falling upon white water lilies as they open out at night. No, this jar is filled with something evil. Listen to the powerful effects it produces. [13] Whoever drinks it will walk with faltering steps in a drunken stupor. He will stumble even where the ground is perfectly level, as his powers of concentration weaken. No longer capable of distinguishing edible from inedible, he will relish everything indiscriminately. Such are the contents of this vile little jar. Buy it, since it is for sale! [14] Thanks to this stuff you will no longer be in control of your own thoughts. You will shamble around mindlessly, like a dumb beast, and make your enemies weak with laughter. Under its influence you will get up and dance in the middle of an assembly, providing your own vocal accompaniment in place of a drum. It is well worth purchasing the contents of this jar, devoid though they are of any good. [15] Whoever drinks this brew will shed his usual modesty and parade the crowded streets naked as a Jain monk, free of the tiresome shackles of clothing. Such are the contents of this jar now up for sale. [16] Those who drink from it will be able to lie asleep and unconscious on a main road, while dogs calmly lick their faces spattered with the food brought up by vomiting. This is the desirable drink that has been poured into this jar. [17] A woman has only to partake of it, and, under its intoxicating influence, she is capable of tying her own parents to a tree, capable of disregarding her husband, be he rich as Kubera[1] himself. This is what is contained in the jar now on offer. [18] When the descendants of Vṛṣṇi and Andhaka[2] became fuddled with drink and, forgetful of their common ancestry, pounded each other with clubs, this was the intoxicating liquor they drank, here in this

jar. [19] When families of the greatest eminence and established position have perished, when wealthy families have been ruined, it has been through addiction to the liquor in this jar now held up for sale. [20] Whoever has been drugged by the contents of this jar weeps uncontrollably or laughs without stopping. His speech becomes slurred, his eyes heavy lidded, as though he had had a seizure. Inevitably he becomes an object of contempt. [21] The aged also become addle-pated and blind to their own good. They babble on to no apparent purpose—all due to the liquor in this jar now offered for sale. [22] It was as a result of drinking this that the primeval gods grew idle and were deprived of their position by Indra. While looking for shelter they drowned in the ocean. This jar is full of that potion. Take it! [23] This jar contains something equivalent to a curse in physical form. It has the power to make a man tell a lie as though convinced that it is the truth, to do something wrong with the joyful certainty that it is right, and to convince himself that good is bad and that bad is good. [24] So buy this chance to experience madness, this basis for evil-doing, this embodiment of bad luck, this begetter of sin, this sole sure road to ruin, this dreadful darkness of the mind. [25] My lord, buy this drink. It robs a man of his senses so completely that he will murder his own innocent parents or a holy ascetic, without a thought for his future happiness. [26] Such is this intoxicating drink, your divine majesty, and it goes by the name of spirits. Go ahead and buy it, whichever of you has no bias toward virtue. [27] Those who are addicted become hardened in their wrongdoing, and in the end they tumble headlong down the dreadful precipice of hell or else are reborn as beasts or hungry ghosts. Is there anyone prepared to give it so much as a glance? [28] Even if drinking spirits has only a mild effect, it destroys the character and intelligence of those who are born as human beings. And, as a further consequence, one is condemned either to live in the burning fiery hell called Avīci or in the realm of the departed or to be incarnated among the lowest beasts. [29] Indeed, to drink this liquor is to blot one's character, to ruin one's reputation utterly, to throw modesty to the winds, and to cloud the mind. In short, it destroys all one's good qualities. How can you still think of drinking it, my lord?"

The king found these arguments so reasonable and convincing that he was persuaded of the evils of drink and lost the urge to satisfy his addiction. He said to Śakra: [30] "What you have expressed so forcefully, in your concern for my own good, would be worthy of a fond father, or of a teacher speaking out of regard for decency, or of a sage who well knows the difference between good behavior and bad. I shall try, therefore, to show my gratitude by positive action; may your holiness deign to accept this token of respect in return for your wise words: [31] I grant you five valuable villages, a hundred female slaves, five hundred cows, and these ten chariots with well-schooled horses in harness. You have spoken for my own good, and for that reason I regard you as my teacher. Should there be anything else I can do for you, be so good as to tell me—you would be doing me a further favor." [32] "I have no need of royal demesnes and the rest of it," answered Śakra. "Understand that I am lord of heaven and that the giver of good advice is best rewarded when what he says is accepted and put into practice. [33] This is the path to glory and bliss and every sort of happiness in the next life. So shake off your addiction to drink, hold fast to what is right, and you will enter my realms."

With these words, Śakra instantly disappeared. And both the king and his subjects gave up drink.

So, then—drinking spirits is a harmful and pernicious habit, which is why decent people not only abstain from it themselves but also discourage others.

18 The Man without an Heir

THOSE WHO CARE FOR THE THINGS OF the spirit chafe at worldly ties, seeing them as so many obstacles to a pure and calm existence.

According to tradition, the Bodhisattva was born into a wealthy family noted for their good conduct and decency. They were much sought after in marriage by those who valued good breeding. Monks and brahmins alike resorted to them, and their treasuries and storerooms were at the disposal of friends and relatives, without distinction. They were patrons to craftsmen, and even the poorest beggars had access to them. Good fortune chose to reside in their home. They enjoyed the king's support and favor and were universally respected.

In course of time the Bodhisattva grew up and applied himself to the approved subjects of study. Nor did he neglect the various branches of the arts. The sight of him gave such pleasure, and he showed such understanding and discretion, that people felt about him as they would about one of their own relatives, [1] for our relatives do not have a claim on our respect simply by virtue of being related to us; nor do we regard a stranger differently from a relative simply because he happens not to be related to us: [2] no, one treats a person with respect or contempt after considering his good or bad qualities—be he a relative or a stranger.

The Great Being then felt a need for renunciation. [3] Worldly life, with its material worries, was, he realized, incompatible with the religious life. What attracted him was not the pleasures of society but the true happiness offered by the hermitage.

When his parents died he was filled with revulsion for the

endless round of birth and death, and he duly distributed the family estate and fortune (which could be reckoned in the hundreds of thousands) to friends and relatives, to the poor, and to monks and brahmins, after which he retired from the world.

In due course, after passing through villages, towns, markets, kingdoms, and capital cities, he settled in a forest hermitage near a town. His constant meditation and devotion to goodness meant that there was nothing false about his serenity: it had become second nature to him. Whatever he said gave delight both to the ear and to the heart. Though he was plainly full of wisdom, there was no hint of condescension in his manner, no trace of petty self-seeking. In its restraint lay its power, with just the right amount of charm and shrewd discrimination between right and wrong. His way of life there attracted notice: its monkish simplicity was delightful and was commended by the good. He was held in even greater esteem when people, in their curiosity, discovered how he had renounced his inheritance. [4] Good qualities are all the more pleasing when they bear the stamp of noble birth, as are shafts of moonlight when they fall on a fine object.

Now, a friend and contemporary of his father heard that the Bodhisattva had retired there and, out of respect for his goodness, went and visited him. After the usual greetings he introduced himself as a friend of the Bodhisattva's father and at a turn in the conversation affectionately remonstrated with him, saying: "Really, didn't your holiness behave a little inconsiderately in renouncing the world at your time of life, without a thought for the family line?[1] [5] Those who live a life of goodness can observe the moral Law in their home as well as in the forest. Why, then, have you abandoned your beautiful home and set your heart on the jungle? [6] You survive only on the alms people give you out of kindness. They care about you as little as they would about a wastrel. Dressed in rags, without friends or relatives, you neglect yourself here in the depths of the forest. [7] How can you embrace this life of poverty and be a willing slave to sorrow? To see you in this state would be enough to bring tears to the eyes of your enemies.

[8] So return to your ancestral home. Even you must have heard how it continues to flourish. There you can fulfil both your religious duties and the wish for a noble son, for that is how the saying goes: [9] even for a slave, it is a comfort to have his own home to go to. How much more so is a home that is yours for the taking and that radiates splendor and wealth."

But the bliss of solitude, like the taste of nectar, had suffused the Bodhisattva's being: his heart was set on it. He well knew the difference between a worldly existence and life in the forest, and this invitation to gratify his desires gave him the same disagreeable feeling as talk about food would give someone who had just had a large meal. So he answered: [10] "I know you are speaking out of affection, and that makes it less painful to hear, but never apply the word 'happy' to the prison house of worldly life. [11] It is a life full of unease, whether one has money or not: either one has the worry of looking after it or the trouble of earning it. [12] It is folly to delight in a way of life that affords not an ounce of pleasure to either rich or poor; rather, such a life is the reward for previous wickedness. As to your claim that even while living in society one can fulfil one's religious duties—that is true enough. But it strikes me as extremely difficult to put into practice. Worldly life presents numerous obstacles to leading the religious life and involves endless troubles. My dear friend, just think—[13] worldly life is not for someone who has no wants, who speaks nothing but the plain truth, who has forsworn violence, and who is incapable of harming others. If someone is set on the pleasures he anticipates from worldly life, he will obviously make every effort to procure them. [14] If one devotes oneself to religion, that precludes worldly considerations. Conversely, if one is taken up with worldly matters, where does religion come in? Tranquility is the essence of the spiritual life, and enterprise of the worldly life. [15] Would anyone who is self-aware choose to lead a worldly life, knowing its serious incompatibility with things spiritual? On the other hand, once the lure of worldly pleasures leads one to disregard spiritual matters, there is nothing to stop one from realizing those pleasures. [16] And the inevitable consequence is a ruined reputation, remorse, and misfortune, which is why sensible people avoid, like the plague, any means of pleasure that goes contrary to the moral Law. Besides, this idea that worldly life is pleasant strikes me as wishful thinking. [17] The worldling is constantly obliged either to earn money or to safeguard it. When it comes to murder, kidnap, or ruin, he is a prime target, and even a king's riches fail to satisfy him—no more can a cloudburst fill the ocean. [18] How, why, or when can one find happiness in worldly life, unless one cherishes illusions about it? To delude oneself that happiness lies in cultivating sensual pleasures is as foolish as scratching a wound. In fact, generally speaking, I would say that [19] wealth usually makes the worldling arrogant, that good birth makes him proud, and that power makes him insolent. Discomfort makes him angry, and misfortune reduces him to despair. When would he find a chance to be calm? That is why I entreat you to realize that [20] in a home lurk the serpents of pride, arrogance, and delusion. In a home all the joy and delight of tranquility are abolished. A home is the abode of sorrows, bitter and plentiful. Who, I ask you, would want to go out and meet such a fate? [21] In the forest, though, people live in contentment, tasting the joys of solitude. There the mind attains such serenity as would be hard to find in heaven itself. [22] Thus it is that, though I keep alive only thanks to other people's kindness and am dressed in mere rags, I am happy here in the forest. I do not want a happiness that involves wrongdoing, like food tainted with poison. My conscience forbids it."

His father's friend was quite won over by these convincing arguments, and expressed his personal esteem for the Great Being by treating him with very special respect.

So, then—those who care for the things of the spirit chafe at worldly ties, seeing them as so many obstacles to a pure and calm existence.

The Lotus Stalks

19

THOSE WHO KNOW HOW TO SAVOR THE bliss of solitude shy away from worldly pleasures as from something deceptive and harmful.

According to tradition, the Bodhisattva was at one time born into an illustrious brahmin family, famed for its goodness and free from blemish. He had six younger brothers who were as good as he was and who always deferred to him out of affection and respect. He also had a sister, which made seven. He applied himself seriously to studying the Vedas, the subsidiary Vedas,[1] and related subjects, thereby gaining a reputation among the learned and universal esteem. To his parents he showed the deep devotion that one shows to the gods, and, like a teacher or a father, he gave his younger brothers instruction. He himself, being a model of wisdom and discretion, took an active part in the affairs of the world.

When, in course of time, his parents died, he felt such revulsion for the endless round of birth and death that, after performing the funeral rites and spending several days in mourning, he gathered together his brothers and said: [1] "Sad and bitter as it is, such is the way things are in this world: death parts us at last even from those we have lived with all our lives. [2] So I want to set off on the glorious path to final bliss in case Death, the enemy, should strike while I am still absorbed in worldly matters. I would therefore like you to know that our family has, by honest means, acquired sufficient capital to support you. You can continue to live here all together, in mutual affection and respect, never relaxing your concern for integrity, honesty, and good behavior, diligent in the study of the Vedas, attentive to the wishes of friends, guests, and relatives, ever intent on what is right. [3] Always

19 · 4 take pride in behaving properly, apply yourselves to your daily study of the Vedas, be generous and thereby maintain your status of householders fittingly. [4] In this way honor will accrue to you, and religious merit, and wealth which is the source of pleasure. You may then expect an easy transition into the next life. So pay constant attention to your worldly responsibilities."

When he mentioned renunciation, his brothers grew alarmed at the thought of being parted from him. Tears of sorrow streamed down their faces as they bowed before him and said: "We are transfixed with grief at the loss of our parents. How can you rub salt into our open wound by causing us a fresh bout of misery? [5] Our hearts have still to recover from the wound inflicted by our parents' death. So please, in your wisdom, give up this idea. Do not apply salt to our wound.[2] [6] But if you are convinced that it is wrong to remain attached to the world or that the way to bliss lies in contentedly living in the forest, then why do you want to leave us to flounder helplessly in the affairs of the world while you retire to the forest by yourself? So, whatever course you adopt will be ours also. We too will renounce the world." To this the Bodhisattva replied: [7] "Not being in the habit of seeing clearly, people are influenced by their passions and desires. On the whole they are apt to regard renunciation as tantamount to throwing oneself down a precipice, which is why I have held back and not spoken to you in favor of leading the homeless life, even though I am well aware of the difference between life in the world and life in the forest. However, if you too are so inclined, let us leave home together."

And so the seven brothers, with their sister making eight, gave up their large family house and fortune, left their numerous friends, their kith and kin, to bewail them, and set out to lead the homeless life of ascetics. One retainer and two servants, a man and a woman—all three devoted to the family—joined them in their renunciation.

There was a large stretch of open country and in it a lake of pure blue water. By day it was ablaze with a mass of red lotus blossom; by night it gleamed with clusters of white water lilies. Swarms of bees hovered busily over it. Here the company settled, each in his separate hut, situated at a distance from one another, enveloped by shady trees, and delightfully secluded. They were intent on their vows and observances and passed their days concentrating their minds on meditation. Every fifth day they went to the Bodhisattva to hear him teach. Each of his sermons was marked by calm and serenity. He would encourage them to meditate, point out the evils of worldly desire, and stir their conscience. He would dwell at length on the pleasures of solitude and would condemn deceit, humbug, sloth, and other such faults. The serving woman continued to attend upon them out of respect and devotion. She pulled up lotus stalks from the lake and laid them out in equal portions on large lotus leaves by the clean-washed shore. Then she announced that it was time to eat by clapping a piece of wood and withdrew. The hermits first prayed and made offerings, then, one by one, in order of seniority, approached the shore, and, each taking his own share of lotus stalks, returned to their separate huts. There they ate the food and resumed their meditation. In this way they never saw each other except when they met to hear the Bodhisattva teach.

This blameless and exemplary life of theirs, this delight in solitude, this whole-hearted dedication to meditation, came to be talked of everywhere, and, hearing of it, Śakra, lord of the gods, decided to visit them and put it to the test. Seeing for himself how absorbed they were in meditation, how innocent of all wrongdoing, how free from regret, and how content in their tranquil life, he admired their goodness all the more and set his heart on putting it to the test. [8] He who lives in the forest without regrets, in complete serenity, excites admiration in the hearts of good men.

One day the serving woman had pulled up the lotus stalks and washed them so that they looked as soft and white as the teeth of a young elephant. She had arranged them in equal portions on the gleaming emerald-green lotus leaves, decorating them with a garnish of lotus blades and filaments. She had sounded the wooden clapper to let the hermits know that

19 · 9 it was dinnertime and had slipped away. At this juncture Śakra, lord of the gods, chose to put the Bodhisattva to the test by making the first portion of lotus stalks disappear. [9] The time to gauge a good man's fortitude is when difficulties arise and comfort vanishes: that is when it blossoms out. The Bodhisattva came to where the first portion of lotus stalks had been put but found the lotus leaf with nothing on it except the garnish, which was in a complete mess. Concluding from this that someone had taken his portion of stalks, he immediately turned round, without a trace of anger or irritation, went back to his hut, and resumed his customary meditations. To avoid upsetting anyone, he did not mention the incident to his brother hermits, who, naturally assuming he had taken his portion, duly took theirs in the usual order of precedence, ate them, each in his own hut, and continued with their meditation.

On each of the four following days Śakra hid the Bodhisattva's portion of lotus stalks, but the Great Being remained as calm and unflurried as ever. [10] Wise men see that death consists not in the extinction of life but in mental confusion, which is why they do not get agitated even when their life is at stake. On the afternoon of the fifth day the hermits met, as usual, at the Bodhisattva's hut to hear him teach, and they saw that he had got thinner: his eyes and cheeks were sunken, his face had lost its color, and his voice its resonance. But though he was physically wasted, there was no diminution in his fortitude, his serenity, or his goodness. His was the frail beauty of the new moon. Approaching him with respect, the hermits anxiously asked him why he was so emaciated. The Bodhisattva told them exactly what had happened, but the ascetics could not suspect each other of such base behavior, and his painful state was so distressing to them that all they could say was "Oh dear, oh dear!" as they stood there bowing their heads in embarrassment. Śakra prevented them using their powers of reasoning, so that they arrived at no explanation as to how this had come about.

Then the brother who was nearest in age to the Bodhisattva gave vent to his feelings and also demonstrated his innocence, by pronouncing this extraordinary curse: [11] "Holy brahmin, may whoever took your lotus stalks get a house whose fine exterior will be a sign of great wealth, a wife who delights his heart, and a full share of sons and grandsons." The next said: [12] "Best of brahmins, whoever it was who took your lotus stalks, may he be powerfully attracted to worldly pleasures: let him wear wreaths and garlands, sandalwood perfume, fine garments, and ornaments that his children will finger." The next said: [13] "May he who took your lotus stalks, even if it was only once, take pleasure in worldly affairs, without a thought for his old age, enjoying the wealth he has earned by farming the land—let him be a family man who takes delight in his children's prattle." The next said: [14] "May he who greedily stole your lotus stalks rule the whole earth as king and be revered by other kings, showing the humility of slaves as they bow down their dangling diadems." The next said: [15] "Whoever it was that took your lotus stalks, may he be family priest to a king, a master of magic spells, charms, and the like, and may he also receive the king's favor." The next said: [16] "May he who coveted your lotus stalks rather than your virtues be revered by people who will gather round him as a teacher fully versed in the Vedas, with the great respect that is accorded to an ascetic." The retainer said: [17] "May he who could not control his greed, even for your lotus stalks, receive, by a king's grant, a prosperous village full of people and rich in grain, wood, and water. May he proceed to enjoy it and die without losing pleasure in life." The manservant said: [18] "May he who ruined his own interests for the sake of those lotus stalks be a village headman, surrounded by friends and lulled by the songs and dances of women, without incurring the king's displeasure." The sister said: [19] "Whoever it was who took the lotus stalks from such a person as you, may she radiate beauty and loveliness so that a king takes her for his wife and gives her precedence over a thousand other women." The maidservant said: [20] "Whoever had an eye on your lotus stalks instead of on doing right, may she eat sweets to her heart's content, all by herself, regardless of what pious people may think, and take delight in receiving attention."

Now, a sprite, an elephant, and a monkey who lived in the

forest had come to that spot to hear the teaching. On hearing this conversation they felt extremely awkward and upset. The sprite, to prove his own innocence, made an oath in front of those present: [21] "He who sinned against you in this matter of the lotus stalks, may he be caretaker and surveyor of the fabric in the great monastery at Kacaṅgalā,[3] and may he make one window every day." The elephant said: [22] "Most excellent of holy men, whoever stole your lotus stalks, may he be bound with six hundred firm fetters, exchange the lovely forest for a place crowded with people, and suffer the painful tug of a mahout's hook." The monkey said: [23] "He who greedily stole your lotus stalks—let him wear a wreath of flowers on his head and a tin collar that rubs against his neck. Let him be beaten with a stick till he is forced to parade in front of a snake's mouth. And let him live in captivity, tied to a leash."[4]

Then the Bodhisattva addressed them all in these kind and gentle words, which showed how long-suffering he was: [24] "Whoever claims he has lost something when he has not, or whoever suspects any of you of such a thing, may he enjoy worldly pleasures to his heart's content, and let him die while still taking part in worldly affairs."

Śakra, lord of the gods, was taken aback by these extraordinary protestations which showed their hostility to worldly pleasures, and a feeling of respect grew in him. He came among the hermits, this time in his own dazzling shape, and said, as if in indignation: "Don't talk like that: [25] those comforts which people are so anxious to secure in their quest for happiness, which allow them no sleep, and for which they are prepared to undergo hardship and suffering—why disparage them by calling them 'worldly pleasures'?" "Sir," replied the Bodhisattva, "worldly pleasures bring endless unhappiness in their train. Listen while I tell you briefly what considerations prevent holy men from approving of them. [26] In satisfying their senses, men suffer bondage and death, sorrow, weariness, fear, and all kinds of misery. To satisfy their sensual appetites kings high-handedly infringe the laws and so fall to perdition when they come to die. [27] When friendship suddenly turns sour and people take to the miry path of cunning and deceit, when they lose their good name while still alive and meet with sufferings after death, worldly pleasures are surely the root cause. [28] My lord Śakra, since worldly pleasures spell the ruin of all men, be their condition high, middling, or low, both in this life and the next, holy men, who care for the things of the spirit, keep clear of them as they would of angry snakes."

Śakra, lord of the gods, greeted these words of the Bodhisattva with approval, and the noble character of the hermits won his heart so completely that he confessed his guilt: [29] "Qualities that are latent come out into the open and are known for what they are only when put to the test. That is why I removed your lotus stalks—to test you. [30] How fortunate the world is to have in it holy men of such renown! You have shown both integrity and firmness, so here are your lotus stalks." Saying this, he handed the lotus stalks to the Bodhisattva who, nevertheless, reproved him, with quiet dignity, for his impudence. [31] "We are neither friends of yours nor relatives, nor are we your troupe of actors or buffoons. So on what grounds do you, lord of the gods, come here to play tricks on hermits?"

At these words Śakra, lord of the gods, hastily discarded the earrings and diadem which lit up his face like lightning, and bowed respectfully before the Bodhisattva, asking forgiveness. [32] "Selfless one, please be like a father or a teacher and forgive the silly trick I played, now that I have explained why I did it. [33] It is natural for those whose inner eye is shut to stumble where it is smooth. Those who are self-aware should be indulgent about such things. So do not take this to heart." With this plea for pardon Śakra vanished then and there.

So, then—those who know how to savor the bliss of solitude shy away from worldly pleasures as from something deceptive and harmful.[5]

20 *The Royal Treasurer*

GOOD PEOPLE ARE SPURRED ON TO acquire the virtues that are falsely imputed to them. So make every effort to acquire virtues.

According to tradition, the Bodhisattva was once a king's treasurer, distinguished alike for his learning, his good birth, and his modest behavior. His mind was lofty and subtle, and he took pleasure in fair dealing. He had applied himself assiduously to numerous branches of knowledge and thereby had become noted for his happy turn of phrase. Prompted by compassion, he showered largesse, in the form of generous presents, all about him, and, thanks to his great wealth, he
was regarded as a model of the wealthy citizen. In short, [1]
being saintly by nature and having acquired such additional assets as learning, he was, for a large number of people, a unique object of respect.

Now one day, when the Great Being had gone to the palace on some business, his mother-in-law came to his house to see her daughter. After asking each other how they were, they settled down to an intimate chat in the course of which the mother questioned her daughter, the Bodhisattva's wife: "I hope your husband appreciates you, my dear, and takes notice of your loving attentions. He doesn't upset you by being irritable, does he?" The daughter bowed her head in embarrassment and, feeling shy and timid, replied softly: "It would be hard to find a character like his, with such goodness and decency, even in an ascetic who had renounced the world."

Old age had impaired her mother's hearing and understanding, and consequently she misunderstood what her daughter was saying in those shy undertones. She caught the word "ascetic" and immediately jumped to the conclusion

that her son-in-law had turned into an ascetic. With loud 20 · 7
sobs she commiserated with her daughter and, quite overcome with emotion, indulged in a long lament. "What sort of goodness and decency is he showing by abandoning his loving family and renouncing the world like this? And anyway, what business has he with renunciation? [2] How is it that someone so young and handsome and sensitive, who is used to comfort and is a favorite of the king, can turn his thoughts to a hermit's life in the forest? [3] There has been no unpleasantness with his family, and age, with its disfigurements, has not yet touched him. What possesses him to abandon, all of a sudden and without a qualm, his home and all its inexhaustible wealth? [4] He is remarkably good-mannered, sensible, dutiful, considerate. How could he act so irresponsibly and with such want of feeling to his own relatives? [5] He has always shown consideration to monks and brahmins, friends and dependents, his own relatives, and anyone who is in distress. His true wealth lies in his good character. Couldn't he achieve what he wants just as well by staying at home as in the forest? [6] Can't he see that, by abandoning, in this excessive zeal for goodness, his innocent, faithful helpmate, he is in fact straying far from the path of goodness? [7] Alas! ah, alas! that by a quirk of fate men can achieve the slightest shred of goodness after abandoning, without any feeling of compunction, their devoted family."

Her mother's miserable and heartfelt lament at the Bodhisattva's supposed renunciation of the world made his wife tremble at heart, as was natural in a woman. She lost her composure, and her face expressed overwhelming despair. The shock of this sudden assault of pain and grief made her quite lose the thread of their conversation. She concluded that her husband had indeed renounced the world—and that on hearing the unpleasant news, her mother had come to the house to comfort her. The poor young thing wept loudly and miserably, then fainted away.

When they came to hear of it, the family and servants, in an access of grief and sorrow, made loud lament, and the news brought all the Bodhisattva's acquaintances to the house: friends and neighbors, relatives and kinsmen, brahmin householders, all who had a tie of affection with the treasurer, as well as the greater part of the citizenry. [8] Just as he had, on principle, remained true to people in good times and bad, so they, as though following his example, remained true to him in good times and bad.

As the Bodhisattva reached home, on his return from the palace, he heard the sound of weeping and wailing and saw that a huge crowd had gathered there. He asked his bearer to find out what was going on. The man soon came back to tell him what the situation was. [9] "There is a rumor that your lordship has renounced your splendid mansion in favor of taking up the life of an ascetic, and, hearing about it, these people in their concern have come from far and wide."

In the innocence of his heart, the Great Being took these words as something of a reproach, and a feeling of shame made him uneasy. "Oh what a high opinion people have of me!" he thought to himself. [10] "Now that I have gained such a flattering reputation from them, it would be weak of me to want to cling on to worldly comforts. [11] That way I would only be inciting people to evil and a way of life that would lack meaning because blind to goodness. People would then lose their respect for me, and life would not be worth living. [12] I shall therefore live up to the high opinion the people have of me, by acting upon it: I shall abandon my home, with all its evil distractions, out of love for a hermit's life in the forest."

With this decided, the Great One turned back there and then and told the king's usher that the treasurer wanted another audience with his highness. He was admitted to the king's presence and approached him with due respect. The king asked him what it was he wanted, and he replied that he wanted to renounce the world and would like leave to do so. The king was taken aback and, in his affection, said to him: [13] "What is wrong, that you should wish to set out for the forest while I am still alive—I who am closer to you than friends or relatives? Surely I can put it right, either with money or through diplomacy or by means of force? [14] Are you in need of money? Then take it from me. Whatever may be the source of your trouble, I will cure it. Or are there other considerations that impel you to leave your relatives and me, though I remonstrate with you here, and to withdraw to the forest?"

To these words, which showed the king's affection and high regard for him, the Great One politely answered: [15] "How can those who cling to your arm for protection have any troubles or be at a loss to think where money will come from? No, I am not withdrawing to the forest because of some misfortune. Listen, my lord, while I tell you the true reason. [16] There is a rumor abroad that I have taken religious vows, and a crowd of people are bewailing the fact with tears and gloomy looks. I want to live in the solitude of the forest because I have been judged capable of such a fine action." "My dear sir," said the king, "you oughtn't to forsake us just because of a rumor. Idle gossip has no bearing on your true worth: it can neither confer nor withhold goodness. [17] All sorts of tales are concocted by wild imaginings. Then they spread unchecked. Anyone who takes them to heart, let alone acts upon them, is ridiculous." "Not at all, your highness," said the Bodhisattva. "If people have high expectations of you, surely you ought to live up to them. Look, my lord, [18] when a person gets a reputation for being good, he cannot, if there really is good in him, fall short of it. He must accept the onus put upon him, if only out of self-respect. [19] For if he is actually seen to be as good as he is supposed to be, then his reputation is confirmed and shines out all the more. Otherwise he is like a dried-up well. [20] A reputation built on false assumptions is shaken by the wind of doubt and, as it topples, shatters a man's good name beyond hope of easy recovery. [21] And so, my lord, you ought not to prevent me ridding myself of things that should be avoided as surely as black adders raising their hoods in anger—I mean family and possessions, which only cause trouble. [22] Though it is kind of you to show affection and appreciation to a servant by offering him money, what use can it be to me now that I have turned my back on the world? Money means possessions and base passions."

With these words the Great Being won over the king and obtained his leave. He straightaway set off for the forest retreat. Thereupon his friends, relatives, and dependents followed him and, with tears of grief filling their eyes, clasped his feet and tried to stop him. Some, with their hands held together respectfully, stood blocking his path. Others tried to coax him homeward with a mixture of fond embraces and gentle persuasion. Others, purely out of affection, swore at him with whatever strong language came to mind. Others pointed out that he ought to feel pity for his friends and relatives. Others, by a combination of reasoning and appeals to holy writ, tried to convince him that the householder's state was full of merit. By stressing the hardships of life in a hermitage, by entreating him to fulfill the remainder of his worldly responsibilities, by casting doubt on the existence of rewards for virtue in the next life, and by adducing various other arguments, they tried to deflect him from his purpose. Seeing how intent his friends were—their faces wet with tears—how opposed to his inclination to renounce the world, how anxious to put a stop to his departure for the forest, he thought: "Clearly, [23] when a person has gone astray, it is right for those who claim to be his friends to insist, however forcefully, on what is best for him. The wise accept that this is the correct way to behave—and even more so when the remedy is pleasant as well as beneficial. [24] But these people, without any qualms, warn me against withdrawing to the forest, as if I were going to be contaminated with something evil, saying 'Better the home than the forest.' How can such an idea arise in sane minds? [25] A dead man, or even someone about to die, or someone who has lapsed morally—each is a fit object of lamentation. But what is the idea of these people bewailing me who am alive and simply want to retire to the forest? [26] If it is being parted from me that makes them so unhappy, then why don't they come and live with me in the forest? But if they prefer their comfortable home life to my company, why bother with such a lavish display of tears? [27] On the other hand, if it is family attachment that debars them from the ascetic life, why didn't the same excuse occur to them on earlier occasions, when conscripted into the ranks of battle? [28] I have witnessed their noble conduct in good times and bad and appreciate that these tears are visible proof of it. Yet, however deeply rooted their friendly feeling, it will seem a sham now unless they follow my example. [29] Just as it is respect for a worthy friend that fills their eyes with tears, chokes their dissuasive pleas with sobs, and bows their heads in reverence, [30] so their affection should make them take the worthy decision to follow my example and become ascetics. Otherwise all this is just playacting, which is something shameful to the truehearted. [31] A worthless wretch can always count on having two or three friends, even in times of disaster. But a man has only to enter on the life of a hermit and, no matter how worthy he may be, it will be very hard for him to get a single companion. [32] In battles crowded with furious elephants, they were ready to oust me from my position in the vanguard. Now they will not even follow me to the forest. Am I the same as I was then? Are they? [33] I don't remember having done them any wrong to make them lose their affection. So this friendly behavior may really be genuine and stem from a concern for my well-being. [34] Or could it be my own lack of virtues that now stops them from following me to the forest? For once hearts are wedded to virtue, what power on earth can draw them to those who do not possess it? [35] But why cast vain suspicions on those who cannot see either the evil of worldly life or the good of ascetic life—both equally transparent? Obviously they have kept the inner eye of wisdom shut. [36] They cannot bear to give up pleasures that cause unhappiness both in this life and the next. Instead, they reject me together with the forest life, which is the reverse of all that. Oh, what delusion! [37] Once I have gained true power by living in a forest retreat, I shall strike with all my might at those very evils which have so ensnared these friends of mine and the whole creation, that they cannot find peace."

[38] With these considerations, the Bodhisattva made up his

20 · 38 mind. He calmly dismissed his friends' well-meaning attempts with a few gently disarming words, and left for the hermitage.

So, then—good people are spurred on to acquire the virtues that are falsely imputed to them. So make every effort to acquire virtues.

Bodhi 21

ONLY BY OVERCOMING ONE'S ANGER can one appease one's enemies. Otherwise one only provokes them further.

According to tradition, the Great Being, while still a Bodhisattva, was once born into a great brahmin family which was renowned for its noble-minded devotion to goodness. Its wealth was assured; the king paid it respect, and people revered it as they did the gods. As time passed, he grew up, received the ritual sacraments, and devoted himself so eagerly to study that he soon earned a reputation in learned gatherings. [1] For a scholar's true worth best manifests itself in learned gatherings, as does a jewel's among connoisseurs of jewels, a hero's in battle.

Now the Great One was thoroughly familiar with the idea of renunciation. Because he had developed his moral sense in previous lives and had purified his mind with wisdom, he could take no pleasure in worldly affairs. He could see that material preoccupations involve one in endless quarrels and disputes, in animosity and nastiness, and also that they are subject to the exactions of kings or of thieves, to the accidents of fire and water, and to unpleasant relatives.[1] And since he could derive no satisfaction from what, in effect, was a boundless source of evils, but cared instead for the things of the spirit, he rejected all worldly concerns as if they were poisoned food, cut off his beautiful hair and beard, exchanged the elegant attire of the householder for the drab, rust-colored robe, and undertook the glorious discipline and self-denial of the ascetic's life. His wife, in her devotion to him, also cut off her hair and no longer bothered about wearing unnecessary ornaments. Adorned only with her own natural beauty and goodness, she wrapped herself in a rust-colored robe and followed her husband on the path of renunciation.

When the Bodhisattva realized that she intended to go with him to the forest retreat, he thought it no fit place for a delicate woman to live in and said to her: “My dear, you have shown how deeply you love me. There is no need to carry on with your decision to accompany me. The right place for you to live is where other women live who have renounced the world. You must realize that conditions are hard in these forest retreats. [2] Homeless ascetics take shelter in cemeteries, empty buildings, mountain caves, and forests haunted by beasts of prey: they spend the night wherever they happen to be when the sun sets. [3] Intent on their meditation, they always go about alone and are averse to the mere sight of a woman. So change your mind. What good will it do you to wear yourself out?” But she had definitely made up her mind to go with him, and tears stood in her eyes as she answered somewhat as follows: [4] “If the joy of going with you seemed like a hardship to me, why then would I torture myself and offend you? [5] But as I simply cannot exist without you, please forgive me for not submitting to your wishes.” Though he urged her two or three times more, she was not prepared to turn back. So the Bodhisattva made up his mind to let her have her way.

Like a devoted shelduck[2] with her mate, she followed him as he wandered through villages, markets, and towns. One day, after the midday meal, he sat meditating in a remote and untouched part of a forest. It was a beautiful place, with all kinds of fine trees whose dense growth cast deep shade. Here and there flecks of sunlight dappled the leaves, while pollen from various flowers covered the ground. As evening drew on, the Great One came out of his trance and sewed some rags together for clothing, while his companion in austerities sat close by, gracing the foot of a tree—and indeed she was lovely enough to be taken for a dryad. There she meditated with the mental concentration taught her by her husband.

It was springtime, when the sprays of leaves look their loveliest. The groves were filled with the hum of bees, moving from one spot to another in a swarm, and cuckoos had begun to call. The lakes and ponds looked attractive with their show of bright lilies and lotuses, and the soft breezes were fragrant with the scent of numerous flowers.

Now the king of those parts was making a tour of the countryside, and came to that very same spot. [6/7] What a delight it is to see the woods become the haunt of Love, when spring seems almost to smother them with its bounty. Bright clusters of flowers blaze out. Cuckoos and peacocks fill the air with their cries, and drowsy bees add their drone. Lotuses cover the ponds, and soft grass pushes up. The king approached the Bodhisattva with respect and, after exchanging greetings with him, sat down in that solitary place. Then he caught sight of a female ascetic of ravishing looks, and his heart was violently disturbed by her beauty. Realizing that she must be the man's companion, and, being lustful by nature, he began to think how he could abduct her. [8] But he had heard how powerful ascetics can be—that their smoldering anger can flame up in a curse—and, though passion had destroyed all self-control, he had no wish to offend the Bodhisattva. His idea was first to discover what powers this anchorite had achieved by his penance. Only then would he know how to proceed. Otherwise there was no hope. If affection for the woman still swayed the man's heart, then obviously he had no supernatural powers. But were he free from attachment or only mildly concerned, then one would have to reckon that he had those powers in full measure.

With this in mind the king addressed the Bodhisattva as though he wished him well, intending to gauge the strength of his spiritual powers: "Hello there, holy father. The world is full of mischief-makers and desperadoes. You ought not to live with this beautiful companion of yours in the woods, where there is no one to call on for help. If any harm came to her, people would certainly put the blame on me. Look—[9] your penances in these lonely parts have made you physically

21 · 10 weak. A man need take no notice of you or of morals and may abduct this lady by force. Then what would you do about it, apart from bewailing her loss? [10] If you give way to anger, you will only disturb your peace of mind, put an end to your pursuit of the good, and so lose your reputation. So let her live in society. After all, what do ascetics want with female company?" "Your majesty," replied the Bodhisattva, "what you say is true. Nevertheless, hear what I would do in such a situation. [11] Were anyone to cross me in this way—be it in an access of pride or without due consideration—he would certainly not escape as long as I were alive, no more than dust can escape a heavy shower of rain." From this the king concluded that the Great Being cared greatly for the woman and therefore had no spiritual powers. Disregarding him and, in his blind passion, heedless of consequences, he ordered the superintendents of the palace women to go and put that lady ascetic in the harem.

When she heard this she felt like a doe in the forest, attacked by a wild beast. Fear and desperation showed in her face, her eyes filled with tears, and her throat choked with sobs, as she lamented her fate: [12] "When people are overwhelmed by catastrophe, a king, like a father, is the best person to resort to. But if the king himself is the source of evil, whom is there to call on for help? [13] Alas! the Guardians of the World have fallen from office, or do not exist, or else have succumbed to death, seeing that they make no attempt to help the afflicted. Even Dharma,[3] I begin to think, is no more than a word. [14] But why speak of the gods when my noble husband is himself unmoved by my fate and keeps silence? Surely, when molested by wicked people, even a stranger has a claim on one's help. [15] He has only to say 'Vanish!' and his curse, like a flash of lightning, could at one stroke turn a mountain into a memory. But even in my present plight he keeps silence. And still, poor wretch that I am, I must go on living. [16] Or am I a wicked person, quite undeserving of pity in such misfortune? Yet surely the proper way for holy men is to treat the afflicted with compassion? [17] I suspect you have still not forgotten how I refused to turn back when you asked me to. Ah! is this the happiness I longed for even at the risk of your displeasure?" Tears and cries and pathetic laments were all that came from her as the men, on the king's orders, put her into a carriage and took her off to the harem.

The Great Being saw it all, but, with great presence of mind, managed to restrain any impulse to be angry and went on sewing rags as before, calm and unperturbed. The king then said to him: [18] "Earlier on, anger and indignation made you burst out with threats loud and bold. But now that you have actually witnessed that lovely woman being carried off, you cloak your frustration with a show of calm. [19] Go on—show what strength you have in your arm or else reveal the power you have gained as a result of your penance. To make vain assertions without taking account of one's limitations shows one up in a poor light." "Your highness," replied the Bodhisattva, "I assure you I made no vain assertion: [20] he who crossed me in this did not, despite his efforts, escape me. I subdued him by force. And so my assertion proved true after all."

The Bodhisattva's calm assurance suggested great reserves of power and aroused in the king some inkling of the special qualities of an ascetic. He began to wonder whether that brahmin had not meant something quite different by what he had said. Conscious that he might have misunderstood him and so have acted rashly, he asked the Bodhisattva: [21] "Who was your other adversary who, despite his struggles, did not escape you? Whom did you subdue just now, as a raincloud smothers rising dust?" "Listen, your majesty," replied the Bodhisattva. [22] "He whose presence makes one blind, whose absence makes one clear-sighted—he stirred within but did not escape me: Anger, I mean, who injures the man who harbors him. [23] He whose presence delights those who wish mankind no good—he stirred within but did not escape me: Anger, the delight of one's enemies. [24] Him whose rising is a bane, him who makes blind, him I suppressed, your highness: Anger is his name. [25] Once anger possesses one, it is farewell to happiness. Even such wealth as one may have acquired slips from one's grasp. Anger, loathsome as a ferocious monster, surged up within me, but I quelled it. [26] Just as fire consumes the stick that kindles it, so anger destroys the man whose false notions give rise to it. [27] Anger—that fever of the heart—breaks out like a raging fire which a man must put out if people are not to despise him. Otherwise their good opinion of him fades, as the light of the moon, that companion of water lilies, fades at dawn. [28] But he who takes no notice of other people's offensive behavior and regards anger as his only real enemy is sure of a reputation that glows as brightly as the lovely halo around the new moon. And there are other reasons why anger is so harmful. [29] A man may wear fine apparel but will still look ugly when anger distorts his features. He may recline on a splendid couch but will not be comfortable if anger has pierced his heart. [30] Anger makes him oblivious of the path to success lying open before him; instead, he strays away from it and so is deprived of fame and success, just as the moon is deprived of its luster in the dark half of the month. [31] Though his friends try to restrain him, he falls headlong to his ruin, all because of anger. Usually he turns stupidly quarrelsome and too dull-witted to discern what is good for him and what bad. [32] Anger incites him to do wrong until doing so becomes part of his nature. Then he will repent in misery for hundreds of years. Could an enemy inflict anything worse even if roused to fury by extreme provocation? [33] Anger is the enemy within. As such, I recognize it. What man worthy of the name will allow anger's insolence to go unchecked? [34] That is why I did not let anger escape me, though it seethed in my heart. For who can afford to disregard an enemy that causes such mischief?"

These convincing arguments, together with the Bodhisattva's amazing equanimity, pacified the king. [35] "Your eloquence matches your serenity," he said. "But why waste words? I failed to understand you and so was misled."

After commending him like this, the king went up to him, fell down at his feet, and confessed his fault. He begged the

lady ascetic to forgive him, let her free, and offered to act as 21 · 35
an attendant to the Bodhisattva.

So, then—only by overcoming one's anger can one appease one's enemies. Otherwise one only provokes them further. One should therefore make every effort to overcome one's anger.

22 The King of the Geese

BAD PEOPLE ARE INCAPABLE OF BEhaving as good people even in misfortune behave, let alone when all is well with them.

According to tradition, the Bodhisattva was once a king of geese, Dhṛtarāṣṭra by name. He ruled over a huge flock, numbering many hundreds of thousands, on the great lake Mānasa.[1] His general, Sumukha, was quick at discerning whether a policy was good or bad and took an active interest in what was going on in distant lands. Conspicuous for his ability, his kindness, and his modest bearing, he graced a family that was already distinguished. He was reliable and honest, of a virtuous disposition, and brave. He could endure fatigue, was ever alert, and proved a tactician of great skill. Above all, he was devoted to his master. Their noble qualities shone out all the more because of their mutual affection. Just as a teacher, assisted by his senior pupil, teaches the rest of his pupils, or a father, assisted by his eldest son, instructs his other sons, so those two gave that flock of geese a thorough initiation into such matters as would be to their advantage in this life and the next. In those who witnessed it—gods, serpents, goblins, sprites, and ascetics—they aroused the greatest astonishment. [1] To sustain the happiness of that flock was their sole duty, as it is the duty of a bird's two wings to sustain its body in the air. As a result of their ministrations, the flock of geese throve greatly, as does the world of men with the spread of moral order and material prosperity. Then too the lake took on an added beauty. [2] When the geese flocked together, with cries that sounded like the soft clang of women's anklets, it looked as though it were covered with a moving mass of white lotuses. [3] And when they scattered in various directions, forming groups large and small, it looked lovelier even than the sky when it is flecked with isolated wisps of cloud.

The heavenly hosts—denizens of the spiritual world—were amazed at the extraordinary qualities displayed by the king of the geese and his general Sumukha in their active devotion to the good of all beings. They gladly seized any opportunity for talking about their prowess. [4] "Their beautiful bodies are the color of refined gold. When they talk, each syllable of their words is clear. Their gentle manners and behavior are rooted in the moral Law. Who are these two creatures, who outwardly are only a pair of geese?" [5] In this way the supernatural beings, proclaiming the virtues of that pair without stint, spread their fame throughout the world, until kings took it to heart and, like a gift presentation, it went the round of the courts.

Now at that time there was a certain king of Benares called Brahmadatta. On several occasions he heard his trusty ministers and brahmin elders in council speaking highly of the outstanding qualities of the goose king and his general, and this sharpened his curiosity to see them both. So he said to his councilors, who were extremely clever thanks to having studied numerous treatises: "Gentlemen, kindly devise a really ingenious plan which will permit me at least a glimpse of these two remarkable geese." The ministers cast about with their mighty intellects for ways and means, then reported to the king: [6] "Your majesty, creatures everywhere are lured by the promise of happiness. If the geese were to hear of some extraordinary attraction that was likely to make them happy, that should draw them. So we suggest that, in some uninhabited part of the country, your highness should create a lake similar to the lake in which those two are said to be perfectly content, but surpassing it in quality and beauty. Then you should grant immunity to all birds by daily proclamation. When the geese hear of those superior attractions, promising greater happiness, their curiosity will be aroused, and most probably they will be lured here. Just think, your highness—[7] happiness, once it is in one's grasp, generally loses its savor and is taken for granted. But while it is not yet in sight and just a pleasant daydream, it captures the imagination."

The king gave his assent, and in a short while a large and beautiful lake was constructed not too close to the outskirts of the city. In its prodigal beauty it vied with Lake Mānasa. Its pellucid waters were smothered with lotuses and water lilies, white, pink, and blue. [8] Trees, covered in blossom and bright with rustling foliage, surrounded the shore, as though they had come for a sight of the lake. [9] Swarms of bees hovered in excitement, attracted by the lotuses that seemed to be laughing as they swayed to the rocking of the waves. [10] At one point the shoreline gleamed with white water lilies that opened out at the touch of moonbeams and looked like splinters of moonlight cut out of the shadow of trees. [11] Elsewhere the pollen from lotuses and water lilies, gathered together by the fingers of the waves, enhanced the lake with golden filigree. [12] With petals and filaments of lily and lotus gleaming everywhere, the lake displayed its beauty like a gift. [13] A further touch was added by the shoals of fish. The water was so still and clear that their bright shapes were as distinctly visible as if they were moving about in the open air. [14] Where elephants blew spray like pearls cascading from a snapped necklace, the waves of the lake seemed to be atomized as the water splashed on the rocks and scattered. [15] In parts it seemed to be perfumed by bathing nymphs, elephants' ichor, and the pollen of flowers. [16] The lake was like a communal mirror for the wives of the moon, the stars, and it echoed with the calls of birds who flocked there happily.

Such was the lake that the king had constructed and that he gave to the whole tribe of birds for their unlimited enjoyment. Then, to inspire their confidence, he had this proclamation, granting them immunity, announced daily: [17] "To all birds the king gladly donates this lake, whose waters are covered with the petals of lotus and lily, and at the same time he grants them immunity."

It was autumn, the season that draws aside the dark veil of clouds to reveal the sky in all its beauty: when lakes charm the eye with their limpid waters and bright masses of full-blown lotus; when the moon's rays seem enhanced as it takes on a youthful splendor; and when the earth is decked with various crops ripe for harvest. This is the time when young geese take wing from Lake Mānasa. Indeed, one pair of geese from that very flock set off and, roaming across distant regions in the autumnal calm, eventually reached the territory of King Brahmadatta. There they saw the lake ablaze with full-blown lotuses and adazzle with white water lilies. Crowds of birds filled the air with a huge din, and bees were swarming busily. Soft breezes, pleasantly cool, were intent on forming rows of waves and wafted the scent of lotus pollen and lily pollen all around.

At the sight of this lake of surpassing beauty, the pair of geese, accustomed though they were to Lake Mānasa, both felt great wonder, and their thoughts turned to the geese they had left behind—if only the whole flock could come here. [18] When people discover a pleasure that can be shared, their first thoughts are naturally of the friends they love.

There the two geese stayed, enjoying themselves, until the start of the rainy season: when louring cloud masses advance like demon armies yet are not so dense that they cannot be slit by the glinting sword thrusts of lightning; when flocks of bright peacocks fan out the fantastic plumage of their tail feathers and perform dances with drawn-out cries and piercing screams, as though to applaud the triumph of the clouds; when small birds begin to chatter; when the gentle, cooling breezes seem like the deep breathing of the forest, fragrant with the scent of flowering trees; when a flight of young cranes flashing across the sky looks like a cloud's row of teeth; when geese in flocks are eager to fly north[2] and warble softly in their longing to be off. So it was that the pair of geese now returned to Lake Mānasa. They entered the goose king's presence, and, when the conversation turned to the subject of foreign lands, they spoke highly of the amazing lake they had found: "Your highness, south of the Himalaya, at Benares, a king called Brahmadatta has given over a large lake for the free use and enjoyment of all birds and has declared it a sanctuary by daily proclamation. The place is extraordinarily beautiful—too lovely to describe in detail—and birds enjoy themselves there without fear or apprehension, as if they were in their own homes. When the monsoon is over, we suggest that your majesty should go there."

Indeed, all the geese grew eager to set eyes on this lake, the moment they heard about it. The Bodhisattva, with an intent look of enquiry, asked Sumukha his commander-in-chief for his view. Sumukha bowed and said: "In my opinion, your majesty ought not to go there, and my reason is that those exquisite delights are just so many enticements. Besides, we lack none of them where we are now. When men appear to have tender compassion in their hearts, it is usually deceptive. They affect charming ways and say nice things, but underneath it all you find a thoroughly nasty character. Just consider, my lord: [19] birds and beasts express what they feel by their cries. Only human beings are clever enough to express the opposite. [20] Of course their language is sweet and smooth and disarming. But, then, merchants also risk some outlay in the expectation of gain. [21] So, my lord, you shouldn't trust any of them in the slightest. If to attain one's ends means running risks and denying good sense, then that cannot be good. However, if we must go there, let us go and enjoy the abundant charms of the lake, but without staying there for long or entertaining any idea of settling. That is my view."

The colony of geese grew ever more anxious to see the lake at Benares, and they never tired of begging the Bodhisattva to go and visit it. So, when autumn came round and the moon was bright and the sky spangled with stars, he gave in to their wishes and set off in that direction, surrounded by the whole vast flock of geese headed by Sumukha, like the moon encircled by a mass of autumn clouds.

[22] When they caught sight of the lovely lake, they were amazed and delighted. But once they had landed on its waters they matched it in beauty and brilliance. [23] Its situation gave it various advantages over Lake Mānasa, so that all memory of the old lake faded as their attention turned to the new. They heard the proclamation of immunity and noticed how all the birds were contented. The prodigal beauty of the lake

gladdened their hearts, and, taking pleasure in it, as in a stroll through a park, they felt pure delight.

Now the superintendents of the lake reported the flock's arrival there to the king, and mentioned one remarkable pair who had exactly the appearance and characteristics attributed to the two famous geese—their wings gleamed bright as gold; the beauty of their beaks and claws outshone even gold; and their well-shaped bodies were larger than normal. With their retinue of many hundreds of thousands of geese, it was as though they had come expressly to adorn the royal lake.

Thereupon the king sought out a fowler who enjoyed a wide reputation for his skill in bird catching, and he keenly urged him to capture the two geese. The fowler promised to do so and, after noting the birds' nesting place and territory, laid strong, well-hidden snares in different spots.

One day the geese were flying around blithely, without a suspicion of danger, so confident were they, when the goose king caught his foot in a snare. [24] Trust can so easily lead to catastrophe. It induces people to become careless and rash by very gradually building up their confidence till they are quite oblivious of danger. To prevent any other member of the flock from meeting a similar fate there, the Bodhisattva let out a special cry to signal the lake's perils. The geese, in alarm at their king being snared, flew up into the sky with a hubbub of terrifying screams, taking no notice of each other, like soldiers when their leader has been struck down. But Sumukha, the commander-in-chief, did not stir from the side of his king. [25] The ties of true affection are such that one will risk one's life without a qualm. They make a friend's distress seem a calamity worse than death.

The Bodhisattva said to him: [26] "Get away, Sumukha, get away. You are a fool to stay here any longer. What chance have you of helping me in my plight?" [27] "If I stay here," replied Sumukha, "I need not necessarily meet my end, and if I go away I still won't escape old age and death. In happy days I was always at your service. How can I abandon your highness in time of distress? [28] Were I to forsake you, king of birds, merely to save my skin, what would shield me from a storm of reproach? [29] It would be quite wrong of me to leave you in this predicament. I am happy to share your fate, whatever it may be, my lord." Against this the Bodhisattva argued: [30] "Is there any fate other than the kitchen for a bird in a snare? How can that appeal to you, who are sane and free? [31] What advantage do you see for me, for yourself, or for the rest of our kin in our both sacrificing our lives? [32] Kindly explain what gain there might be in laying down your life in circumstances that make any such gain as impossible to discern as rough and smooth in the dark?" [33] "Most excellent of birds," replied Sumukha, "how can you be blind to the advantage of doing what is right? Due respect for the moral Law brings the very highest advantage. [34] And so, with an eye to that Law and to the advantage that comes from respecting it, out of devotion to you, my master, I do not cling to life." [35] "In truth," said the Bodhisattva, "decent people are in duty bound not to desert a friend in trouble, even at the cost of life. By being mindful of this duty [36] you have shown respect for the moral Law and have demonstrated your devotion to me. Now do what I ask you this last time: get away! I give you leave. [37] Besides, now that things have taken this turn, it is for you, my wise councilor, to fill completely the gap I leave among our friends."

[38] As the two of them were exchanging these words inspired by their mutual love, the bird catcher appeared, rushing up like Death incarnate. The two magnificent geese fell silent the moment they saw him approaching, and, when he saw that the flock of geese had flown off, he was sure that one of them must have been trapped. He made a round of the snares he had laid and caught sight of the two splendid geese. He marveled at their beauty as he closed up the snares next to them, assuming they were both caught. Then, when he noticed that only one was caught while the other, though free, stayed by him, he was even more astonished. Going up to Sumukha, he said: [39] "This bird is prevented from getting away by a large trap, which is why, even when I come close, he cannot fly up into the sky. [40] But you haven't been caught: you are safe and sound—your winged chariot is at the ready.

So why, even when I come near, do you not quickly take to the air?"

On hearing this, Sumukha replied in human speech, pronouncing each syllable of every word distinctly, his powerful voice showing the firmness of his character: [41] "The reason why I do not go, though able to do so, is this: there is a bird who has had the misfortune to be snared. [42] With this large trap you hold him fast by the leg. But he has me tied by the heart with bonds that are stronger still, his virtues." The hunter was so astonished that he felt his whole body tingle as he spoke again to Sumukha: [43] "The other geese were scared of me and flew up to the sky and deserted him. But you do not forsake him. What does this bird mean to you?" [44] "He is my king," answered Sumukha, "a friend as dear to me as life itself. He to whom I owe my happiness is in difficulty, which is why I cannot possibly desert him, not even to save my own life." As he spoke, he noticed that the bird catcher was overcome by admiration mixed with sympathy. So he continued:[45] "My friend, if only this conversation of ours could have a happy outcome—if only you could gain a reputation for saintliness by releasing us today." [46] "I certainly wish you no ill," said the bird catcher. "Besides, I haven't caught you. You can go as you please and see your relatives and make them happy." To which Sumukha replied: [47] "If you do not wish me ill, then grant me a request. If you are satisfied with one victim, then release him and take me. [48] Our height and girth are identical, and we are of the same age. You can be sure that by taking me as a ransom for him you would not be the loser. [49] Please think it over, and then I hope you will be keen to have me. You can tie me up first and release the king of the birds afterwards. [50] That way you will have achieved just as much; you will have fulfilled my request, made the flock of geese happy, and also earned their friendship. [51] So set the king free and allow the whole host of geese the pleasure of seeing him shine out in the clear sky like the moon released by Rāhu."[3]

Now the fowler, though his cruel profession had made him hard-hearted, was completely won over by these words, which showed tenderness as much as firmness, gave strong proof of gratitude, and evinced a proud attachment to one's master without regard for one's own survival. Overpowered by admiration and respect, he joined his hands in reverence and said to Sumukha: "Excellent, excellent, you blessed creature! [52] The goodness you show in sacrificing your life for your master would be accounted a miracle among men or even among gods. [53] I shall therefore do your king the honor of releasing him. For who could injure him whom you value more than your own life?" With these words the bird catcher, regardless of King Brahmadatta's orders, paid honor to the king of the geese and, moved by pity, released him from the snare. Sumukha, the commander-in-chief, was absolutely delighted at the release of his king and, with a tender look of affection, said to the bird catcher: [54] "You are a joy to your friends. Just as you have made me happy today by releasing the goose king, so, my friend, may you find eternal happiness with all your kindred. [55] Now, so that your efforts do not go unrewarded, take me and the king of the geese, and let us perch on a shoulder pole, free and unfettered. Then show us to the king in his private apartments. [56] No doubt the king will be pleased to see the goose king and his companion and will reward you with riches beyond imagination, which will bring you happiness."

As he was insistent, the bird catcher thought the king really ought to see this extraordinary pair of geese. So he took them on a shoulder pole, free and unfettered and showed them to the king. [57] "Your grace," he said, "deign to behold the marvel I present. I have brought you the king of the geese together with his commander-in-chief." The king was filled with delight and amazement when he saw the two chief geese, like two heaps of gold, radiant and captivating. [58] "Tell me in detail how you who are earthbound have laid hold of this pair of birds without harming them or tying them up," said the king to the bird catcher, who bowed and then replied: [59] "I laid a huge number of horrible traps in the places where the birds disport themselves, beside lakes and ponds. [60] Then this fine goose came along and, lulled by a sense of security, caught his foot in a hidden trap. [61] This other one was not caught but stayed at his side and then implored me to accept him as ransom for the goose king's life. [62] He used human speech and pronounced every syllable clearly and melodiously. Such self-sacrifice had a strong effect on me. [63] His fine words and determined effort on behalf of his master so melted my heart that I relaxed my grip both on his lord and on my harshness. [64] He was overjoyed at the release of the king of the birds and thanked me profusely. Then he urged me to come on this visit to you, so that, as he put it, my efforts should not prove wholly fruitless. [65] So it is that, in recognition of the release of his king and for my sake, this saintly being, whoever he may be—he who, in the guise of a splendid bird, momentarily aroused some tenderness even in my hard heart—has come of his own accord, together with his master, to your private apartments."

The king heard the story with amazement and delight and assigned to the goose king a golden throne fit for a king to sit on, together with a footstool. It had beautiful feet which glinted with the luster of various gems, was covered in the richest fabric, and was plumped out with luxurious soft cushions. To Sumukha he assigned a cane chair befitting a prime minister. Judging that now was the moment to return the king's greeting, the Bodhisattva spoke to him in a voice melodious as the ring of anklets: [66] "I trust that your body—that abode of brightness and beauty—enjoys the health that you deserve. And your spirit, is that also intact, and does it, so to say, exhale words full of bounty? [67] You who are dedicated to looking after your subjects, bestowing favor or inflicting punishment according to circumstance—are you increasing the luster of your fame, the affection of your people, and the common good? [68] I trust that, with devoted and capable ministers who are too upright to resort to underhand methods, you consider what is best for your subjects—you can hardly be indifferent to such things? [69] When vassal kings, their power curbed by your wise policies and prowess, beg for mercy, are you disposed to treat them leniently without, however, being so gullible as to relax your vigilance?

22 · 70 [70] No doubt men applaud your conduct which contradicts none of the accepted aims of life—spiritual, sensual, or material—and word of it spreads abroad thanks to your solid reputation. Only your enemies, I imagine, take it ill and sigh over the fact?"[4]

The king showed by his happy looks that his conscience was clear on these matters and said to the Boddhisattva in reply: [71] "Now that the wish I have had for so long has come true and I have met a holy being, I shall always be happy, dear goose. [72] When you were in the grip of the snare, I hope this fellow didn't grow giddy with delight and do you an injury by maltreating you with his stick? [73] For that's how it is with these louts the moment they see a bird in distress: the excitement of it goes to their heads and induces them to commit some ugly deed." [74] "Your highness," said the Bodhisattva, "despite the dreadful situation, we felt quite happy, and this man was not at all hostile toward us. [75] Indeed, when he saw Sumukha, in his affection for me, staying there as though caught while in fact free, he was both surprised and curious and spoke most kindly. [76] Then Sumukha's frank words won him over. So he released me from the trap and treated me with polite respect. [77] Because of this, Sumukha wanted him to get some good out of it. So may our coming here bring him some reward too." [78] "You are welcome here, both of you," said the king. "I have been longing for you to come. The pleasure of seeing you gives me great joy, [79] and this bird catcher will straightaway receive a large reward. He has treated you both kindly and so deserves great kindness himself." So saying, the king rewarded the bird catcher by bestowing a huge fortune upon him. Then he spoke again to the king of the geese: [80] "This residence you have come to, treat it as your own and drop all constraint with me. Tell me how I may be of use: my riches are at your disposal. [81] A friend can give the rich man far greater satisfaction by his frank request than the rich man can give the friend by his money. Among friends a request is a positive kindness."

The king then felt moved to speak with Sumukha. With a look of admiration he said: [82] "Before one is on a firm footing with a new acquaintance, one is naturally not too forward in one's demands. But one can at least have friendly and courteous conversation, [83] which is why, simply by talking to me, your honor can fulfill my hope that you will ask for something and increase the affection I already feel." At these words Sumukha, the commander-in-chief of the geese, bowed politely and said to him: [84] "To speak with you who are Indra's[5] equal is a rare delight, and such a show of friendliness is surely beyond anyone's wildest dreams. [85] When the king of men and the king of birds were talking together amicably, it would hardly have been right for a servant to interrupt them rudely in the middle of their conversation and to talk himself. [86] That is not the way one is taught to behave, and, knowing as much, how could I butt in? So I kept quiet, your highness. If that requires forgiveness, then forgive me."

The king, with delight and admiration lighting up his face, congratulated Sumukha: [87] "How right people are to enjoy hearing about your good qualities! How right that the king of the geese should choose you as his friend! Only the spiritually mature can behave so unassumingly and with such sound sense. [88] Now that it exists, may this bond of affection between us never be severed, and may you both put your trust in me, for true friendship is everlasting." Realizing how much the king wanted to be friends and how ready he was to show his affection, the Bodhisattva approvingly said to him: [89] "You have treated us as one would treat one's best friend. Though we are but newly acquainted, you have followed your own generous instinct. [90] Who could fail to be captivated by such honor as your highness has shown us? [91] Of what use can I be to you? and what value can you see in it? Nonetheless, one thing is certain, your gracious majesty: the hospitality you offer comes as a matter of habit from one who is devoted to goodness. [92] Nor is this surprising in someone with your self-mastery, who performs his royal duties for the betterment of his subjects and is as devoted to penance and meditation as a holy man. Simply by following your natural disposition you have become a repository of virtues. [93] Virtue brings happiness and has a happy way of earning such praise as this, while there are no advantages to be found in the evil haunts of vice. Knowing that this is the nature of virtue and vice, what man of sense would choose to stray from that which is to his own advantage? [94] Neither enterprise, nor powerful reserves, nor successful diplomacy will serve to get a king to the position he can reach, effortlessly and without expense, by following the path laid out by virtue. [95] Even the king of heaven in his majesty has a regard for virtue, while the virtuous are themselves humble. Virtue alone engenders fame, since the panoply of power rests upon virtue. [96] Virtue is lovelier than moonlight. It can soften the hearts of enemies though they bristle with intolerance and wanton pride, no matter how set they may be in their envy, which grows out of hostility. [97] Therefore, sovereign lord, ruler of the earth whose proud kings are humbled by your prowess, inspire a love of virtue in all creatures by your own practice of self-discipline, as well as by your other virtues, which are of no mean brightness. [98] A king's chief concern is his subjects' welfare, and that is the way for him to be happy in this life and the next. As long as the king values what is right, it will be so. For people model themselves on their king. [99] So rule the earth with justice, and may Śakra grant you his protection. Though your company is a benison to those who share it, the plight of my relatives drags me away."

The king and his entourage appreciated this speech, and, after saying a few kind words to show his respect, he gave both of those excellent geese leave to depart. The Bodhisattva flew up to the sky, which, in its calm autumn beauty, was deep blue like a spotless sword blade. Sumukha, the commander-in-chief of the geese, followed behind, like his shadow. At the sight of their king approaching, the flock of geese was overjoyed. [100] In due course, that goose, in his passionate concern for others, came back with his flock and preached the Law to King Brahmadatta, who, humbly submissive, honored him in turn.

So, then—bad people are incapable of behaving as good people even in misfortune behave, let alone when all is well with them.

Bodhi the Wandering Ascetic

23

For those who have helped them in the past, good people feel a sympathy that subsequent ill-treatment can do nothing to weaken. This comes of gratitude and ingrained patience.

According to tradition, the Lord, when still a Bodhisattva, was once incarnated as a wandering ascetic called Bodhi. While still living at home he had acquainted himself thoroughly with the scope and method of the various branches of knowledge that people consider important. He had also been keen to master the fine arts. Then, as a result of his choosing to renounce the world and his ambition to be of help to his fellow creatures, he gave special attention to the moral codes, on which he became an authority. His store of merit from previous lives, his profound wisdom, his understanding of men, and his excellent conduct made him, wherever he went, an object of respect, attracting both the learned and the patrons of learning—kings, chief ministers, and brahmin householders—as well as homeless ascetics belonging to different sects.

[1] Good qualities take on a special brilliance when founded on a store of merit, and, when they irradiate one's whole manner, people appreciate them. Even one's enemies, who have to consider what others will think of them, are forced to concede good qualities a peculiar respect.

In his desire to be of help to the world, the Noble One passed through villages, towns, markets, country districts, kingdoms, and capital cities, until he reached the realm of a certain king. This king had heard of his multifarious qualities and was delighted to hear that he was on his way, though still far off. He had a rest house made for the Bodhisattva in lovely woodland within his own park, then went out to meet him and paid his respects before formally bidding him enter his realm. After that he treated him with the honor a pupil shows to his teacher, by serving him and attending to his needs.

[2] It is an exceptionally happy occasion for a lover of virtue when a man of virtue favors him with a visit to his fine residence.

Every day the Bodhisattva graciously discoursed to the king on spiritual matters, which gave pleasure to both heart and hearing. In this way he gradually set the king on the path to final bliss.

[3] The devout have an altruistic desire to preach the good word even to those who show no sign of being disposed toward it—how much more to someone who, like a spotless vessel, is ready to receive what is good for him and who is open to the power of love.

The king's ministers continued to receive the honor due to their learning, and the members of the court circle were still treated with consideration, but they could not bear the way greater and greater deference was paid every day to the Bodhisattva because of his many virtues. Jealousy had clouded their minds.

[4] A man who shows he can attract people by his reputation for outstanding virtue kindles the fire of resentment in those others who are valued solely for their practical accomplishments.

In learned disputes, the ministers were quite unable to get the better of the Bodhisattva, and they resented the king's attachment to religion. They therefore tried in various ways to prejudice the king against the Bodhisattva. "Your majesty ought not to trust that monk Bodhi," they said. "Some neighboring king has obviously heard of your highness's love of virtue and penchant for the Law and is making clever use of this fellow as an agent who, with his soft, deceitful words, will inveigle you into some evil and who meanwhile serves as a means of transmitting intelligence. For the fact is that, posing as a holy man, he instructs your highness always to show compassion, to cringe with modesty, and to assume a moral stance that is at odds with the pursuit of profit and pleasure,[1] that is alien to the role of a king, and that can only lead to misguided policies. Ostensibly it is out of concern that he takes it upon himself to tell you your duty by way of these exhortations. But he also likes mixing with the envoys of foreign kings and is far from ignorant of the contents of treatises on statecraft. This is what makes us feel apprehensive."

A large number of people constantly urged the king to break with the Bodhisattva, as though it were for his own good. And the effect was that his unbounded respect and affection shrank. He grew suspicious, and his attitude changed.

[5] Be it the terrifying crash of thunder or the lightning flash of calumny, was there ever anyone who could stand up to it unperturbed, armed only with a man's courage?

As the king lost confidence in the Great Being, his love and respect waned, and he was less ready than he had been to show hospitality. But the Bodhisattva, in his innocence, thought nothing of it, knowing that kings are preoccupied with their many duties. But when he noticed that the royal entourage had grown less polite and obliging, he realized that the king had become estranged. So he collected his triple staff,[2] his water pot, and the rest of a wandering ascetic's gear and made ready to depart. When he heard of this, the king, prompted by lingering affection and a wish to be considerate and polite, went to the Bodhisattva and, with a show of concern, made as if he wanted to dissuade him: [6] "Why are you set on going away and leaving us all of a sudden? Have you perhaps found us guilty of some careless slip which has aroused your misgivings?" [7] "I have my reasons for wanting to be off," replied the Bodhisattva, "but it is not that I have taken offence at some trifling incivility. It is you who, by being false, have ceased to be receptive to the Law. And so I am leaving."

At that moment the king's pet dog came bounding up, barking fiercely and baring his teeth. Pointing to it, the Bodhisattva continued: "Your highness, this hound proves what I am saying: [8] he used to imitate his master and fawn on me

23 · 9 abjectly. But now, not knowing how to dissimulate, he betrays your real feelings by barking. [9] He must have heard you say something unpleasant which showed that your attachment to me was over, and he has obviously reacted like this to please you. That is the way dependents behave." At this reproof the king hung his head in shame. He was overwhelmed by the Bodhisattva's keen perception and, conscience stricken, concluded that it was no longer right to go on pretending. With a bow to the Bodhisattva, he said: [10] "Indeed there were arrogant people in my council who spoke in some such terms about you and, in the press of business, I acquiesced. Forgive me, and stay. Please do not go away." "Your highness," replied the Bodhisattva, "I can assure you it is not because I was slighted that I am going. Nor is it resentment that impels me. But I don't think this is the right moment for me to settle down, and so I am not staying. Look, my lord—[11] now that I am considered a mediocrity, I am no longer treated so handsomely. Supposing I didn't leave of my own accord—either because I felt attachment or, through apathy, because I had nowhere to go to—wouldn't it end up in my being hauled out by the scruff of the neck? [12] In the circumstances this is the right thing to do, and so I shall go, but without any resentment. To be fair, a single affront does not cancel out all the kindnesses that went before. [13] Yet, it is no good paying court to someone who is not well-disposed, any more than going to a dry well for water. Success will be hard won, and the gains meager and not unmixed. [14] The obvious and usual course for anyone who wants to be happy and to avoid unpleasantness is to apply to someone who is as welcoming and approachable as a large pool of water in autumn. [15] He who rebuffs someone eager to show devotion, or who finds it demeaning to have his approaches rebuffed, or is slow to remember past favors—he may appear to be a man, but it is hard to be sure. [16] One can destroy friendship by neglect, by being overattentive, or by making persistent demands. I am now going in the hope of saving what is left of our affection. That too would be spoiled were I to stay." "Your holiness," said the king, "if you have decided that you really must go,

then perhaps you will do us the favor of returning here one day. As you yourself say, one must take care that friendship does not suffer from neglect." "Your majesty," replied the Bodhisattva, "our earthly life is beset with obstacles: we are faced with so many possible misfortunes. I cannot, therefore, give you a firm promise that I shall return. But should there be sound reasons for my doing so, I hope to see your highness again."

In this way the Great Being appeased the king and, with his approval and blessing, set out from his realm. Mixing with worldly people had upset his inner balance, and so he retired to a lonely spot where he applied himself to meditation and before long attained the four stages of trance and the five kinds of transcendent knowledge.[3] As he relished the sweet savor of tranquility, he felt concern for the king and wondered how he was getting on. He could see him being inveigled by his ministers into whichever false theory each of them adhered to.[4] One minister urged on him the doctrine of noncausality, giving instances where it is difficult to discern a cause. [17] "What," he asked, "is the cause of the shape, the color, the structure, the softness, and so on of the stalk, the petal, the filament, and the pericarp of a lotus? Who is responsible for the variety in birds' plumage? And so with everything in the world: it is clearly the result of spontaneous development." Another minister favored the idea of God as first cause and expounded it to the king: [18] "This universe cannot exist without a cause. Above everything on earth is some Being, One and Eternal, who, by concentrating his extraordinary will, creates this wondrous world, then destroys it again." Another minister tried to prejudice the king with the doctrine that everything, good and bad alike, is the result of previous actions and that no effort of ours can avail to alter things: [19] "How can one being possibly create simultaneously the endless different kinds of living things, each with its own distinct form? No, the universe is the outcome of previous actions, which is why even those who take pains to secure their own happiness nevertheless come to grief." Another minister, with arguments in support of the theory that there is no afterlife, tried to inveigle the king into becoming a hedonist: [20] "Pieces of wood which differ greatly in color, quality, and shape do not owe their existence to previous actions, yet they do exist. And once they have ceased to exist, they will not reappear. The same goes for the world in general. Therefore, pleasure should be one's sole object in life." Another minister claimed that a king's rule of conduct lay in the devious practices of diplomacy prescribed by the science of statecraft, even though they go contrary to the moral Law and are tarnished with ruthlessness. So he instructed the king accordingly: [21] "Avail yourself of men as you do of shady trees. Show you appreciate them and thereby earn popularity, as long as there is nothing to be gained by putting them to use. But the moment something needs doing, use them as you would beasts for a sacrifice." This was how the ministers, each by means of his own false theory, tried to lead their king astray.

Now the Bodhisattva saw that the king was ready to fall headlong into some heresy, both because of the bad company he kept and because his trust in others made him gullible. He was overcome with pity for the king and wondered how he could stop him.

[22] Good people, because of their ingrained virtue, remember any kindness, while any wrong slips from their mind as water from a lotus petal.

After deciding what was the right thing to do in the circumstances, the Bodhisattva conjured up a large monkey in his hermitage, then used his magic power to strip off its skin and make the rest of the body disappear. Wearing this large monkey's skin that he had conjured up, he appeared at the gate of the king's palace. His arrival was announced by the gatekeepers, and he then gradually made his way through the outer courts, where soldiers were posted to keep guard, to the king's council chamber. Here there were attendants, armed with swords and staves, stationed at the doorway, and inside it was filled with ministers, brahmins, military commanders, envoys, and leading citizens, all seated according to rank. In the midst of this refined, sober, and distinguished-looking company sat the king on his throne.

The king rose to greet the Bodhisattva and showed him every courtesy due to a guest. After enquiring about his health, he offered hospitality and invited him to be seated. Then, succumbing to curiosity, he asked how the Bodhisattva had come by the monkey skin. "Who conferred a great blessing on himself by presenting your holiness with this monkey skin?" "Your highness," answered the Bodhisattva, "I got it myself: it wasn't given me by someone else. Sitting or sleeping on the hard ground, with only grass or straw for a mattress, makes one's body ache, and then it is difficult to perform one's religious exercises. I saw this big monkey in my hermitage and thought to myself 'Aha! the skin of this monkey could help me to fulfill my religious exercises. If I could sit or sleep on that, I could perform them easily. Then I would not covet even the couches of kings, covered with the richest fabrics!' So I took this skin of his and did away with him."

When the king heard this, he was too courteous and discreet to make any reply. He bowed his head slightly in embarrassment. But his ministers, who already bore a grudge against the Great Being, looked at the king, and their faces lit up with smiles at this opportunity to speak their mind. Pointing to the Bodhisattva, they said: "Ah! the sole thing that delights the heart of the Blessed One is his devotion to the Law. What dedication! What strength of purpose! It is a wonder that, wasted as he is by penance, he could single-handedly despatch such a big monkey the moment it came into his hermitage. May his penance prove wholly successful!" Without getting at all angry at this sarcasm, the Bodhisattva replied: "Gentlemen, you ought not to criticize me without bearing in mind your own fair arguments. That is not the way to win a reputation among the wise. You must realize, gentleman: [23] anyone who, in his antagonism toward another, says things that undermine his own arguments, as good as destroys himself in his desire to discredit that other person."

23 · 24 After administering this general rebuke to the ministers, the Noble One wanted to criticize them individually. So, addressing the one who denied causality, he said: [24] "You boldly assert that the world is the result of spontaneous generation. If that is the case, why blame me? How is it my fault if the monkey met his natural end? In fact, I did right to kill him. [25] Now, if I am guilty of killing him, surely that proves his death had an external cause? So, either abandon your claim for noncausality or else say what it is that you apparently find wrong in my argument. [26] And if the arrangement, color, and so on of the different parts of a lotus were not caused by anything, surely they would occur under any conditions. But we know that they are produced from seeds in conjunction with water and other things. They come into being under those conditions but not otherwise. And I would ask you to give serious thought to this too, your honor: [27] he who states causes[5] for denying causality must surely abandon his thesis! On the other hand, if he is loath to adduce any reasons, what value is there in merely making an assertion? [28] And he who fails to discern a cause in some isolated instance and on that basis alone claims that nothing has a cause, won't he, when he realizes that the thing after all clearly does depend on a cause, take a dislike to it, and curse it for not fitting his theory? [29] If in some instance a cause is not apparent, why then assert dogmatically that it does not exist at all? It exists, but for some secondary reason it is invisible, like the bright disk of the sun at close of day. [30] Surely, sir, you procure such objects as you desire for your own happiness, and you have no wish to pursue those which go contrary to it? That is why you are in the king's service. And yet you say there is no causality. [31] And if, even so, you consider that everything happens without a cause, then obviously the death of the monkey has no cause. So why blame me?"

With this clear reasoning the Noble One discomfited the advocate of noncausality. Then he turned to the theist and said: "Your honor, you too really ought not to be criticizing me. For in your opinion God is the cause of everything. Now look—[32] if it is God who does everything, then God killed the monkey, didn't he? How can you be so unfriendly as to besmirch me with another person's crimes? [33] If, on the other hand, God was moved by pity not to murder that valiant monkey, how can you proclaim aloud that he is the cause of everything on earth? Besides, my friend, believing as you do that God is at the root of everything, [34] how can you hope to propitiate him with hymns and prostrations and all that sort of thing when he himself, the Self-Existent, is performing those very actions of yours? [35] You may claim that it is you who do the worshipping. Even so, you cannot deny that he is the true agent: he who acts by virtue of his own supreme power is the true agent. [36] If it is God who commits all sins, without exception, then what good quality of his do you visualize when you direct your devotion to him? [37] But if, abhoring such wickedness, God does not commit them, then it is wrong to say that everything is done by him. [38] Now, his supremacy must either originate in the Law or in something else. If in the Law, then God could not have existed before the Law. [39] 'Dependence' is what it should be called when one thing is created by another. Otherwise you may as well predicate 'supremacy' of any cause at all. Even so, should you have been prevented, by passionate devotion, from weighing up right and wrong [40] and so still consider an all-pervading God to be the cause of everything in the world, surely you ought not to charge me with the murder of that fine monkey, which was ordained by God?"

With this close[6] reasoning the Noble One quite dumbfounded the theist. Then, turning with great address to the determinist, he said: "You too, sir, hardly show yourself in a good light when you reproach me, since in your opinion everything results from previous actions. In that case, let me tell you: [41] if everything were a consequence of previous actions, then I was certainly right to kill this monkey. He was consumed by the blazing fire of his former actions. What fault of mine is there in that to criticize? [42] On the other hand, if I am guilty of killing the monkey, then it is I who am responsible, not his former actions. And if you consider that one action inevitably gives rise to another, then, in your sys-

23 · 43 tem, no one will achieve final release from this world. [43] Should there be a case of someone being happy in circumstances that cause misery or miserable in circumstances conducive to happiness, then one would certainly infer that happiness and misery depend entirely on former actions. [44] But since this is not the case with happiness and misery, former actions cannot be their sole cause. Suppose no new karma were created: how can you account for old karma in its absence? [45] If, nevertheless, you consider everything to be the result of previous actions, what has made you decide that I am the cause of the monkey's death?"

With this irrefutable reasoning the Noble One appeared to have imposed a vow of silence on the man. Smilingly he said to the nihilist: "Why is your honor so anxious to put the blame on me if you really believe there is no 'beyond'? [46] If there really is no afterlife, why avoid doing evil, why have a foolish respect for good? Any intelligent person would follow his whims in that case. And so there was nothing wrong with killing the monkey. [47] If it is only fear of scandal that makes a man such as you steer clear of evil and keep to the path of good, he will still not escape people's scorn, because he will not be practicing what he preaches. [48] And, because of this fear of what people will think, he will find no happiness as he lives out his life. So, to be deluded by such a futile theory is surely the crassest folly! As to your saying that [49] pieces of wood which differ greatly in color, quality, and shape do not owe their existence to previous actions yet exist nonetheless—that once they have ceased to exist they do not reappear and that the same goes for the world as a whole—I should like to know what reason you have for saying so. [50] But if, even so, you persist in your leanings toward nihilism, then why blame someone who kills a monkey or, for that matter, a man?"

With this series of clear and sparkling rejoinders the Great Being silenced the nihilist. He then addressed the minister who had a shrewd knowledge of statecraft: "You too , sir, why do you reproach me like this if you approve of the methods prescribed by the *Arthaśāstra*?[7] [51] For it approves any act, good or bad, that is to one's advantage: only after a man has set himself up should he use his wealth to do good. So what I say to you is this: [52] if, in the attainment of one's ends, one need not bother about treating even one's loving relatives decently, how can you find fault with me for killing this monkey for his skin—a sensible procedure actually prescribed by your treatise? [53] If, on the other hand, you consider such a deed reprehensible because it is ruthless and fraught with evil consequences, why do you blithely accept a doctrine in which such a thing is approved? [54] Now if this is a fine example of prudence according to your system, what sort of an aberration must it call imprudence? Oh! the effrontery of those who despise people so much that they cite treatises to preach error! [55] Now if you claim that what I have done is quite harmless—its implications are, it seems, clearly set out in a treatise—then I am not to blame for killing the monkey, since I was only following the course prescribed in the treatise."

In this way the Noble One crushingly defeated the ministers, though they dominated the assembly and were used to having their own way. He realized that he had completely won the hearts of both king and assembly, and he spoke to the king with the intention of dispelling any repugnance he might still feel about his killing the monkey: "Your highness, of course I didn't kill a live monkey. I simply produced a magical illusion of one, then took his skin to spark off these exchanges. So do not misjudge me." With these words he dissolved the magic monkey skin, and, aware that the king and the whole assembly were now entirely on his side, he said: [56] "Can anyone kill a living creature if he sees that every result stems from a cause, if he behaves responsibly and is aware of a future existence, if he acknowledges goodness and is sensitive? Consider, your highness—[57] how could anyone who accepts the doctrine of an ordered universe commit a crime that neither the advocate of spontaneous creation, nor the determinist, nor the materialist, nor the adept in political science would do even for a brief glimmer of fame? [58] True or false, it is one's outlook that determines the way one chooses to behave, your excellency, for, by choosing to do this or that according to what one believes, one illustrates one's belief by what one says or does. [59] For this reason one should act upon a good doctrine and give up a bad one that only showers one with misfortunes. By consorting with good people and keeping one's distance from the bad, one can achieve this. [60] There are loose people who roam the world as they please, impersonating the truly disciplined—demons masquerading as monks. With their false doctrines they are the ruin of simple people, like snakes who can poison with a glance. [61] The ranting style in which they preach noncausality and other such heresies is as characteristic as the howl of jackals. Therefore, if he is wise, a man will not frequent their company. Instead he should work for their reform, if he has the strength to do so. [62] Even for practical purposes one should not make friends with someone unsuitable, however high his reputation may be in the world. Even the moon loses its beauty at the onset of wintry gloom. [63] Shun those who shun virtue. Cultivate those who cultivate virtue. And thereby kindle a blaze of glory by destroying evil tendencies among your subjects and by arousing in them a love of good. [64] With you observing the moral Law, the greater part of your subjects may be inclined to live good lives and to keep steadily to the road that leads to heaven. Your people need looking after, and you have the will to do it. Therefore, live according to the moral Law, following its fine code of discipline. [65] Keep your character spotless; earn a reputation for generosity; think as kindly of strangers as of your own relatives; and long may you rule the earth, with justice and vigilance. That way you will attain happiness, bliss in the afterlife, and fame. [66] For if a king does not look after the country people who pay him taxes—farmers and stockbreeders who are like trees that bear fruit and flowers—the plants in his country will be blighted.[8] [67] Likewise, if a king does not look after those who earn their livelihood by buying and selling different sorts of merchandise—traders and townspeople who help him with the duties they pay—the resources of his treasury will fail. [68] Likewise, if a king is carelessly unappreciative of his army when it is renowned for its skill in arms and, so far from showing itself inadequate, has proved itself in the field, he will surely be balked of victory in battle. [69] Likewise, if the king is so corrupt as to disdain holy men who are notable for their moral purity, their learning, or their supernatural powers and whose noble nature is evident, he will be deprived of the joys of heaven. [70] As he who picks unripe fruit kills the seed and finds it without flavor, so a king who levies unfair taxes ruins his country and gets no good out of them. [71] Conversely, just as a tree provides an excellent crop of fruit as and when it is ripe, so a country protected by its king brings him both spiritual and material well-being. [72] Helpful ministers with a sharp eye for promoting your interests, honest friends, and your own relatives—these you should bind to yourself by their heartstrings, with kind words and with wealth offered graciously. [73] These are the reasons why you should give prominence to the moral Law and should set your heart on making your subjects happy. Govern your people by administering justice without malice or favor, and thereby secure a happy afterlife for yourself."

In this way the Noble One kept the king from the error of false doctrines and set him and his court on the right road. Thereupon he flew up into the sky. All those present bowed respectfully and, with hands held out together, saluted him one by one, while he returned to his solitary retreat.

So, then—for those who have helped them in the past, good people feel a sympathy that subsequent ill treatment can do nothing to weaken. This comes of gratitude and ingrained patience.

24 The Great Ape

WHAT MAKES GOOD PEOPLE SUFFER is not so much any harm that is done them as the moral failings of those who inflict it.

According to tradition, the Bodhisattva was once a great ape who lived by himself in a beautiful region on the slopes of the Himalaya. There, bright veins of ore provide the various tints necessary for its cosmetics, and deep forests clothe it in a mantle of silk. The variety of color and contour and the picturesque undulations lend a beauty to the mountainsides such that one might think it had all been laid out with special care. Water pours down from numberless cascades. Everywhere there are deep caves, chasms, and cataracts, and the air vibrates with the drone of bees. The trees bear all kinds of fruit and blossom and are fanned by pleasant breezes. The mountain spirits make this place their playground.

Though only an ape, the Bodhisattva had not lost his awareness of what is right; he never forgot any favor done to him; there was nothing mean in his nature; and he showed great patience. Nor did compassion ever leave him—as though bound by affection! [1] Earth with its forests, noble mountains, and seas may perish a hundred times by fire, water, and wind, as each eon comes to an end, but the great compassion of a Bodhisattva never.

The Great One lived in that lonely place like an ascetic: his sole subsistence was the leaves and fruit of the trees that grew wild in the forest. And to such creatures as happened to cross his path he showed sympathy in whatever way he could.

One day a man, attempting to find a stray cow, had wandered about in every direction and eventually missed his way.

He had lost his bearings and went round in circles till he reached the very spot we have described. He felt faint with hunger and thirst, heat and exhaustion, while inwardly he was consumed by a gnawing despair. He sank down at the foot of a tree as if the weight of despondency were more than he could bear. Looking around, he noticed some russet-colored fruit which, being ripe, had dropped off an ebony tree. He ate them with relish, and so famished was he that he found them deliciously sweet. This made him all the more eager to discover where they came from. So he peered around and caught sight of an ebony tree that was growing on the brink of a cataract. The tips of its branches were russet colored with the ripe fruit that weighed them down. Drawn by his craving for the fruit, he climbed the mountainside and scrambled along a branch of the ebony tree that hung, with its load of fruit, over the cataract. Such was his greed that he went on to the very end of the branch. [2] Then, with a loud crack, the branch suddenly snapped, as though lopped with a hatchet: it was too slender to bear the extra weight that made it bend. The man fell with it down the great mountain gorge, enclosed on all sides by a wall of stone, like a well. But thanks to the mass of foliage and the depth of the water below, he managed not to break any bones. He got out of the water and crept around, but nowhere could he see a way of escape. Realizing that he would inevitably die soon, his will to survive weakened; tears of grief streamed down his face, crumpled in misery; the searing shaft of despondency pierced him to the quick; faintheartedly he bewailed his fate in some such words as these: [3] "Here I have fallen into this wild gorge, far from the haunts of men. However carefully he search, who, I ask, will find me, apart from Death? [4] My friends and relatives are out of reach. Swarms of mosquitoes have made me their exclusive resort. Who will haul me out, as one would a wild beast that has plunged into a gaping pit? [5] Ah! this night of doom, dense and dark as a night of the waning moon, it blots out all the beauty of the world I know—park, forest, arbor, and river—and the sky with its brilliant scattering of jewels, the stars." With these lamenta- 24 · 5 tions the man went on for several days, keeping himself alive on water and the ebony fruit that had fallen down with him.

Now the great ape happened to pass through that forest in search of food and came to the place as though beckoned by the tips of the branches of that ebony tree, stirring in the wind. He climbed the tree and, looking over the cataract, caught sight of the man writhing there in a desperate plight: his eyes and cheeks were hollow with hunger, and his body was pathetically pale and thin. The ape was overcome with pity for him in his wretched state and, setting aside his quest for food, looked intently at the man and said, in human language: [6] "How comes it that you are in this gully which is inaccessible to men? Do please tell me, sir, who you are and how you come to be here." The man in his misery prostrated himself before the great ape, then looked up, and, holding out his hands in supplication, said: [7] "I am a man, your honor. I got lost on my way through the forest and landed myself in this trouble while trying to pick fruit from that tree. [8] You who look after the tribe of apes, come to my rescue too: I have no friend or relative in my hour of need."

When the Great Being heard this he felt extremely sorry for the man. [9] Someone in distress, without friend or relative, clasping his hands and looking up piteously, can make even his enemies feel compassion. The compassionate he cannot fail to arouse. The Bodhisattva felt pity for him and comforted him with tender words which in his plight the man had hardly expected. [10] "Do not despair and imagine that this fall has left you helpless and all on your own. Whatever a relative would do for you now I will do just as well, never fear." And with this reassurance the Great Being brought him fruit from the ebony tree and elsewhere. Then he went off and practiced with a rock that was the weight of a man, so as to be able to haul the man out of the gully. After taking the measure of his strength and being sure that he could lift the man out of the gully, the Great Being went down to the bottom of it and, stirred by pity, said to him: [11] "Come, climb on to my back and hold on tight while I bring out both you and my body's true worth. [12] For good people would say that the sole worth of one's otherwise worthless body is that a wise man can turn it into an instrument for helping others." The man readily agreed, bowed with respect, then mounted on his back. [13] The extra weight of a man on top of him was a severe handicap. But because of his great goodness he did not lose courage and managed to rescue him, albeit with great difficulty. [14] He was extremely glad to have got the man out but was so exhausted that he tottered about dizzily, then lay down to rest on a slab of rock, dark as a rain cloud.

Having just done the man a service, the Bodhisattva, in his innocence, did not expect any harm from him and trustingly said: [15/16] "This part of the forest lies open on all sides, and there is nothing to stop beasts of prey from coming in. So guard us both, and cast a wary eye all around, in case someone comes and does away with me and his chances of future happiness while I lie asleep exhausted. I feel utterly weary and want to sleep just a while." "Sleep as long as you like, sir, and wake up refreshed," said the man with false courtesy. "I will stand guard over you, I promise."

As soon as the Bodhisattva sank wearily asleep, evil thoughts occurred to the man: [17] "How can I keep my wasted body alive, let alone build it up again, with roots obtained only with immense effort or with wild fruit that I may chance upon? [18] And how can I get across this almost impassable wilderness if I haven't the strength? But there is enough meat on this animal to enable me to escape that peril. [19] He may have done me a service, but even so I can eat him, since that is how nature made him. And certainly this is a standard procedure in emergency. So he must serve as my provisions.[20] But I can only kill him while he is sound asleep and all unsuspecting. Once he is ready to put up a fight, even a lion might expect to be worsted in an encounter with him—in which case I have no time to lose." The scoundrel could reach this decision because he was perverted by the sin of greed, felt no gratitude, had no conscience, and had lost all pity and tenderness. Despite his extreme weakness he had an overpowering urge to commit that crime and, picking up a large rock, hurled it at the head of the great ape. [21] But such was his eagerness to get it done that he threw the stone hastily and with a hand trembling with weakness. So, though intended to send the monkey to sleep for good, it served only to banish sleep from him. [22] It did not hit him with full force and so did not smash his head to bits but only wounded it with its sharp edge, then fell to earth like a thunderbolt. [23] The Bodhisattva, whose head had been split open by the impact of the rock, jumped down quickly, wondering who had hit him. He looked around but saw no one except that man, shamefaced and [24] cringing, who looked sick with embarrassment and had changed color in his abject dismay. The man's throat had gone dry with terror, he was pouring with sweat, and he dared not look up.

As soon as the great ape realized that it was the man who had done it, he gave no thought to the pain from his injury but was moved to intense pity by this vile deed, done without any regard to the man's own future well-being. He felt neither anger nor blind rage, but, with tears in his eyes, he looked at the man, felt sorry for him, and said: [25] "My dear friend, how could you, a man, do such a thing? How could you think of doing it, let alone bring yourself to do it? [26] You were supposed to be barring the approach of any enemy bent on doing me harm and to display the courage of a hero in my defense. [27] It was presumptuous of me to imagine I had performed a difficult feat. But you have banished any such notion by doing something even more hard to do. [28] You were reprieved from the life to come, virtually snatched from the jaws of Death, yet no sooner are you dragged out of one chasm than you fall into another. [29] Oh! a curse on vile ignorance, harshest of evils, which takes people as they strive pathetically for happiness and engulfs them in misery. [30] You have condemned yourself to an evil destiny, afflicted me with burning sorrow, tarnished your reputation, gone counter to your worthier instincts, [31] destroyed your credibility, and are now a target for reproach. Whatever did you hope to gain by this? [32] My wound certainly does not hurt me as much as the painful thought that I am the cause of your having done wrong and yet am powerless to expiate the sin. [33] So please follow me closely and be sure to keep in sight, since you are obviously not to be trusted. I shall guide you out of this jungle with its many dangers, on to the path that leads to a village, [34] before someone attacks you as you wander in the forest, alone in your weak state and not knowing the way. If you came to harm, all my efforts will have been vain."

Sorrowing over the man in this way, the Great One brought him to a place that was inhabited and, setting him on his way, spoke again: [35] "My dear friend, you have reached the haunts of men. Leave behind the forest region, with its dangerous wilderness, and go in peace. Try to avoid doing evil, because the consequences, when they occur, are invariably unpleasant."

Thus the great ape, in his compassion, instructed the man as though he were a pupil. Then he returned to his part of the forest. But the man who had committed that dreadful crime was consumed with burning remorse. Suddenly he was struck with a severe form of leprosy. His whole appearance changed: white spots came out on his skin, pus from suppurating sores oozed over his limbs, and his body smelled disgusting. He was hideously deformed—one could hardly believe he had a human body—and his voice had altered distressingly, so that, wherever he went, people, the moment they saw him, were sure he must be the Evil One in person. Whereupon they would pick up clods and sticks and drive him away with harsh threats.

One day a king was passing by on a hunt and saw him wandering about in the open, looking like a hungry ghost with filthy, tattered rags covering his loins—a really horrible sight. With mixed feelings of alarm and curiosity, the king asked: [36] "Your body is deformed by leprosy, your skin flecked with white spots. You are pale, thin, and wretched. [37] And your hair is grimy with dust. Who are you? A hungry ghost or a goblin, an embodiment of the Evil One or a vampire? You are afflicted by such a number of ills—perhaps you are yourself a disease?"

Prostrating himself, the wretch replied in a febble voice: "I am a man, your highness, not a demon." The king then asked

how he had reached that state, and the man revealed his
wicked deed, adding: [38] "So far this is only the flowering oc-
casioned by that treachery. The fruit will be something else
again, and obviously far worse than this. [39] You should therefore look upon treachery as a foe and regard with affection
friends who are affectionately disposed toward you. [40] Such is
the state that people reach already in this life when they behave in an unfriendly manner toward their friends. From this
you may infer the destiny in the next life of those whose
minds are so muddied by greed and other evil tendencies that
they betray their friends. [41] On the other hand, he who feels
kindly and affectionate toward his friends earns their goodwill and their trust and also benefits by their help. He is possessed of the virtue of humility and great gladness of mind.
His enemies will find him hard to assail, and when he dies he
will go to heaven. [42] Your highness, take note of these powerful consequences of good and bad behavior toward one's
friends and keep to the path that good people choose, for
good fortune attends him who follows it."

So, then—what makes good people suffer is not so much any harm that is done them as the moral failings of those who inflict it.

The Ibex

25

THE TRULY COMPASSIONATE TAKE PITY even on their would-be murderers. If they find them in distress they do not ignore them.

According to tradition, the Bodhisattva was once born as an ibex in a remote forest region. In the absence of man it was a peaceful place, inhabited by all sorts of animals. Trees and shrubs grew in plenty, their roots smothered by dense undergrowth. Neither the paths nor the borders of the forest showed any trace of travelers' footprints or wheel ruts. It was a landscape of riverbeds, anthills, gullies, and rough ground.

The ibex had a robust body, was strong, swift, handsome, and bold. So inveterate was his compassion that he bore the other creatures no malice, and so modest his contentment that he lived entirely off grass, leaves, and water, delighted with life in the forest. Like a yogi in his love of complete solitude, he was an ornament to that wild region. [1] An animal in appearance but with the intelligence of a man, he treated all creatures with sympathy, as a hermit does. He lived in that lonely forest as a yogi, content to eat the tips of grass.

Now, one day the king who ruled the realm came to that spot. He was mounted on a fine horse and held his bow and arrows at the ready, eager to test his marksmanship on the game. In his enthusiasm he pursued the wild beasts on his swift charger till his host of elephants, horse, chariots, and infantry was left far behind. The moment he caught sight of the Great Being in the distance, he determined to kill him, and, fixing a sharp arrow to his taut bow, he spurred on his steed toward the Great One. But when the Bodhisattva noticed the king rushing toward him on horseback and brandishing his bow, he sprang away with alacrity. Though ca-

25 · 2 pable of offering resistance, he had no wish for violence. With the horse in pursuit, he came to a gully which lay in his path. Quickly he leaped over it, as though it were a little puddle, and bounded away. The horse chased after the ibex at top speed along the same path until it reached the gully, hesitated about leaping over it, and stopped abruptly in its tracks. [2] The king, bow in hand, was tossed off the horse's back and fell straight into the gully, like a demon warrior falling into the ocean.[1] [3] With his eyes fixed on the ibex, he had not noticed the steep fall, so that when the horse suddenly halted, he was quite unprepared, lost his seat, and fell headlong.

When the sound of the horse's hoof-beats ceased, the Bodhisattva began to wonder whether by any chance the king could have turned back. Twisting his head round, he looked carefully and saw that the horse was riderless and had come to a halt where the deep hole was. He realized that the king must have fallen into the chasm, for there was no tree thereabouts to whose dense shade he might have retired for rest, nor any lake into whose clear waters—blue as the petals of a water lily—he could have plunged. He could not have turned his horse loose anywhere once he had penetrated to the heart of the forest, which was infested with beasts of prey. Nor could he be taking a rest or be pursuing the game on foot. Nor was there any deep grass here in which he might be hidden. So, obviously the king must have fallen into the gully.

On coming to this conclusion, the Noble One felt extremely sorry for the man, despite the fact that the man had intended to kill him. [4] "Only today this king was attended by a host of chariots, horse, infantry, and elephants, resplendent with bright banners, glinting with shields and weaponry, and marching to the stirring strains of music. [5] He was enjoying all the privileges of being king: a splendid parasol, shimmering chowries, and the homage of crowds of people holding out their hands in humble devotion, as though he were lord of the gods. [6] And now he has dropped into this deep pit and, with the violence of the fall, doubtless broken a limb. Either he is unconscious or else in extreme pain. Oh!

what anguish he must be suffering. [7] Because their hearts have in some way grown callous through hardship, common people, when calamities come, are not so affected as are men of higher rank, who in their pampered existence have not experienced hardship. He will never be able to get out of there by himself. If he has survived at all, it is not right to abandon him."

With these thoughts the Noble One, swayed by pity, went up to the edge of the pit, and there he saw the king struggling desperately. His armor was tarnished with dust, his clothes, turban, and accoutrements awry, and he was suffering agonies of pain as a result of being violently jolted into the pit. [8] To see the king writhing there brought tears to the Noble One's eyes. Overcome with pity, he no longer thought of him as an enemy and shared in his suffering. [9] He spoke to him kindly, thereby demonstrating his innate goodness. In clear language he comforted him, gently, politely, and pleasantly: [10] "I trust your majesty has not injured yourself by falling into this hellish pit? You haven't broken any limbs, I hope? And perhaps the pain is already easing? [11] I am no demon, your excellency, just a wild animal living in your domain and thriving on your grass and water. So you can put your trust in me. [12] Don't lose heart because you have fallen into this pit. I can rescue you from it, sir. If you are prepared to trust me, then just give the word and I'll come."

The king was overcome with astonishment at this extraordinary pronouncement of his. He began to feel ashamed and to reflect seriously. [13] "How can he possibly feel pity for me when I have shown my hostility to him by the way I have behaved. And how could I have committed such a sin against this innocent creature? [14] Oh! how sharply his gentleness puts me to shame. It is I who am the animal, the brute rather, and he is an ibex only in appearance. He certainly deserves the honor of my accepting his offer." On coming to this decision, the king said: [15] "My body was encased in armor. So I wasn't too seriously hurt. And I can put up with the pain caused by crashing into the pit. [16] But the pain from my fall distresses me far less than my blunder with regard to such a noble-hearted being as you. [17] Do not take it to heart that I trusted to appearances and took you for a wild beast, without discerning your true nature."

The king's pronouncement seemed to indicate goodwill, and the ibex inferred from it that he was permitted to rescue him. So he took a rock that was the weight of a man and practiced lifting it up. After he had taken the measure of his strength and was sure he could rescue the king, he went down into the pit, approached respectfully, and said: [18] "In view of the circumstances I hope you won't mind coming into contact with my body for a moment, while I give myself the pleasure of seeing an expression of affection and goodwill come over your face. Now, your highness, climb up onto my back and hold on tight."

The king complied and mounted him like a horse. [19] Then, with the king on his back, the ibex reared and sprang up with amazing speed and energy, looking like a carved leogryph[2] supporting an arch up in the air. [20] After rescuing the king from this difficult situation, the ibex gladly reunited him with his charger, pointed out the way to the capital, and turned to go back to the forest. But the king was overwhelmed by this kind service and, in his gratitude, embraced the ibex, saying: [21] "Ibex, my life—and, needless to say, whatever lies within my power to give—is yours. So do come and see my capital and, if it is to your liking, make it your home. [22] It would surely be wrong of me to return home alone and leave you in this dreadful forest where there are hunters all around and where you are at the mercy of heat and cold, rain, and other troubles. So come, let us set out together."

The Bodhisattva thanked him with gentle humility and replied: [23] "Your excellency, such an offer is only to be expected from a devotee of virtue, such as yourself, for, by constant practice, virtues come naturally to good people. [24] But if you think that I who am used to the forest would consider it a favor to live in a palace, you are mistaken: one kind of thing gives pleasure to human beings, and another suits the animal creation. [25] But if you want to do something to please me, sir, then give up hunting. One should pity the poor brutes whose animal nature makes them dull-witted. [26] You must understand that all creatures are like-minded in their pursuit of happiness and in their avoidance of what is unpleasant. It is therefore wrong to do to others what you would not like to have done to yourself. [27] Knowing that doing evil entails loss of face, criticism from good people, and unhappiness, you should root out evil as though it were an enemy. You should no more disregard it than you should illness. [28] By devoting yourself to doing good, you have earned the status of king, something that people greatly respect and in which good fortune inheres. Redouble your efforts. For there must be no thinning of the ranks among those who do good. [29] Accumulate merit, which is a means to fame and happiness, by generous gifts—all the more welcome for being timely and given with good grace—by moral integrity which gains strength through intimacy with good people, and by showing the same concern for other beings as you do for yourself."

In this way the Noble One helped the king in matters relating to this life and the hereafter. And the king welcomed his words and gazed after the ibex with respect as he entered the forest.

So, then—the truly compassionate take pity even on their would-be murderers. If they find them in distress they do not ignore them.

26 *The Antelope*

It is other people's suffering which makes good people suffer: it is that which they cannot endure, not their own suffering.

According to tradition, the Bodhisattva was once an antelope who lived in a vast forest region, far from the haunts of man. There the trees—date palms, flame trees, teak, acacia, and many others—grew in profusion, among dense thickets of reeds, grasses, and bamboo. All kinds of creeper draped their tendrils over the crisscross of branches, and animals roamed the forest in large numbers: deer, spotted antelopes, and waterbucks; yaks, elephants, gayals, and buffaloes; antelopes, muntjaks, boars, leopards, hyenas, tigers, wolves, lions, bears, and yet others.

The coloring of this antelope was as bright as pure gold, and its coat was downy and brightly dappled with spots the color of rubies, sapphires, emeralds, and beryls. His large, liquid eyes were dark and clear. With the soft gemlike luster of his horns and hoofs, he was of surpassing beauty, like a moving mass of jewels. But knowing how attractive his body was and how slight other people's compunction, he preferred to stay in the depths of the forest, avoiding human contact. Also, his sharp senses warned him to keep right away from the places where hunters set traps, spikes, nets, snares, pits, lime-twigs, and scattered bait. Like a teacher he alerted the herd of deer that followed him, and like a father he exercised authority over them. [1] Nowhere on earth does the combination of beauty and intelligence, crowned by worthy behavior, fail to inspire respect in people who care for their own good.

One day, while in the jungle, the Noble One heard a man shouting for help. The river that flowed nearby was in spate, and he was being swept away by the strong current. [2] "Come quickly if you have any pity for those in distress. Save me in my plight. The swollen river current is carrying me off, and without a boat I am helpless. [3] My arms are no use to me: I'm too exhausted and can't last out much longer. I can't find any shallows. So please come: there's no time to lose."

The Bodhisattva was smitten to the core by this piteous cry for help and called out "Don't be afraid! Don't be afraid!" in human language that had been perfected, in the course of a hundred incarnations, to banish fear, despair, and fatigue and which he now repeated in strained but clear tones. Then he bounded out from the depths of the forest and caught sight of the man, in the distance, being carried along by the stream as if he were some precious offering. [4] The Bodhisattva was determined to rescue the man and, without a thought about the danger to his own life, plunged into the frightful river race like a warrior striking confusion into an enemy army. [5] Barring the way with his body, he told the man to cling on to him, and the man, in a paroxysm of fear, trembling all over with exhaustion, climbed onto his back. [6] Such was his exceptional presence of mind and magnificent, unflinching bravery that, despite being weighed down by the man and whirled round by the racing current, he reached the haven of the river bank. [7] Weariness disappeared in a great surge of joy as he got the man ashore and warmed him up with the heat of his body. Then he showed him the way, said goodbye, and sent him off.

Such amazing readiness to be of help is hardly to be expected even in an affectionate relative or friend. The man was touched to the heart by it. And the deer's outward beauty aroused his wonder and respect. Bowing before him, he said several kind things: [8] "No friend devoted to me since childhood—or even a relative—would have done what you have done for my sake. [9] Therefore, my life is in your hands. Should there be anything, however small, in which my life could be of use to you, that would give me the greatest pleasure. [10] So please do me the kindness of employing me in whatever capacity your honor may judge fit."

26 · 11 The Bodhisattva thanked him: [11] "There is nothing remarkable about gratitude in a decent man: it is a natural instinct in him. But when one sees the world and its rampant perversity, one begins to count even gratitude a virtue, which is why I say to you: should you ever recall this incident, do not divulge it to anyone and say what a special sort of animal it was that saved you. Being so attractive, this body of mine is, I know, vulnerable. There is, on the whole, little tenderness in the hearts of men, who are unbridled in their greed. [12] Therefore, have a care for your own character as well as for my safety: no good ever comes of betraying friends. And please don't get upset or angry at my talking to you in this way. We animals are unpracticed in the smooth manners and evasiveness of human beings. Besides, [13] it is the fault of clever tricksters, masters of hypocrisy, if a genuinely honest creature is looked at askance. So I would like you to do me this kindness."

The man agreed to do so, bowed before the Great Being, circled round him respectfully, and set off home.

Now at that time the queen consort of the realm had prophetic dreams. Whatever she dreamed, however outlandish, came true. Once, at daybreak, while still fast asleep, she dreamed about an antelope, resplendent in beauty like a mass of every kind of jewel, sitting on a throne and surrounded by the king and his court. It was preaching the Law in a human voice, clearly pronouncing the syllables of each word. She woke up in amazement just as the drums were sounding to awake her husband.[1] At the first opportunity she went to the king, who honored her with his confidence. [14] Her beautiful eyes were wide open in wonder, her lovely cheeks shivering with joy, as she visited the king and regaled him with the story of her marvelous dream as with a gift. And after relating her extraordinary dream to the king, she respectfully added: [15] "So my lord, please take steps right away to capture this beast. In that way your inner apartments will be radiant with this jeweled deer, as is the sky with the constellation of the Deer."[2]

The king had learned to trust what his consort saw in her

dreams, and he agreed to her suggestion, partly because he wanted to please her, partly because he was eager to get hold of this jeweled deer. He accordingly gave orders for all his huntsmen to go in search of the antelope, and he had the following proclamation made daily in the capital: [16] "A deer with golden skin and dappled as if with hundreds of jewels has been mentioned in reports and sighted by some. The king will reward the man who locates it with a fine village and no less than ten beautiful women."

Now, the man who had been rescued heard this proclamation over and over again. [17] When he took into account all the ills of poverty, he felt desperate, but at the same time he remembered what a great service the antelope had done him. Torn between greed and gratitude, his mind was in the balance as he thought first one thing then another. "What on earth am I to do?" he wondered. "Should I have an eye to virtue or to riches, cherish the favor done me or my family ties? Should I consider this world or the next? Should I follow those who set a good example or behave like everyone else? Should I seek my fortune or behave with the modesty that saintly people approve? Which am I to think of, the present or the future?" Then greed clouded his mind, and he thought: "If I acquired a large fortune, I could not only live comfortably myself but also treat my family, my friends, guests, and dependents properly and thereby gain happiness in the next life too." With this conviction he forgot about the great service done him by the antelope, gained access to the king, and said: "My lord, I know that extraordinary deer and where it lives. So tell me whom should I show it to?" The king was delighted at what he heard and replied: "My dear fellow, show it to me in person." The king put on suitable clothes for going out hunting, gathered a large body of troops around him, and left the capital. Guided by the man, he came to the banks of the river. He then surrounded the dense forest with his entire force, took up his bow and hand guard, and entered the jungle with a resolute and trusty escort and with the man still acting as guide. The man then caught sight of the antelope standing there without suspicion, and showed it

26 · 18 to the king. "Here it is, my lord, this fabulous deer. Look at it, my lord, and take care." [18] Then, as he raised his arm to point out the deer, his hand dropped from his wrist as though severed by a sword. [19] If one makes an attempt on such a creature, sanctified as it is by exceptional deeds, the consequences develop rapidly, and, if there is within one only a feeble counterpoise of good, retribution comes at once.

The king, in his anxiety to get a glimpse of the antelope, cast his eyes in the direction indicated by the man. [20] And in the forest, dark as a fresh rain cloud, he saw a form radiant with the splendor of a hoard of jewels—the deer, dear on account of his good qualities, like a flash of lightning in that cloudlike thicket. [21] Its radiant body impressed the king deeply, and he longed to get possession of that animal. Fixing an arrow so that it bit into the bowstring, he advanced toward the deer, with the intention of shooting it.

Meanwhile the Bodhisattva had heard people making a noise all around him, and concluded that he must be entirely surrounded. He then noticed the king advancing to shoot him, and knew he had no chance of escape. So he addressed the king in human language, clearly articulating his words. [22] "Stop a moment, your highness! Do not hit me, paragon among men. Please satisfy my curiosity first: [23] who was it who told you where I was to be found, living happily in the unpeopled jungle?"

That the deer should use human speech left the king even more amazed, and he pointed out the man with the tip of his arrow, saying: "There is the man who has shown us this marvel of marvels." The Bodhisattva recognized him and said reproachfully: "Poor wretch, [24] how true the saying is that one does better to haul a log than an ungrateful man out of a torrent. [25] So this is how my efforts are rewarded. Can't he see that he is ruining his own chances of happiness?"

The king began to wonder about the reason for these complaints and, in some alarm, said to the antelope: [26] "I shudder to hear you make these reproaches without any discernible reason. Your meaning escapes me. [27] So tell me, marvelous beast, whom are you referring to when you talk in this way? Is it a man or a demon, a bird or a beast?" [28] "Your majesty," replied the Bodhisattva, "it is not that I want to blame him, but, when I realized he had behaved contemptibly, I spoke as sharply as I did in the hopes that he would resolve never to do so again. [29] For who wants to sprinkle salt on a wound by speaking harshly to those who have erred? Yet, when his son falls ill, a doctor will apply whatever remedy is necessary, however much he loves him. [30] He whom I, in my pity, rescued as he was being carried away by the powerful river current—he is the cause of the peril I now face myself, dear sovereign. Certainly, no good comes of mixing with bad people."

The king gave the man a sharp look, and his features hardened with menace as he asked: "Is it true, you wretch, that this deer rescued you once when you were in distress?" The man was overcome with terror and abject despair. He broke out into a sweat, changed color, and faltered out in shame: "It's true." "Shame on you!" said the king in a threatening tone and, putting an arrow to his bow, went on: "This really won't do—[31] anyone whose heart is not softened when such efforts are made on his behalf is an open disgrace to his fellow men. What right has such a mean specimen to go on living?" With these words he tightened his grip and drew his bow to kill the man. But the Bodhisattva, disturbed at heart by a feeling of great pity, intervened and said: "Stop, your highness! Do not strike one who is already stricken. [32] The moment he succumbed to the enticements of that enemy Greed, in all their vileness, he was as surely doomed in this world by forfeiting his good name as he was in the next by canceling out his good works. [33] It is when their minds are steeped in unbearable misery that men—attracted by the prospect of great gain as silly moths are attracted by the light of a lamp—take to evil ways. [34] Therefore feel pity, not anger, for him. And whatever it was he hoped to gain by acting as he did, grant it, so that his desperate attempt may not prove fruitless—for, see, I bow my head and await your command."

This mercy toward the man who had wronged him, this genuine desire that he should have some reward, filled the king with amazement and won him over. Looking at the marvelous antelope with great respect, he said: "Excellent! excellent! you blessed creature. [35] Such compassion for one who openly threatened you with grievous harm shows true humanity: we are men only in outward appearance. [36] However, since you think this rascal deserves pity, and since it is thanks to him that I have seen a saintly being, I grant him the wealth he desired, and I grant to you free passage throughout this realm." "I accept this royal favor," said the antelope. "It is not given in vain. But first say what I can do for you, so that your coming here may be of some profit to you."

The king, treating him as his mentor, then made the antelope mount the royal chariot, and brought him with great pomp to his capital and, after showing him due hospitality, seated him on his royal throne. Then, with his wives and a group of ministers gathered around him, the king asked about the Law, giving the antelope a kind look which showed both love and respect: [37] "People differ greatly in their notions about the Law, whereas you are quite clear about it. So please explain it to us." Whereupon the Bodhisattva explained the Law to the king and his court in language whose words were clear, pleasant, and well chosen. [38] "It can be defined as refraining from doing injury, from theft, and so on, and there are three ways of putting it into practice,[3] but compassion to living creatures is, I think, the quintessence of the Law. Just think, your majesty—[39] if one felt the same compassion for others as one does for oneself or one's family, who would there be so evil-hearted as to desire what is contrary to the Law. [40] But, because they lack compassion, people go completely wrong in the way they think, talk, and behave toward their own family as well as toward other people. [41] For this reason, whoever wants to follow the Law should not neglect compassion, from which spring all the good things that one wants, since it produces virtues as a good rainfall does crops. [42] Once compassion enters the heart, one loses any impulse to harm others. And when the heart is pure, neither word nor deed can go awry. In fact, a man's pleasure in doing good to others springs from love, and as it grows it gives birth to other good qualities, such as generosity and patience, which make for a fine reputation. [43] Because he is calm, the compassionate man does not make other people anxious. And, since he is compassionate, everyone is ready to trust him as one of the family. No disturbing emotion takes hold of a heart made firm by compassion. For the flames of anger cannot burn in a mind bathed by the waters of compassion. [44] This is why the wise, who do not waver in their compassion, believe that it is the essence of the Law. And, indeed, is there a virtue that good people cherish which does not follow on from compassion? Therefore treat people with the same intense compassion as you would show to your son or to yourself. Capture people's hearts by your good behavior and thereby magnify your royal dignity."

The king applauded these words of the antelope and, together with his subjects, townsmen and countrymen alike, become devoted to the Law. He also granted safety to all beasts and birds.

So, then—it is other people's suffering that makes good people suffer: it is that which they cannot endure, not their own suffering.

27 *The King of the Monkeys*

THOSE WHO MAKE A PRACTICE OF GOOD behavior can win over the hearts even of their enemies.

According to tradition, the Bodhisattva was once king of a tribe of monkeys in a beautiful vale of the Himalaya. The ground there was covered with a profusion of plants, each with its own special properties and efficacy, and trees in their hundreds spread their branches, decked with all sorts of flowers, fruits, buds, and foliage. Through the vale flowed a torrent of clear water like slivers of crystal. And the air resounded with the various calls of birds as they flocked together. Though the Bodhisattva was only a monkey, renunciation and compassion were a habit with him, and consequently such things as jealousy, selfishness, and cruelty never entered his mind, as though prevented from doing so by his devotion to their opposites. He lived in a huge banyan tree, which scraped the sky like a mountain peak and seemed to lord it over the forest. The dense foliage of its branches spread darkness like a mass of clouds, and its boughs were always bending under luscious fruit, much larger than palm nuts, of a delicious sweetness and with lovely scent and color.
[1] The good, even when reduced to the status of animals, still have a residue of good fortune which can be a source of happiness; like the possessions that people leave behind when they go abroad, it can be of use to their friends.

Now one branch of this tree hung over a river that flowed nearby. And, being farsighted, the Bodhisattva had been careful to warn his troop of monkeys that, unless that particular branch of the banyan tree were kept free of fruit, there would be no fruit at all for any of them to enjoy. They did as he said, but once it happened that the monkeys failed to notice a fruit that, being newly formed, was not very big and was concealed by a leaf which some ants had curled over. Gradually the fruit grew, took on color and scent, and became soft and juicy. When it was completely ripe, it came loose from its stalk and dropped into the river. It was duly borne downstream until it caught against a screen of netting behind which a king was disporting himself with his ladies in the waters of the river. [2] As the deliciously fragrant aroma of the fruit spread, it smothered even the heady combination of the strong drink, garlands, and perfumes of the women. [3] They were instantly intoxicated by it and narrowed their eyes as they inhaled it deeply. Then they darted eager looks in every direction. And as they glanced around keenly, they noticed the banyan fig, which was bigger than a fully ripened palm nut, stuck to the screen of netting. It caught the eye of the king as well, and they all wondered what it was. The king had someone fetch the fruit and, after reliable doctors had examined it, tasted it himself. [4] He was amazed by its wonderful flavor, as one is by the feeling of wonder that grips one during a play.[1] [5] He marveled at its unique color and scent, but its taste sent him into an ecstasy of astonishment. Though he was used to eating things with a sweet taste, the king, in his passionate addiction to the taste of this fruit, thought: [6] "If one cannot enjoy this fruit, how can one enjoy the fruits of being king? Anyone who has this to eat is a king indeed and without the cares of being king." He made up his mind that he would find out where it came from, and, by reasoning with himself, he deduced that the special tree from which the fruit had come was obviously not very far away and somewhere on the banks of the river. For neither the fruit's color nor its scent or flavor had been spoiled. Nor was it damaged or decaying. So it could not have been in contact with the water for long. Therefore the king felt sure that one could trace its source. Drawn on by his yearning for a taste of that fruit, he abandoned his water sports, took proper precautions for the safety of his capital, and set out along the river with a large escort of troops equipped for an expedition. As he gradually cleared his way through the thick jungle which teemed with

27 · 7 wild beasts, he enjoyed a variety of experiences—seeing forests of great natural beauty and scaring away the wild animals with the noise of kettledrums—until eventually he reached the tree in a spot all but inaccessible to humans. [7] From afar it looked to the king like a mass of clouds weighed down with water. Though there was a mountain nearby, it seemed like a mountain itself. This lord of the forest was looked up to by the other trees as though indeed it were their king. It exuded a heady and pervasive scent that smelled sweeter than ripe mangoes and that seemed to be coming out to welcome him. He was sure that this was the tree, and he went up to it. Then he saw that its branches were full of monkeys—several hundred of them—busily devouring the fruit. The sight of them robbing him of the objects of his desire incensed him. "Kill them, kill them!" he commanded his men in a harsh voice. "Destroy them, do away with every one of these vile monkeys." The king's men fitted arrows to their taut bows and threatened the monkeys loudly, while others, with clods of earth, sticks, and weapons at the ready, advanced on the tree as though intent on assaulting an enemy stronghold.

Now the Bodhisattva had seen the king's forces streaming forward in a tumult, like the waters of the sea stirred up by a gale, and making a confused and restless din. He saw the great tree smothered on all sides with a hail of arrows, clods, and sticks, like a shower of thunderbolts. And when he saw the tribe of monkeys unable to do more than give hoarse screams of panic, as they looked up at him with desperation in their strained faces, he felt a great surge of pity in his heart. Being himself free from despair, anxiety, or fear, he rallied the troop of monkeys and set his mind on rescuing them. So he climbed to the top of the tree, with the intention of leaping across to the mountainside nearby. Now although it took several leaps to reach, the Great Being, by virtue of his extraordinary power, sailed up to the mountain slope like a bird. [8] Even in two leaps other monkeys could not have spanned it, but he boldly crossed the gap in one swift bound, as though it were a mere nothing. [9] Pity strengthened his resolve, and courage gave it edge. He made a special effort, so intense that he got there in a moment. Climbing to a higher spot on the mountainside, he found a tall cane, full-grown and sturdy, deeply and immovably rooted, which was longer than the gap between the tree and the mountainside. He fastened the top of it tightly to his feet, then jumped back to the tree. But because the gap was wide and because he was hampered by having his feet tied, the Great Being only just caught hold of the tip of a branch of the tree with his hands. [10] Then, clinging fast to the branch, he tautened the cane with an effort and, with a recognized signal, ordered the troop of monkeys to leave the tree immediately. The moment they found a way of escape, the panic-stricken monkeys made a wild rush for it and, without worrying about stepping on their leader, easily got away along the cane. [11] As a result of being incessantly trampled by the panic-stricken monkeys, the Great Being's body lost some of its flesh, but his heart lost none of its exceptional endurance.

At the sight of this, the king and his men were overcome with utter amazement. [12] Simply to hear of such wisdom and courage, such selfless concern for others, let alone to witness it with one's own eyes, is enough to arouse one's wonder. The king then gave his men the following orders: "This monkey king has had his body bruised and battered by the feet of that band of monkeys in their blind panic. Clearly he must be absolutely exhausted from staying in that one position for so long, and he cannot extricate himself from it on his own. So be quick and spread a cloth sheet underneath him, then with two arrows shoot down the cane and the banyan branch simultaneously." The men did as he told them, and the king had the monkey gently lifted off the sheet and placed on a soft couch. As a result of exhaustion and pain from his wounds, a stupor invaded his senses. Clarified butter and other salves for alleviating fresh wounds were applied, and the pain abated. When the monkey revived, the king approached and, with mixed feelings of curiosity, amazement, and respect, first asked him how he was, then said: [13] "Without a thought for your own life, you made yourself into a bridge for these monkeys and saved them. What are you to

27 · 14 them? What are they to you? [14] If I am fit to hear it, then tell me this, my lord monkey. To be able to do such a thing, one's heart must be bound by no mean friendship."

The Bodhisattva, wishing to show honor to the king in return for his readiness to be of help, made himself known in an agreeable manner, saying: [15] "These monkeys, who are prompt to act on my orders, charged me with the burden of kingship, while I, who am attached to them as though they were my children, undertook to bear it. [16] This, your royal highness, is the kind of relationship that exists between them and me. It has grown over a long period, and, as a result of our living together, the friendly feeling that exists between animals of the same species has developed into a genuine affinity." The king was truly amazed when he heard this, and he continued: [17] "Ministers and others exist for the king, not the king for them. Why, then, did you sacrifice yourself for the sake of your own servants?" "Your highness," answered the Bodhisattva, "although political science proceeds on that assumption, I find it difficult to comply. [18] It is extremely hard to disregard someone who is in unbearably serious difficulty, even if he is unknown to you. How much more is this so in the case of people who tender their hearts' devotion and have become as dear to you as relatives. [19] So when I saw the monkeys getting more and more desperate in their wretched predicament, I was instantly overwhelmed with sorrow, which left no room for any personal considerations. [20] At the sight of bows being bent and of sharp arrows shooting out, I quickly jumped off the tree over to the mountain, shutting out of my mind the terrible twang of the bowstrings. [21] But I was drawn back by the thought of my comrades, who were overcome with acute terror. There was a remarkably tall cane with strong roots. This I tied to my feet. [22] Then I leaped from the mountain back to the tree, to rescue my comrades, and just caught hold of the tip of a branch, which stretched out like a hand to catch me. [23] Then, by means of my body, held taut between the cane and the tip of the branch, my comrades, without a scruple about stepping on me, got away safely."

That the Great Being should be full of joy even in his present condition surprised the king greatly, and he questioned the monkey further: [24] "Sir, what good have you gained by disdaining your own happiness and taking upon yourself the misfortune that befalls others?" The Bodhisattva replied: [25] "Your highness, though my body be shattered, yet my spirit has attained perfect well-being, inasmuch as I have relieved the distress of my subjects whom I have ruled for so long. [26] Just as heroes who have conquered their proud foes in battle bear the distinguished marks of their valor on their bodies like a badge, so I gladly bear this pain. [27] Now I have repaid the debt I owe for the whole series of blessings I have enjoyed as king over my fellow creatures, who have treated me not only with courtesy and kindness but with devotion also. [28] That is why it is no torment to me to suffer pain, to be separated from my friends, or to forgo happiness. And now that death draws near as a consequence of what I have done, it is like the eve of a festival. [29] Requital of former services, satisfaction for myself, calming of anxiety, and a spotless reputation; respect from a king, calmness in the face of death, and a feeling of gratitude among the worthy—[30] these are the benefits I have gained by my suffering, O you who are a roosting place for virtue. But the king who shows no concern for his dependents will meet with the reverse of these. [31] A king devoid of good qualities and who has ruined his reputation and become a familiar haunt of vice can surely expect no fate other than the flaming fires of hell. [32] That is why I have demonstrated, to you whose own power is far-reaching, the power inherent in good and evil. Therefore govern your kingdom with justice and remember: fortune is as fickle in her favors as any woman. [33] Beasts of burden, army, country people, townsmen, ministers, the helpless poor, monks, and brahmins—the king should, like a father, endeavor to procure for them all a fruitful happiness. [34] By increasing your merit, your wealth, and your fame in this way, you will earn happiness both in this life and in the next. Therefore, lord of men, may your reign be marked by the glory of the royal sages of old, which is achieved by showing compassion to your subjects."

27 · 35 [35] After delivering these precepts to the king, who, like a pupil, received them with devout attention and respect, the Bodhisattva left his body, which was paralyzed with overpowering pain, and went to heaven.

So, then—those who make a practice of good behavior can win over the hearts even of their enemies. With this in mind, he who wants to win people over completely should follow the ways of the good.

Kṣāntivādin 28

THOSE WHO HAVE MADE FORBEARANCE part of their nature and have great powers of judgment can endure anything.

According to tradition, the Bodhisattva once came to the conclusion that worldly life, because it is beset with pettiness, leaves little room for matters of the spirit. It seemed to him that living in society involves one in endless trouble and nuisance. Nor is it conducive to a tranquil state of mind, as one tends to concentrate purely on the material and sensual. Besides, one is exposed to the taints of passion, hatred, delusion, impatience, anger, arrogance, pride, selfishness, and other sins. Worldly life undermines one's sense of shame, one's awareness of what is right, and instead serves as a breeding ground for greed and caprice. On the other hand, he regarded the homeless life of a wanderer as something blessedly free from all these ills, because it does away with possessions and things of the senses. He therefore became an ascetic, noted for his integrity, his learning, his serenity, modesty, and self-possession. Because he never faltered in his vow of forbearance, was always preaching that virtue, and had a way of teaching the Law in the light of it, people disregarded his real name and that of his family and invented the suitable nickname Kṣāntivādin—Preacher of Forbearance. [1] Any outstanding achievement, be it in power, knowledge, or penance, any extravagant devotion to the arts, any quirk of speech, physical peculiarity, or mannerism can earn a man a nickname. [2] So it was with him. Knowing what power there is in the virtue of forbearance and wishing to instill it into others, he used to discourse on the topic constantly and, as a result came to be known as Kṣāntivādin. [3] The great forbearance that was part of his nature and that remained unaltered when others wronged him, together with the remarkable sermons he gave on the subject, earned him the reputation of a saint.

The Noble One lived in a delightfully secluded area of forest. With its abundance of fruit and flowers all the year round and with its pellucid lake adorned with white lotuses and blue water lilies, it was like a lovely park. And by residing there he endowed the place with the sanctity of a hermitage. [4] For, wherever a holy man of outstanding character chooses to settle, the place becomes auspicious and delightful—it becomes an object of pilgrimage, a hermitage. The various forest deities who lived there revered him, and people seeking salvation, lovers of virtue, visited him constantly. And he gratified the gathered crowd by giving sermons on the subject of forbearance, which were a delight both to their ears and to their hearts.

One day the king of those parts[1] thought he would like to have a water party—a particularly attractive idea since it was the height of summer—and with the ladies of his court he went to that same part of the forest, which had all the qualities of a park. [5] Crowded with court beauties, the forest looked as lovely as Nandana, the garden of the gods, but the king seemed to embellish it further as he strolled through it, amusing himself with that gorgeous bevy of wantons. [6] In pavilions and bowers, under trees bright with flowers, and in the water where the lotuses were wide open, he delighted in the spontaneous exuberance of the women. [7] With a smile he watched how gracefully some reacted in their alarm at the bees who were confused by the fragrance of their garlands, their intoxicating drinks, their scented water and ointments. [8] Though their ears were adorned with flowers of fresh beauty, and though their hair was wreathed with many a garland, the women were no more sated with flowers than the king was with their graceful movements. [9] He watched how the young women's eyes settled first on the pavilions, then lingered over the clusters of lotuses, then hovered like bees about the flowering trees. [10] Even the bold mating calls of the cuckoos, the dancing of the peacocks, and the hum of the bees were outshone by the chatter, the dancing, and the singing of those women. [11] The royal drums sounded like the dull rumble of thunderclouds and roused the peacocks to scream and fan out their tails:[2] they looked like actors practicing their art in the service of their king.

In the company of his women the king thoroughly enjoyed his outing to this park. But the never-ending round of amusements had made him weary, and he was feeling the effects of drink. So he lay down on a magnificent couch in a beautiful pavilion and surrendered to sleep.

When the women noticed that the king was otherwise occupied, they set off together in friendly groups, since the beauties of the forest had captured their hearts and they had not yet seen enough of it. As they rambled about with typical restlessness, the confused jangle of their jewelery mixed with the sound of their chatter. [12] Behind them came their maids, bearing the umbrella, fly whisk, throne, and other insignia of royalty, all brightly decorated with gilt. [13] Deaf to their maids' protestations, the women rushed up and greedily picked from the trees any blossom that was within easy reach, and the tender shoots as well. [14] Though they themselves were covered in flowers woven into wreaths and ornaments, if they encountered on their way a bush with pretty flowers or a tree with trembling buds, they could not pass it by without greedily stripping it.

Now, as the royal ladies wandered through the forest, captivated by its natural beauty, they came upon Kṣāntivādin's hermitage. Those in charge of the women, though aware of the saint's holiness and of the power he had acquired by his austerity, nevertheless dared not prevent them from approaching him, because the king liked to indulge their whims. Besides, the women were by now out of reach. It was as though they were drawn by the beauty of the hermitage, which was further enhanced by its aura of magic power. And no sooner did they enter it than they saw the great saint sitting cross-legged at the foot of a tree. His expression was calm and gentle but of such extreme profundity that he was hard to approach. He seemed positively ablaze with the radiance that came from his austere life.[3] Through constant meditation he contemplated the highest objects and yet had that beauty in repose which is a sign that the senses are unruffled. He was, in fact, like an embodiment of the Law, a blessed and auspicious sight.

The king's women felt the power that he had acquired by his austerity pervading their whole being, and, the moment they saw him, all frivolity, playfulness, and arrogance dropped away. They approached with proper humility and attended upon him reverently, while he greeted them, made them welcome, and gave them as good a reception as any guest could wish. Then, as their enquiries about religion gave him the opportunity, he entertained his guests with a religious address whose point women could easily grasp, illustrating it with plenty of examples.

[15] "Anyone born in the human condition—which is not to be despised—who is of sound constitution and has acute senses, who, though death inevitably awaits him, is yet so feckless that he fails to do a good deed every day, must be under some misconception. [16] A man may have a good pedigree; he may be handsome and in the prime of life; he may be extremely powerful or prosperous. But to secure happiness in the next life none of these avail: he must also have perfected himself in such virtues as generosity and integrity. [17] Even without a good pedigree and other advantages, a man has only to refrain from evil and to possess those virtues of generosity and integrity for happiness to be his in the next life, as surely as rivers flow into the sea in the rainy season. [18] A gold chain only shows that one is rich. The true ornament in this present life, of one who is wellborn, handsome, in the prime of life, exceptionally powerful or wealthy, is a regard for virtue. [19] Trees are adorned with blossom, low-hanging rain clouds with streaks of lightning, lakes with lotuses and their drunken bees, and human beings with virtues that have

been brought to perfection. [20] Whether it be health, age, wealth, beauty or birth, three different degrees can be distinguished: high, low, and middling. This threefold distinction is by no means due to a person's natural disposition, nor to outside influences, but rather to how he has behaved in the past. [21] Once one has realized that this is the immutable law of existence and that life is transient and prone to decay, one should desist from evil and feel disposed to do good. This is the path to fame and happiness. [22] On the other hand, a corrupt heart acts like a fire, burning up both one's own and other people's good completely. If, therefore, one is afraid of evil, one should take pains to avoid such corruption, by cultivating its opposite. [23] Just as a fire, however fierce, is quenched when it meets a large river brimful of water, so a raging heart grows calm if one inclines to forbearance, that mainstay in this life and the next. [24] Practice forbearance and you will avoid evil by cutting it off at the root. The result will be that you arouse no ill feeling because of your friendly disposition. You will be loved and honored for it and thereby win happiness. Finally you will enter heaven as though it were your own home—all because of your attachment to virtue. And what is more, dear ladies, this quality of forbearance is [25] the crowning glory of a fine character, the full flowering of virtue and good reputation. It is purification effected without contact with water, great riches attained by a host of different virtues. [26] It is the pleasing imperturbability of the stouthearted that ever remains impervious to the affronts of others. That which goes by the fair name of Forbearance is the result of special qualities. It is imbued with compassion and benefits everyone. [27] Forbearance is the distinguishing mark of the powerful, the culminating strength of ascetics. A torrent of rain on the raging fire of malice, forbearance allays all ills in this life and the next. [28] The shafts of abuse hurled by the wicked are blunted by the armor of forbearance worn by the good. Mostly they turn into flowers of praise and become part of the garland that celebrates their good name. [29] They say forbearance destroys the delusion that is at odds with the Law and that it is also a fine means of attaining salvation. Who, then, would choose not to persevere in forbearance, which invariably conduces to happiness?"

Such was the sermon with which the Great One entertained the ladies.

Meanwhile the king had slept off his weariness and awoken. His eyes were heavy with the lingering effects of drink. His thoughts turned to lovemaking, and he frowningly asked the chambermaids where the royal ladies had got to. The maids told him that they were now gracing another part of the forest and were admiring its splendors. On hearing this, the king was eager to watch the ladies at their ease, laughing, chatting, playing, and disporting themselves without constraint. So he rose from his couch and wandered off through the forest with young women carrying his parasol, his fly whisk, his fan, his shawl, and his sword. In his train came those attached to the women's appartments, dressed in their tunics and holding their canes of office. The trail that the young ladies had made in their wayward ramblings was strewn with all sorts of flowers, sprays of blossom, and twigs and was picked out with the red juice of chewed betel. By following it, the king came to the hermitage. But the moment he set eyes on Kṣāntivādin, that noble sage, surrounded by the royal harem, he became extremely angry, partly out of hatred, because he had long borne a grudge against him, and partly because his brain was fuddled with drink and his thoughts were warped by jealousy. And as he was completely lacking in calm judgment, his good breeding and refined manners vanished as his vile temper got the better of him. He broke into a sweat, grew pale, and started to tremble. Under a frowning brow his eyes squinted, rolled, stared, and became bloodshot. His charm and good looks disappeared as he wrung his hands, crushing together the rings on his fingers and shaking his golden bracelets. Then, hurling abuse at the great sage, he said something to this effect: "Huh! [30] Who dares to affront our majesty by setting eyes on our royal ladies? Who is this sly seducer masquerading as a holy man?"

At this the eunuchs grew alarmed and said to the king:

"Your majesty, please, please don't. This is the holy man Kṣāntivādin who has purified his soul with a long course of vows, restraints, and penances." But because his mind was disturbed, the king took no notice of what they said, and he continued: "Good heavens! [31] How long have people been taken in by the hypocrisy of this twisted character who gives himself out to be no ordinary ascetic! Let me be the one to expose the man's deceitful nature, full of guile and duplicity, which he conceals behind the garb of an ascetic." So saying, he snatched his sword from the hand of the female attendant who was carrying it and advanced upon the holy saint as though he were an enemy whom he was determined to kill.

The royal ladies had been informed by their attendants that the king was coming. But when they saw that his gentle mood had been dispelled by anger, they grew sad at heart. Their eyes flickered with distress and agitation, as they stood up and took leave of the great sage. Then they went to meet the king, lifting their cupped hands to their faces in homage. They looked like lotuses in autumn with their buds bursting out from the sheath. [32] But neither their respectful attitude, nor their charm, nor their gentle manners availed to calm his mind, which was enflamed with anger. His violent change of mood was apparent in his rough bearing as, with a fixed scowl and with his sword at the ready, he advanced upon the holy man. Seeing him do so, the court ladies grasped at this last opportunity to plead, gathered around him, and said: "Please, your majesty, please don't do anything rash. This is the blessed Kṣāntivādin." But the king, in the wickedness of his heart, grew all the more angry, feeling sure that the man had already won their affection. His puckered brow and sharp, sidelong glances full of indignation were clear signs of menace that silenced their daring plea. In a rage he turned on those in charge of the womenfolk, and, shaking his head so that his earrings and the tassels of his crown trembled, he said, with a glance at the women: [33] "This man preaches forbearance but does not practice it. As you see, he couldn't resist the desire to have contact with women. [34] His words are one thing, but his actions and his wicked thoughts are another. What is this dissolute character doing sitting in a hermitage, boldly trumpeting aloud his fraudulent vows?" The king was so intensely angry that his heart grew hard, and the court ladies found their request rejected. Since they knew how ferocious he could be, and how inflexible, their spirits sank into despair, and their superintendents, equally anxious and distressed, made signs with their hands to motion them away. Deeply sorry for the holy man, the ladies bowed their heads in shame and retired.

[35] "It is our fault that this mild ascetic, blameless though he be, and famous for his virtues, has incurred the king's displeasure. Who knows what quirky impulse he will follow, what course he will take? [36] Any injury the king may do to the holy man's body, already wasted by penance, would at the same time be a blow to his position as king, to the renown that accrues from it, and to our own innocent hearts." Such was the lament of the royal ladies as they went away, helpless to do anything but sigh deeply and commiserate. The king went up to the saint and threatened him. In his blind fury, he drew his sword to cut him down with his own hand. But seeing the Great Being remain calm and impassive, maintaining a cool and unruffled composure even in the face of attack, the king, in an even greater passion, said to him: [37] "What a fine art this fellow has made of playing the monk: he even looks at me just as a holy man would, flaunting his hypocrisy!" The Bodhisattva's patience was so habitual that he remained unruffled. After the initial shock, he immediately realized, from this rude outburst, that it was a fit of anger that was making the king behave so unnaturally that he had dropped all semblance of politeness and good manners—and that he had lost the power to discern what was good for him and what was not. Feeling sorry for him, he tried to soothe him by speaking in earnest somewhat as follows: [38] "One meets with disrespectful behavior in life, and, since it may be part of one's fate or even due to some fault of one's own, I do not care about that. But I am sorry not to be giving you the usual welcome due to visitors—not even a greeting. Besides, your highness, [39] it is not fitting for someone such as you,

intent on setting miscreants aright and working for the good of the world, to act in haste. You would do far better to reflect first. [40] A thing can seem bad though in fact it is good. Equally, something bad may appear otherwise. The right way to behave is not immediately obvious. First one must consider the various factors involved. [41] But if he reflects on what to do, arrives at the truth, and then proceeds in the proper manner according to the rules of statecraft, the king will secure great blessings, both spiritual and material, for his people and will not lack them himself. [42] You should therefore purge your mind of rashness and devote yourself to work that will do you credit, because any unwonted breach of conduct among persons of distinction causes great scandal. [43] Since you would not tolerate someone else behaving in a way that would disrupt the forces of good in this hermitage, protected by the might of your arm, how can you yourself, the lord of the land, be ready to do something of which no decent person would approve? [44] If your women happened to come to my retreat together with their attendants, what fault could that be of mine to transform you with rage like this? [45] But just supposing it were my fault, it would, even so, become you better, my lord, to show forbearance in the matter, since forbearance is the greatest mark of distinction in a powerful man: it shows he can maintain his good qualities. [46] Nothing—neither dark-blue earrings whose glint plays upon the cheeks nor crest jewels of varied luster—can adorn kings so well as forbearance. So please do not disdain it. [47] Get rid of your impatience: it can never give solace. Cultivate patience instead, as you do your lands. For kings usually behave toward holy men with noble and tender respect."

Despite the saint's conciliatory words, the king, his judgment still distorted, persisted in his false suspicions and replied: [48] "If you are not merely disguised as an ascetic and are set on keeping your vows of restraint, why are you begging me for safety on the pretext of a sermon on forbearance?" "Your highness," said the Bodhisattva, "deign to hear why I have made the attempt. [49] It was to prevent you being branded as the murderer of an innocent brahmin ascetic and thereby ruining your good name because of me. [50] All beings are doomed to die, in the natural order of things. So I am not frightened of dying, even as I look back on my life. [51] It was to prevent you from infringing the Law, which holds out the reward of happiness, that I commended forbearance to you as a sure means of attaining bliss. [52] I speak of forbearance with joy at having something so incomparable to offer: it is a rich source of other virtues and a sure defence against wrongdoing." But the king took no notice of the saint's lofty words—kind and true though they were—and angrily interjected: "Now let us see how devoted you are to forbearance." So saying, he aimed his sharp sword at the saint's right hand, which, with its long, delicate fingers upraised, was slightly outstretched in an attempt to restrain him, and he severed it from his arm as a lotus from its stalk.

[53] Even with his right hand cut off, the Bodhisattva, keeping true to his vow of forbearance, felt less pain than sorrow as he envisaged the frightful and inexorable suffering in store for the pampered king who had cut it off. "Alas!" he thought. "He has gone beyond the point where he can still be helped and is no longer amenable to gentle persuasion." He felt sorry for the king, as for a sick man deserted by his doctors, and kept silent. But the king continued his threats. [54] "Unless you give up your hypocritical austerities and this mischievous charlatanism, I shall go on hacking at your body till it finally succumbs." But the Bodhisattva said nothing to him, knowing that he could not be won over and that he was set in his obstinacy. The king then duly proceeded to lop off his other hand, both his arms, his ears and nose, and his feet. [55] But as the sharp sword fell upon his body, that perfect saint felt neither grief nor anger: he knew full well that the mechanism of the body must have an end, and he was well used to exercising forbearance toward people. [56] Even as he silently looked on while his body was hacked to pieces, his spirit remained unbroken in its constant forbearance. And, because of his kindly disposition, he felt no sorrow. But to see the king fallen from the path of virtue caused him anguish. [57] Compassionate souls, who have great powers of judgment, are not so

much troubled by the hardship they themselves experience as by that which befalls others. [58] But, the moment the king had committed his foul deed, he was attacked by a burning fever, and no sooner had he left the bounds of the wood than the earth gaped wide and swallowed him up. The ground opened up with a terrific noise and was ablaze with leaping flames. As the king sank into it, a great din arose on all sides, and the courtiers were shaken and bewildered. The king's ministers knew the great power of the saint's spiritual energy and realized that it was thanks to it that the king had sunk below ground. They became terribly afraid that the holy man would shortly burn up the whole country because of the king's crime. Accordingly they approached him, bowed low, and, with hands held out, begging his pardon, made an appeal: [59] "The king is quite thoughtless. He is the one who in his blindness has reduced you to your present state. Let him alone serve as fuel for the fire of your curse. Do not burn down this city. [60] Please do not burn the innocent people in it: the women and children, the old, the sick, the holy men and the poor. You are on the side of the good. So kindly preserve both the king's country and your own religious merit." The Bodhisattva reassured them, telling them to have no fears. [61] "As to him who has cut off my ears and nose, hands and feet with his sword—maiming an innocent being who lives in the forest—[62] how could someone such as I wish him any ill at all? Long live the king! And may no evil befall him. [63] A being oppressed with death, sickness, and sorrow, obsessed with greed and hate, eaten up by his own evil life, is someone who deserves pity. How could anyone be angry with such a person? [64] But were such a thing feasible, I would it were I who suffered retribution for the king's crime, since the taste of suffering, however brief, is intolerably bitter for those who are accustomed to an easy life. [65] Now, as I cannot save the king who is ruining his own well-being in this way, why should I compensate for my own helplessness by harboring malice against him? [66] Quite apart from the king, every born creature has to suffer death and its concomitant ills. In such circumstances the really unendurable thing is the fact of birth. Without that, what suffering can there be, and from what source? [67] Through countless eons this wretched body has perished time and again in a long succession of lives. Why give up being patient now, simply because it has been maimed? It would be like giving up a precious jewel in exchange for a piece of straw. [68] Living in the forest, keeping the vows of an ascetic, preaching forbearance, and soon to die, why should I want to lose my patience? So do not fear: I wish you well. Now go."

[69] In this way the saint instructed the ministers and at the same time initiated them as disciples in goodness. He himself remained resolute to the end, relying as he did on his forbearance. Then, leaving his earthly abode, he mounted up to heaven.

So, then—those who have made forbearance part of their nature and have great powers of judgment can endure anything.

29 The Inhabitant of Highest Heaven

SINCE THE EVILS OF FALSE BELIEF ARE so unspeakable, good men should feel a special sympathy for those who have fallen into such error.

According to tradition, the Lord, when still a Bodhisattva, was at one time born in the highest heaven. This was the potent effect of good karma, accumulated by his constant practice of meditation. But he had been so used to showing pity in his previous births that even the great felicity of the highest heaven—the reward for his exceptional meditation—could not quell his urge to be of active help to others. [1] Sensual pleasures make people extremely uncaring, whereas the pleasures of meditation do not interfere with the desire, which good men have, to be of use to others.

Now, on one occasion the Great One was gazing down at the sphere of the senses[1] that is plagued with endless woe and suffering and, with its elements of intense malice, cruelty, and sensuality, is a proper object of pity. There he saw the king of Videha,[2] who was called Aṅgadinna, astray in the jungle of false belief. This was due partly to his keeping bad company and partly to his chronically evil mentality. He had reached the conclusion that there is no otherworld and questioned whether one's acts, good or bad, have any consequences. This put a stop to any desire to keep religious observances and deterred him from cultivating such virtues as generosity and good behavior. He felt a growing contempt for the devout and, in his unbelief, had a scathing opinion of the religious codes. He was inclined to make fun of stories about the next life and showed scanty respect to monks and brahmins, whom he treated with little honor or politeness. He devoted himself instead to sensual pleasures. [2] Once a man has formed the conviction that good and bad deeds definitely have a pleasant or unpleasant outcome in the next life, he will reject evil and strive for good, whereas the unbeliever is the sport of his desires.

That the king should have succumbed to the fatal sin of apostasy, a source of endless misfortune to his people, filled the Great One, the divine sage, with compassion. In a blaze of light he descended from the highest heaven into the presence of the king, who was titillating his senses in the seclusion of a beautiful pavilion. At the sight of him blazing like a mass of fire, shining like sheet lightning, and emitting intense brightness like a cluster of sunbeams, the king was overpowered by such radiant energy. In some alarm he rose to greet him, humbly joined his hands, and, looking up at him respectfully, said: [3] "Your lotus-like feet seem to rest on air as if on solid earth. You shine out with the radiance of the sun. Who are you, your lordship, that your appearance so gladdens the eye?" [4] "My lord king," answered the Bodhisattva, "recognize in me one of those divine sages who, through intense concentration, have attained to the highest heaven, after subduing both love and hatred as one would subdue two proud enemy leaders in battle. At this the king welcomed him with kind words, then offered him hospitality with the ritual water and with water to wash his feet. Looking at the Bodhisattva with wonder, he said: "Great sage, your magic power is indeed miraculous: [5] without clinging to the walls of the palace, you walk about in the air as though on the ground. Tell me how you come to have this supernatural power, you who are as bright as a lightning flash." The Bodhisattva replied: [6] "Such an attainment as this, dear king, is the result of meditation, spotless integrity, and perfect restraint of the senses—all of which I have made part of my nature in the course of other existences." "Is it really true that there is another world?" asked the king. "Yes, there certainly is, your highness," answered the visitor from heaven. "But, your holiness, how could I, too, believe in it?" asked the king. "Your highness," replied the Bodhisattva, "it is a solid fact which can be recognized by applying the usual means of proof, such as direct perception, inference, and so on. Reliable people have demonstrated what happens, and it can be certified by means of tests. Just look at [7] the heavens above, adorned with sun, moon, and stars, and at the many different species of animal. There you have another world before your very eyes. Do not allow yourself to be blinded by skepticism. [8] Besides, there are people, here and there, who, through intense meditation and a vivid memory, remember their previous lives. This is another reason for inferring that there is a world beyond. And surely I myself provide evidence to prove it? [9] You may also deduce the existence of another world from the fact that a developed intellect presupposes the prior existence of that intellect. For the rudimentary intellect of the fetus is the direct continuation of the intellect in the preceding life. [10] Now, intellect is defined as the perception of the knowable. Therefore, there must be a sphere in which intellect can operate from the very beginning of one's existence. But it cannot be in this world, owing to the absence of eyes and other sensory organs at the fetal stage. In effect, the place where it is to be found is that other world. [11] One can observe how children diverge from their parents in character, behave differently, and so on. As this is not accidental, it must owe something to the habits of other existences. [12] The fact that a newborn child, though his mental powers are unfocussed and his senses still inchoate, tries to suck the breast without being taught [13] shows that in other existences he has had to concern himself with how to get food, for practice makes perfect and increases one's ability to do various things. Now because you are unfamiliar with the notion of another world, you might object to this and say that [14] the way lotuses open and shut is surely a proof of their having practiced doing so in other existences—and that, if I do not accept this, then why do I claim that the instinct to suck the breast has its origin in efforts made in other lives? This objection carries no weight once one realizes that in one case there is a necessity, in the other not, and that while one makes an effort, the other does not. [15] For the opening and shutting of lotuses it is evident that there is a fixed time. But this does not apply to the effort to suck the breast. The lotus makes no effort; the suckling clearly does. It is the sun's power that makes the lotus open. Thus it is, your majesty, that, after examining the evidence, one can believe in the existence of another world."

Now the king, because of his deep-seated attachment to the claims of false doctrine, and because much evil had accumulated in him, felt uneasy when he heard this account of the other world and said: "Great sage, [16] if the other world is not just a child's bugbear, or if you think I ought to accept its existence, then lend me five hundred gold pieces now, and I will pay you back a thousand in the next world."

The king's ill-mannered quip, spoken with his usual careless effrontery, was like a poisonous discharge from his false belief. But the Bodhisattva answered it in a truly fitting manner. [17] "Already in this world people who want to accumulate wealth certainly do not lend money to a bad man, to a glutton, to a bungler, or to a lazybones, for once their money gets into the hands of such a person, that spells their ruin. [18] But if they see someone who is calm and discreet and astute in business, they give such a person a loan without even bothering about witnesses, for money entrusted to him brings prosperity. [19] Your highness, just such a procedure should be followed in the case of a loan to be redeemed in the next world. But there can be no question of lending money to you, who, because of the evil doctrine you hold, do not know how to behave. [20] For when you are cast into hell through your own vile deeds—all deriving from your sinful error—who then would come and press you to repay a thousand gold pieces as you lie there dazed and racked by pain? [21] There the skies are not bright with the rays of sun and moon but are veiled in dense darkness. Neither can one see the heavens adorned with clusters of stars, like a lake with full-blown lilies. [22] Thick gloom prevails in the afterworld of unbelievers, and a wintry wind, which causes terrible pain as it pierces to the marrow. Who in his senses would enter there simply to retrieve some money? [23] Some wander endlessly in the bowels of hell amid thick darkness, murky with acrid fumes. Hampered by their trailing thongs and tatters, they howl with pain as they stumble over each other. [24] Others rush around ceaselessly in the hell of blazing chaff, wearing their feet away. They long for release, but neither their suffering nor their life comes to an end. [25] Others are held fast by Yama's[3] fierce henchmen, who, like woodcutters felling fresh timber, hack at their bodies and gleefully carve them up with their sharp, vicious knives. [26] Some suffer the agony of being flayed, then being completely stripped of their flesh so that they are left as mere skeletons. Yet, they do not die: their evil deeds keep them alive in the same way as those others who are chopped into pieces. [27] Others, with broad, flaming bits choking their mouths, submit to fiery-red harness and goad and endlessly draw blazing chariots across plains of molten iron. [28] Some get in the way of the mountains of Saṃghāta[4] and are crushed to pieces. But though their bodies are pulverized by their onrush, and despite great and unremitting suffering, they do not die until their evil karma comes to an end. [29] Others are put into flaming hot troughs where they are pounded by huge metal pestles, also ablaze. Yet, though this lasts a full five hundred years, they do not give up the breath of life. [30] Others are slit open on red-hot trees that look like coral but that bristle with blazing spikes of sharp iron. With bloodthirsty screams the demonic servants of Yama drag them around upside down. [31] Others taste the fruit of their actions on large heaps of live coals, the color of molten gold, and are powerless to do anything but writhe and scream. [32] Others lie on the ground, which is fearsome with rings of flame, and have hundreds of sharp spikes stretched over their tongues. They shriek at the searing pain inflicted on their bodies. And it is then that they are convinced that another world does exist. [33] Some are wrapped in fiery copper bands and then boiled down in copper caldrons, while others are wounded by streams of sharp weapons and then have the skin stripped off their flesh by packs of ravening beasts. [34] Others, in their exhaustion, enter the alkaline waters of the Vaitaraṇī,[5] but these are as searing as flames to the touch and the flesh completely dissolves in it—but the breath of life, which is sustained by the force of their evil acts, does not. [35] Those who, suffering agony from the heat, come to the hell of unclean corpses, as to a pool of water, undergo the unparalleled torment of having their bodies consumed to the bone by hundreds of worms. [36] Others are enveloped by flames, their bodies a continuous blaze, going through the tortures of being burned alive. Like iron, they are subjected to fire but, preserved by their past deeds, do not turn to ash. [37] Some are slit open with flaming saws, others with sharp razors. Others groan in anguish as their heads are smashed under the impact of hammers. Others are cooked over a smokeless fire, their bodies transfixed by broad skewers. Others are made to drink liquid copper, the color of glowing fire, and scream aloud. [38] Others are attacked by ferocious spotted dogs,[6] who with sharp fangs strip the flesh from their bodies. Lean and lacerated they collapse, moaning in misery. [39] Such is the horrible suffering in the various hells. When your own deeds will have forced you to experience it for yourself, when you suffer agony and are overwhelmed with exhaustion and despair, who could possibly claim his debt from you then? [40] Who, I ask, would claim his debt from you as you wander helplessly amid copper caldrons, whose leaping flames make them unapproachable and which seethe with the corpses of wicked people being sucked into the boiling mixture. [41] Or, when your body is tied down by blazing wedges of iron, to the ground that is red with smokeless fire, and when you weep pitifully as the flames consume you—who, I wonder, would claim his debt from you then? [42] Who would claim his debt at a time when you had met with humiliation, were subjected to great sufferings, and were incapable of giving even a reply? [43] Who could possibly claim his debt in the next world, while you are being cut to shreds by a wintry wind, powerless even to moan, or howling in a hundred agonies as your bones are torn apart? [44] Who would press you with a demand for money in the next world while you are being tortured by Yama's servants or else writhing in a fierce fire, or having your flesh and blood devoured by dogs and crows? [45] Besides, while you undergo various torments, such as being hit, cut to pieces, beaten and slashed, burned, carved up, crushed, and split apart, how could you repay me your debt then?"

Now when he heard this horrifying description of the different hells, the king was conscience stricken and abandoned his false beliefs. Firmly convinced of the existence of another world, he bowed to the holy man and said: [46] "Now when I hear of the torments of hell my heart almost melts with fear. And yet I feel a burning anxiety about what is to become of me when I meet with them myself. [47] For I have been improvident and have followed evil ways, my wits fuddled by false doctrines. Now my sole recourse is your noble self: you are my last resort, my refuge, holy sage. [48] Since you have rid me of the darkness of error, as the rising sun banishes the darkness of night, so now, great sage, you must tell me the way in which I can avoid an evil fate after this life."

The Bodhisattva saw that the king had undergone a change of heart, that his false beliefs were now set right, and that he had become receptive to the Law. And, feeling sorry for him, he instructed him, as a father his son or as a teacher his pupil. [49] "When kings of old behaved like good pupils toward monks and brahmins by showing their love of virtue and were true to their own station by showing compassion for their subjects, they trod the glorious path to heaven. [50] Therefore, master your bad habits, which are extremely hard to master, overcome greediness, which is hard to overcome, and enter in splendor the city of the Lord of Heaven, with its golden gateway and blazing mass of jewels. [51] May the beliefs cherished by good people continue to appeal to you despite your long attachment to false views. What you must renounce is that commitment to evil preached by people who wish to ingratiate themselves with the ignorant, [52] for, now that your highness is ready to behave in a manner approved by the true doctrine, you have banished from your mind all harsh feeling toward virtue, and the very same moment you have set foot on the right road. [53] So use your money for virtuous ends and show compassion to people, which is both kind and to your own advantage. Continue to keep good control of your senses and conduct. That way you will meet with nothing unpleasant in the next world. [54] My lord king, let your rule blaze out with the splendor of your worthy deeds and earn the respect of good men. May its integrity give delight. Use it for your own good and advantage, while at the same time relieving all creatures of distress, and thereby achieve fame. [55] Here you are in a chariot. Let respect for the virtuous be the driver, and your own body, begetting virtue, the chariot. Let tenderness be its axle, self-control and generosity its wheels, and the devout wish to acquire merit its shafts. [56] Let your restrained senses be its horses, bridled with attentiveness. Make intelligence the whip, and the whole range of sacred learning the weaponry. Let modesty be the chariot's trappings, humility its lovely rail, forbearance its yoke, and dexterity its motion, steadied by your willpower. [57] Curb harsh words, and it will go without creaking. Use pleasant language, and its sound will be deep and rumbling. Its joints will never come loose so long as there is no break in your self-restraint. Provided you shun the tortuous paths of evil, it will go straight. [58] With this vehicle that radiates awareness, whose flag is renown, whose lofty ensign is tranquility—with compassion in its train, you will journey for the good of others as well as of yourself and never will you go to hell, dear king."

In this way the Great One dispeled the darkness of the king's false beliefs with the bright beams of his words, and showed him the way to bliss. Thereupon he disappeared. And the king, having now grasped the true facts about the next world, accepted the true doctrine wholeheartedly and, together with his ministers and his subjects—from both town and country—devoted himself to charity, self-control, and restraint.

So, then—since the evils of false belief are so unspeakable, good men should feel a special sympathy for those who have fallen into such error.

The Elephant

30

GOOD PEOPLE REGARD EVEN SUFfering as being of profit if it results in happiness for others.

According to tradition, the Bodhisattva was once a huge elephant. He lived in a forest that was the haunt of elephants—a beautiful place with the fresh green of magnificent trees whose tops could be descried, laden with fruit, blossom, and sprays of leaves. The ground was covered with all kinds of shrubs and grasses. Mountain and upland presided serenely over this forest, as though captivated by its beauty. The place was a refuge for wild animals, and in it there was a broad, deep lake. A large desert, without trees, bushes, or water, isolated the forest, on every side, from human habitation. Here the Bodhisattva lived a solitary life. [1] Like an ascetic, satisfying his needs with a leaf from a tree, a lotus stalk, and some water, he enjoyed peace and contentment.

Now one day, as the Great Being was wandering at the borders of the forest, he heard the sound of human voices coming from the direction of the desert, and he wondered what this could possibly mean. In the first place, there was no road that passed that spot, leading elsewhere. Nor was it likely that people should have crossed such a large desert to go hunting, much less that they should have troubled to mount a major expedition to capture his fellow elephants. [2] Clearly these people were lost, their guides having missed the way, or else they must have been banished either at the angry whim of a king or owing to some misdemeanor of their own, [3] for the sound he heard was feeble, quite without joyful exuberance—in fact, full of distress, as though the people were actually weeping.

30 · 4 The Great Being decided he would find out straightaway who they were and, drawn on by a feeling of compassion, went in the direction from which the sound of human voices was coming. The moaning became more distinct, and he heard cries for help that had an unpleasant ring of desperation and hopelessness. The Great One hurried on, his heart moved by compassion. At the point where he came out of the jungle there were no trees or bushes, and so he had a wide view. He immediately caught sight of as many as seven hundred men coming in the direction of the forest. Hunger, thirst, and exhaustion had slowed them down, and they were crying out for help. The men also noticed the Great Being advancing in their direction like a peak of the Himalaya on the move, or a thick mist, or an autumn cloud driven toward them by a strong wind. In their despondent and miserable state they panicked at the sight, thinking that now at last they were done for. Yet they made no attempt to escape: hunger, thirst, and fatigue had so sapped their energies. [4] Overwhelmed with despair and afflicted with hunger, thirst, and fatigue, they made no attempt to escape, even when danger was imminent. The Bodhisattva realized they were frightened. "Don't be afraid! Don't be afraid! You have nothing to fear from me," he assured them, raising his trunk with its broad tip, soft and dark red, and drawing near. Then, with pity in his voice, he asked: "Who are you, sirs? And how do you come to be in this state? [5] Dust and exposure to the rays of the sun have turned you pale and gaunt. You are suffering from pain and exhaustion. Who are you, and why have you come here?"

When they heard him speak in a human voice, assuring them they were safe and showing he was ready to be of help, the men took heart and, prostrating themselves, said: [6] "Lord of elephants, an outburst of stormy temper from our king has, before the very eyes of our grief-stricken relatives, whirled us away to this spot. [7] And yet we must still have some good luck left—Fortune must surely be favoring us—in that you have noticed us, you who are better than any friend or relative. [8] And we know, from the joy of seeing you, that our troubles are over, for who could fail to surmount difficulties once he had seen someone like you, if only in a dream?"

Then that lordly elephant asked how many they were. [9] "Graceful creature," replied the men, "there were a thousand of us abandoned here by the king, but since then many, never having experienced hardship before, have perished—victims of hunger, thirst, and grief. [10] Now there must be seven hundred men left, sinking slowly into the jaws of death. To these you have appeared as an embodiment of Relief."

On hearing this, the Great Being was moved to tears, with his usual compassion, and, feeling sorry for them, he spoke with earnestness, somewhat as follows: [11] "Alas! That king certainly does not have a tender conscience: he is quite shameless and unconcerned about the next life. Oh! How blind to their own good people are, once they are hypnotized by the splendor of being king, which lasts no longer than a flash of lightning. [12] He is, I suppose, unaware of how near death is, or else he pays no heed to the fact that wickedness leads to a bad end. Woe to those godforsaken kings who are so weak in judgment that they are impatient of advice. [13] This cruelty to other beings is all for the sake of one body, itself a prey to illness and doomed to perish. Oh! What folly!"

Then, as the elephant lord looked at those men with tender feelings of pity, the thought occurred to him: how were people so physically weakened by the torments of hunger, thirst, and exhaustion going to get across a waterless desert stretching for many hundreds of miles without any shade, unless they had provisions for the journey? Besides, what was there in the forest where the elephants lived that could sustain them even for a day and that did not require a great effort to collect. On the other hand, if they took his flesh as provisions and used his entrails as water bags, they might be able to get across this desert. Otherwise it was impossible. [14] So he decided he would make his body—that repository of countless ills—a raft that would ferry these men, beset with suffering, across the sea of misfortune. [15] Being born as a man gave one the chance to attain the bliss of heaven and of final release and was not easy to achieve. So these men ought not to squander it like this. [16] Also, their coming there made them by rights his guests, since he was on his own territory. And, as they were in distress, beyond the reach of their relatives, they had all the more claim to his pity. [17] At long last this receptacle of countless ills, this resort of all manner of affliction brought on by perpetual suffering, this host of evils that goes by the name of 'body,' would finally be put to use in the service of others.

Then some of the men, ravaged by hunger, thirst, fatigue, and heat, held their hands together in supplication. With tears in their eyes, they prostrated themselves and begged him for water, making signs with their hands—such was their sorry state. Others appealed to him pathetically: [18] "You are a kinsman to us who have none. You are our refuge and defense. Blessed creature, please care for us as you think best." But others of a hardier temperament asked him where one could find water and which route would bring them out of that dreadful desert: [19] "If there is a pool nearby, or a river with cool water, or a waterfall, or a shady tree, or a grassy spot, tell us, lord of elephants. [20] Take pity and please show us in which direction you think we should go to get out of this desert. We have been astray here for a good many days. So please, master, come to our rescue."

These piteous pleas pained the Great One's heart all the more, and, since it was indeed possible to cross the desert, he lifted his trunk, which was as thick as the coils of a big snake, and with it he pointed out a mountain range, saying: "Under that mountain range there is a large lake whose clear blue waters are adorned with lotuses and water lilies. So go that way, and when you have recovered from the heat and from thirst and exhaustion, you will discover, not very far from there, the body of an elephant that has fallen down the mountain. Use its flesh as provisions and its entrails as water bags to collect water. Then continue in the same direction. In this way you will get across the desert with little difficulty."

With these words of encouragement the Great One set the men on their way. Then he went as quickly as possible by another route and climbed up to the summit of that mountain. As he was about to sacrifice his own body in the hopes of saving those people, he earnestly affirmed this vow[1] [21] "This is not an attempt to earn myself a happy destiny, or the majesty of a universal monarch, or heaven with its unadulterated joys, or the bliss of Brahma's world, or even the happiness of final release. [22] But whatever merit may be mine in thus wishing to extricate these people who have foundered in the desert, may it help me to become the savior of mankind wandering in the wilderness of endless birth and death."

Such was his resolve, and in his elation the Great One thought nothing of the agonizing death he would suffer by being shattered on the steep cliffs but hurled himself down the mountainside, as he intended. [23] His falling body looked like an autumn cloud, or like the orb of the moon toppled from the Western Mountain, or like the snow-covered peak of that mountain flung down by the strong rush of air from Garuḍa's[2] wings. [24] With a massive roar, as of a whirlwind, he fell to the ground, jolting the earth and the mountains and also Māra's[3] power-obsessed mind. The forest creepers were prostrated by the weight of his fall, and the forest spirits by admiration. [25] Certainly the gods that dwelt in that forest showed utter amazement at what had happened. Their hair bristled with excitement, and they threw their arms in the air, each finger like a twig pointing upward. [26] Some covered him with a ceaseless stream of flowers, sweet smelling and tinted with sandal powder, while others covered him with ornaments or cloaks brilliant with patterns of gold and not woven of cloth. [27] Others likewise did him honor with hymns of praise devoutly composed, stretching out cupped hands that looked like lotus buds. Or else they bowed their heads, crowned with lovely diadems, and did obeisance. [28] Some fanned him with a fragrant breeze, scattering pollen and forming ripples on water, while others used thick clouds to make a canopy for him in the sky. [29] Some were prompted by devotion to honor him by making the sky laugh aloud with the roll of heavenly drums, while others decked the trees of the forest with buds, blossom, and fruits—all out of season.

[30] The sky grew radiant with an autumnal beauty, the sun's rays seemed to lengthen, and the ocean's swelling waves seemed astir with eagerness to pay him a joyful visit.

Now, in due course those men reached the lake, and in its waters they dispeled heat, thirst, and fatigue. Nearby they noticed the corpse of an elephant not long dead, just as the Great One had told them, and they remarked its resemblance to the lordly elephant. [31] Could it be the brother of that mighty elephant, they wondered, or a relative, or one of his sons? Even in its mangled state, this body, bright as a snowy mountain, certainly resembled his. [32] It looked like a mass of white lilies, or like compacted moonlight, or rather like his own reflection in a mirror. But some of them looked more carefully. As far as they could see this splendid elephant, who in his exceptional appearance rivaled the mighty elephants at the world's four corners,[4] was indeed the very same elephant. He had thrown himself down the mountainside hoping to save them who in their distress were without friends or relatives. Realizing this, they said: [33] "That noise we heard, like a whirlwind, which seemed to rock the earth. Obviously it was this elephant falling down. [34] Of course this is his body: it has the same pale coloring, like a lotus stalk; its hair is as white as moonbeams; it is flecked with small spots; these are the same tortoise-like feet with white nails; and this is the same backbone gracefully curved like a bow.[5] [35] This is the very same face, long and broad, adorned with streaks of ichor, fragrant and beautiful; and this the head, erect, magnificent, untouched by any goad, and set on a massive neck. [36] This is the same pair of honey-colored tusks with their proud mark, the fine dust of the mountainside. And this is the same trunk with whose tip, like a long finger, he showed us the way. Oh! This is truly a marvel of marvels! [37] What kind of affection must he have shown his friends or relatives when—knowing nothing of our family, our character, or our faith and not even having heard of us before—he has been so friendly to us, who were battered by fate? All honor to this blessed being, the soul of compassion! [38] He who came to help people like us, when we were in the midst of disaster and overcome with fear and anguish, must surely be someone disguised as an elephant, who somehow sustains the flagging spirits of living beings. [39] Where did he learn this extraordinary power of bringing luck? What teacher did he attend in the forest? Here is visible proof of the popular saying 'Beauty without virtue gives no delight.' [40] Oh! How well this creature of exceptional character has proved his true auspiciousness by this culminating act. Indeed, even in death, with his body bright as Himalaya, he seems to be smiling happily at the perfection of his soul. Who now will feel able to feed on the flesh of this creature who has behaved with such surpassing goodness? In his readiness to come to our aid and in his concern to be of service to us even at the cost of life, he showed greater love than affectionate friends or relatives would have done. We ought rather to pay our debt to him by cremating his body with full honors."

Such thoughts inclined them to indulge their grief, with tears in their eyes and their throats choking with sobs, as though it were a relative of theirs who had died. Observing this, others, of a tougher mentality, who saw matters in a different light, said: "By doing this we would certainly not be greatly honoring this excellent elephant, nor would we be treating him fitly. In our view we should honor him by carrying out his wishes. [41] For this unknown friend, with the object of saving us, sacrificed his own dear body, holding his guests to be dearer still. [42] His intention ought therefore to be followed. Otherwise, wouldn't this magnificent feat of his be pointless? [43] Indeed, in his affection he has offered his guests all that he has. Now who would wish to make such hospitality fruitless by not accepting it? [44] Therefore, by acceding to his command as if it came from a superior, we can show him proper respect and at the same time do what is right for ourselves. [45] Once we have escaped this peril we can honor him either individually or all together: we will perform every rite for this good elephant, as for a departed relative."

Now these men were anxious to escape from the desert and remembered what the elephant lord had intended. And so, without opposing his orders, they took the Great Being's

30 · 45 flesh and used his entrails as water bags. Then, going in the direction he had indicated, they came safely out of that desert.

So, then—good people regard even suffering as being of profit if it results in happiness for others.

Sutasoma 31

ASSOCIATING WITH GOOD PEOPLE, however this may come about, brings lasting joy. Whoever wants to attain such joy should consort with good people.

According to tradition, the Lord, when still a Bodhisattva, was once born into the illustrious royal family of the Kurus, a dynasty of brilliant renown. Its passion for acquiring virtues had earned it the constant devotion of its subjects, while it humbled the pride of its vassals by its splendor. The child's father named him Sutasoma[1] because he looked as lovely as the moon, his numberless virtues radiating from him like a halo. Like the waxing moon, he grew daily more beautiful and charming. In course of time he became proficient in the Vedas, the subsidiary Vedas, and the ancillary sciences.[2] He also mastered the arts and other accomplishments and became an object of love and respect to the people. His readiness to be of real assistance, his ever-increasing attentiveness, and his self-imposed vow of guardianship gave him almost a family tie with the Virtues. [1] Good character, learning, generosity, compassion, self-control, ardor, patience, wisdom, resolution, humility, modesty, shame, majesty, beauty, fame, courtesy, intelligence, strength, and integrity—[2] such excellent qualities as these did he harbor. His youth seemed to enhance them further, and his purity and nobility lent them charm. They were like the different phases of the moon. And in consequence the king conferred on him the rank of heir apparent, both because he had the capacity to govern the people and because there was so much goodness in his nature. [3] In his love of wisdom the boy particularly appreciated religious maxims and therefore treated with special honor anyone who came and recited such maxims to him.

31 · 4 It was the flowery season of spring, and the parks surrounding the city were decked with beautiful sprays of fresh leaves. The burst of bloom gave them a dazzling charm. Fresh grass covered the ground, like a carpet, and the ponds of clear water were strewn with the blue and white petals of lotus and lily. The place was ahum with swarms of roving bees, and cuckoos and peacocks flocked together busily. Cool breezes, soft and fragrant, wafted through these parks, which were a balm to the heart.

One day, as he was strolling there with a small escort, the Great One entered one of the groves to pass his time in pleasure. [4] The place resounded with the call of male cuckoos and was further beautified by a delightful garden pavilion. Its various trees bowed under the weight of blossom. Here he wandered about, accompanied by his ladies, just like a man in paradise, enjoying the reward for his virtuous life. [5] He delighted in the sound of the women's songs blending with the mellifluous strains of musical instruments, in their subtle allure and graceful sequence of movements as they danced, and in their wanton exuberance under the influence of drink. Also he enjoyed the beauty of the grove itself.

While there, the Great One was approached by a certain brahmin who had some wise sayings to recite. After being given a polite welcome, the brahmin sat down, entranced by the prince's physical beauty. And though the Great Being was in the act of enjoying these youthful pleasures, which were the direct consequence of his great store of merit, he nonetheless felt honored by the brahmin's visit. But the brahmin himself got no reward out of coming to recite his words of wisdom, for there was a sudden uproar, which drowned the music and singing and ruined the pleasure they were getting from their lighthearted pursuits. It alarmed the womenfolk and made them anxious. And when the crown prince heard it, he was concerned and asked the attendants of the harem to find out what it was. Then the sentries rushed up in a panic, with fear and dismay in their faces, and reported: "Your highness, it's the cannibal Kalmāṣapāda, Sudāsa's son, who is even more bloodthirsty than the demons. He goes on destroying men by the hundred, as though he were Death himself. His power, his energy, and his insolence are superhuman, and he looks as fierce and terrifying as a demon. He could be the Great Bogy, and he is on his way here. Our forces have scattered. Fear has drained them of courage. And with the chariots, the cavalry, and the elephants all amok, the troops are in disarray. So your highness must be ready to resist or else decide on the appropriate action to take."

Though he knew perfectly well, Sutasoma asked them who was this person called Kalmāṣapāda, Sudāsa's son. "What," they replied, "your highness doesn't know about King Sudāsa? Once, while he was out hunting, his horse bolted, and he reached the depths of the jungle. There he coupled with a lioness. She became pregnant and after a while gave birth to a boy. The foresters took him and presented him to Sudāsa who, not having a son, adopted him. And when his father went to heaven, he became king in his own right. But from his mother he inherited the unfortunate craving for raw meat. Once he had tasted human flesh and decided that he liked its flavor, he proceeded to kill numbers of people in his own capital city and then devoured them. When the townspeople took measures to do away with him, Kalmāṣapāda took fright and promised the goblins, who delight in offerings of human flesh and blood, that, if he got out of this scrape, he would sacrifice a hundred royal princes to them. Well, he did get out of it, and since then he has abducted many princes. Now he has come to abduct your highness. You have heard the facts. Your highness must judge what is best."

The Bodhisattva already knew of the perverted and evil habits of this Kalmāṣapāda, and he felt sorry for him. So he set his mind on curing him. He sensed he had the power within him to put a stop to this aberration, and so, when it was announced that Kalmāṣapāda was approaching, he felt as happy as though it were good news and earnestly said: [6] "A man who has fallen from power because of his craving for human flesh, who is as out of control as a lunatic, who has abandoned his duties and ruined his good reputation, is surely in a pitiable state. [7] There is no call for me to use force nor to feel frightened or disturbed by someone in such a condition. I will completely eradicate this man's evil habit without any effort, agitation, or violence. [8] And now this very man, who would deserve my pity even if he had gone elsewhere, has, of his own accord, entered my territory. It is therefore proper that I should show him hospitality: that is how decent people treat visitors." Then, turning to those in charge of the harem, he ordered them each to attend to his duties. The young women made ready to block the path. Their eyes flickered, then stared wide in despair. Their throats quavered with sobs. The prince reassured them and made them turn back. Then he set out in the direction of the frightful noise and caught sight of Kalmāṣapāda in hot pursuit of the fleeing army. His filthy clothes were tightly hitched up with a belt. His disheveled hair hung down stiff with dust and was held in by a headband made of bark. A tangled growth of beard covered his face and darkened it. His eyes rolled wildly in rage and fury, as he brandished sword and shield.

Without a trace of fear, the prince boldly called out: "Hey there! I am Sutasoma. Come back here. Why are you so intent on slaughtering these poor people?"

At the sound of this summons Kalmāṣapāda felt a stir of pride and bounded back like a lion. When he saw the Bodhisattva standing there by himself with neither sword nor shield and looking his naturally gentle self, he exclaimed: "You are the very person I am looking for." And without hesitation he rushed up in excitement, lifted him onto his shoulder, and ran off.

The Bodhisattva noted with concern that Kalmāṣapāda was in a frenzy of pride, that his mind was bewildered and confused, and that he was brimming with arrogant delight at the rout of the king's forces. As this was not the moment to teach him better, he calmly bided his time. Kalmāṣapāda, on the other hand, had got what he wanted and so returned home to his stronghold in high spirits, as though he had captured an important prize. [9] The place was littered with the corpses of men he had killed, and the ground was horribly spattered with blood. The eery howl of jackals and the crackling fires seemed to be harsh threats made in anger. [10] And the dense trees were discolored by the smoke of countless funeral pyres, their rusty leaves soiled by the crows and vultures who perched there. When travelers caught sight of it from afar, their eyes would glaze over with horror, for that unquiet spot was as loathsome as the burial grounds where demons and phantoms perform their dances.

Setting the Bodhisattva down there, Kalmāṣapāda took a rest and watched him intently, his eyes riveted by such remarkable beauty. Meanwhile, the Bodhisattva remembered about the brahmin who had come with his offering of wise sayings. He had received no hospitality and must still be waiting, with hope in his heart, for him to return to the park. "Oh dear!" he thought, [11] "that brahmin came a long way to offer those wise verses and was full of expectation. What on earth will he do when he hears I have been carried off? [12] The failure of his hopes will be a burning torture to him, and despondency will make him feel his exhaustion all the more acutely. Either he will pity me and sigh deeply, or else he will curse his own fate." Thinking of how unhappy the man must be, the Great Being suffered greatly. Pity was so deeply ingrained in him that tears welled up.

Seeing the tears in his eyes, Kalmāṣapāda burst out laughing and said to the Bodhisattva: "Stop that! [13] What about all those good qualities of yours, and your reputation for being wise? No sooner do you fall into my hands than you start shedding tears. How very true is the saying [14] 'In calamity, fortitude is of no use. In grief, no learning can avail. There is no creature in existence who, under attack, does not quail.' So tell me the truth—[15] what is it that you are bewailing: your own precious life, your wealth which procures you comfort, your relatives, or your crown? Or is it the thought of your loving father or your weeping children that has reduced you to tears?" [16] "No," replied the Bodhisattva, "it is not that I am thinking of my own survival, or even of my parents, children, relatives, and wife. Nor is it the recollection of pleasures I enjoyed as a prince that brings me to tears. But there is a brahmin who with high hopes brought me some verses of wisdom. And when he hears that I have been kidnapped he is certain to be consumed with despair. That is what was in my mind and the reason for the tears in my eyes. [17] So please, let me go and revive the spirits of that poor disappointed brahmin by sprinkling them with the water of appreciation, and let me gather the honey of his wise words. [18] Then, when I am no longer in debt to the brahmin, I shall honor my debt to you too by returning here, once more to be seen by your eyes that will have been eagerly awaiting that pleasure. [19] And do not be uneasy and suspect that this may just be a ploy of mine to get away: people like me, O king, follow a path that is different from others." To this Kalmāṣapāda replied: [20] "This suggestion you are making in all seriousness quite passes belief. After escaping from the jaws of Death, who, I ask, would return there again when he is free to do as he pleases? [21] Once you have survived the danger of death, which is not easy to avoid, and are comfortably installed in your beautiful palace, what possible reason could there be for you to return here to me?"

"What," said the Bodhisattva, "doesn't your lordship understand that there is indeed a very serious reason why I should return? Have I not given my word that I will? That should be enough to stop you treating me with the same suspicion as you would some trickster. After all, I am Sutasoma. [22] It is true that some people, out of greed or in fear of death, don't care a straw about what they have once promised. But, for decent people, their word is something of value, is life itself, and therefore they do not betray it even when the situation is desperate. [23] Neither life nor the pleasures of this world can save a man from an evil fate once he has deviated from his word. Who, then, for the sake of these, would repudiate his word, the source of contentment, renown, and happiness? [24] If a person is clearly on the path of evil or is not noticeably zealous in the cause of good, then one doubts whether he will do anything decent. But what have you noticed to make you suspicious of me too? [25] Now if I had really been afraid of you, or were a slave to pleasures, or if I had had no pity in my heart, surely I would have gone out to meet someone as notoriously savage as you, like a hero, brandishing sword and shield? [26] But might it not be that I really wanted to make your acquaintance? After rewarding that brahmin for his effort, I shall come back to you of my own accord. People like me do not make vain promises." Kalmāṣapāda thought the Bodhisattva was just boasting when he talked like this, and in his annoyance the idea came to him—"This fellow certainly does brag about being so truthful and virtuous. Alright then, let's see how faithfully he keeps his promises and how much he loves virtue. What would it matter to me even if I did lose him? Thanks to the mighty strength of my right hand, I already have a full complement of one hundred princes in my power. With these I shall make my sacrifice to the demons as promised." With this in mind he said to the Bodhisattva: "Off you go, then! Let's see how true you are to your word and how virtuous you are. [27] Go and do whatever that brahmin wants. Then come back quickly. In the meantime I shall prepare your funeral pyre."

The Bodhisattva gave his word and, on arriving at his palace was welcomed back by his household. He sent for the brahmin, who then recited a set of four verses to him. Hearing these words of wisdom put the Great Being into a benign mood, and he thanked the brahmin with kind words and showed him honor. Then, reckoning each verse as worth a thousand gold pieces, he rewarded him with the riches he longed for.

Now his father, who was anxious to prevent any lavish or misplaced expenditure, waited for a suitable moment and then gently remonstrated with him: "My boy, you ought, really, to recognize some limit when rewarding wise sayings. You have a large household to support, and the majesty of a king depends on the resources of his treasury. That is why I am telling you: [28] to reward a wise saying with a hundred gold pieces is already a very high valuation. But to go above that is wrong. For if one is overgenerous how long can one maintain the outward show of wealth, though one be Kubera[3] himself?

[29] Wealth is the chief means to success, and an effective one, since it is quite impossible to live as one likes without it. Once a king no longer has a full treasury, Fortune, like a harlot, does not spare him a glance." [30] "But your majesty," protested the Bodhisattva, "were it at all possible to measure the worth of wise sayings, I am sure I would not incur your displeasure even if I bartered my crown for them. [31] When something you hear calms your mind, reaffirms your yearning for salvation, enlarges your wisdom so that the gloom of ignorance vanishes, surely you would pay for it with your own flesh and blood if need be? [32] Sacred knowledge is a lamp that scatters the darkness of delusion. It is the best kind of wealth, beyond the reach of theft or anything else. It is a weapon to foil that enemy of ours, confusion. With its advice on the sensible course to take, it is the perfect counselor. [33] It is a staunch friend even when one is in trouble, and a painless cure for the ills of grief. It is a mighty power that crushes the forces of evil, and a priceless store of honor and glory. [34] Indeed, the riches contained in sacred knowledge are also the principal ingredient of that eloquence which in good company has the charm of a gift and which in learned assemblies gives pleasure. Such eloquence throws a flood of light on rival doctrines and destroys the vainglory of the contesting parties. [35] The bright eyes and glowing cheeks even of strangers vouch for its superior merits—rapturously they twirl their fingers in intense approval. [36] It enables one to express one's meaning with clear logic, illustrating it from various treatises and traditional doctrines. In its grace, perfection, and charm it is like an unspoiled wreath of flowers. [37] It shines like a steady bright light and is a sure harbinger of fame. Put to use, the riches contained in sacred knowledge are a clear means to success, [38] and those who take heed of them pursue the three objects of life[4] along a path free from besetting sins. They behave in strict conformity with the sacred precepts and surmount the difficulties of life with ease. [39] This sacred wisdom, renowned for so many merits, has come to me as a gift. How can I not treat it with honor when it is in my power to do so? On the other hand, how can I

disregard your command? [40] I shall therefore go to Kalmāṣapāda. I want neither the cares of kingship nor those which I would bring upon myself were I to follow the path of evil and recklessly compromise my character."

His father, because he was so fond of him, grew anxious and said to him earnestly: "My boy, I was only thinking of your own good when I spoke as I did. So do not take it to heart. May your enemies fall into the hands of Kalmāṣapāda! But you have promised to return to him, and, being someone who keeps his word, you want to fulfill that promise. Nevertheless, I will not allow you to do so. Perfidy is no sin if one has to resort to it to save one's life or for the sake of one's elders—those who know the Vedas say so. So why make things difficult for yourself by disregarding them? Besides, political experts regard it as misguided and perverse of kings to hold to moral considerations when these obviously clash with material interests and personal happiness. So stop being so obstinate: it pains my heart, and you are being blind to your own interests. My dear boy, you cannot bring yourself to break your promise because you think it would be disgraceful and immoral, and because you are not accustomed to doing so. Even so, here I have a grand army—elephants, cavalry, chariots, and infantry—fully equipped and all ready to come to your rescue. The troops are loyal and well-tried—warriors skilled in arms, who have many times been through the ceremony of lustration before battle. They are as terrifying as a huge flood. Set off with these as your escort and make Kalmāṣapāda submit, either to you or to death. In this way you would both fulfill your promise and save your life."

"Your majesty," replied the Bodhisattva, "I cannot promise one thing and do another. Nor can I strike a blow at people like him who have sunk into the mire of vicious habits, are bound for hell, and are therefore to be pitied—who have been abandoned by their own families and friends and are helpless. Besides, [41] that cannibal did something both difficult and noble in my case: though I was in his power, he let me go, because he trusted my word. [42] It is thanks to him that I learned these wise sayings, father. He did me a favor and therefore deserves my sympathy all the more. And, my lord, do not worry about my being in danger from him. For how can he possibly do me any harm if I return to him, as I will?"

In this way the Great Being won his father over and turned aside his dependents who were set on restraining him, dismissing the devoted troops also. Then, without fear or misgivings, true to his word, he went all by himself to where Kalmāṣapāda lived, hoping, for the sake of the world, to reform him. Kalmāṣapāda caught sight of him from afar, and in his astonishment he felt even greater respect and goodwill toward him. Though his mind was clouded by a cruelty that by dint of long practice had become ingrained, his reaction was definite: "Ah ha ha ha ha! [43] Wonder of wonders! What a miracle indeed! The way this prince honors his word is something more than human, more than divine. [44] That he should master fear and anxiety and, of his own accord, return to me when I am by nature as savage as Death—oh! what strength of character, what real integrity! [45] How right that he should be famous for being true to his word, seeing how he has sacrificed his life and his royal rank to keep faith."

While Kalmāṣapāda was overcome with this feeling of amazement and respect, the Bodhisattva came up to him and said: [46] "I have discovered the riches contained in those wise sayings. I have rewarded the petitioner. And joy has entered my heart. All this because of you. So now I have come back. Eat me if that is what you want, or else condemn me to serve as a victim in your sacrifice." [47] "It is not yet the moment for me to eat you," said Kalmāṣapāda, "especially as this pyre is too smoky, and flesh tastes good only when cooked on a smokeless fire. So let us hear these wise sayings of yours." "Why does someone in your state want to hear wise sayings?" asked the Bodhisattva. [48] "Your belly has made you what you are, and you have lost all feeling for your subjects. These verses are in praise of virtue, and virtue does not go together with wickedness. [49] You lead the loathsome life of a monster. You have forsaken the paths of honest men. You have nothing to do with truth, let alone virtue. What use can you make of sacred knowledge?"

Exasperated by this rebuke, Kalmāṣapāda replied: "You are wrong. [50] Tell me what king does not raise his bow to kill the beloved companions of the hinds in his park. In the same way I kill men to keep myself alive. But apparently I am in the wrong while those who kill deer are not." [51] "Certainly they are not in the right either, drawing their bows against deer as they flee in terror," said the Bodhisattva. "But someone who devours men is far more to blame than they are, because human beings are a higher form of existence and are not there to be eaten."

Now although Kalmāṣapāda had had some very harsh things said to him, his savage nature was overcome by the Bodhisattva's great friendliness. So he still remained in a good mood and, laughing at what the Bodhisattva said, continued: "My dear Sutasoma, [52] I set you free and you went home to revel in all the trappings of being king. Then you came back to me, from which I deduce you are not well-versed in the ways of the world." "Not so," said the Bodhisattva. "I am perfectly well-versed in the ways of the world. And that is precisely why I have no wish to put them into practice. [53] After all, what is the point of being expert in something that involves total abnegation of what is right when it does not even assure one of happiness? And, what is more, [54] those who are clever at putting worldly wisdom into practice usually suffer miseries after they die. I have rejected the tortuous ways of the world, kept my word, and returned here. [55] It is I who am well-versed in worldly wisdom insofar as I have forsworn untruth and delight in truth. Indeed, those who know about such matters declare that no action that does not bring fame, happiness, and fortune in its train is wise."

Then Kalmāṣapāda questioned him: [56] "You have surrendered your own life, left your family in tears, given up all the delightful pleasures associated with being king. What advantage do you see in keeping your word that makes you come back to me because of it?" "Many fine things follow from holding to the truth," answered the Bodhisattva. "Listen while I tell you in brief: [57] Truthfulness is more beautiful than

31 · 58 a garland of flowers, sweeter to taste than anything else, and, because it earns merit without trouble, it is better than any penance or wearisome pilgrimage. [58] Fame is ready at any moment to spread among men, and truthfulness is the means whereby it penetrates all three worlds. It is the gate that admits one to paradise. It is the bridge that leads one across the perilous stream of repeated existences." "Excellent! absolutely right," exclaimed Kalmāṣapāda, bowing down before him. Then with an admiring look he continued: [59] "Others who fall into my clutches give up in despair, and fear robs them of all composure, whereas you never cease to be magnificently imperturbable. I presume you have no fear of death, my lord." [60] "What good is cowardly terror? It is a futile remedy for something one cannot evade even by taking enormous pains. Yet, even those who know this and have reflected on the human situation [61] are paralyzed by a fear of death. Remorse for evil proclivities, a conscience about their apathy in doing good, anxiety about retribution in the next world—all contribute to this. [62] But I do not recall ever having done anything about which I could feel remorse: I have made a habit of behaving with integrity. And if one holds to what is right, why need one fear death? [63] Nor do I remember a suppliant whose coming was not a delight to me, as well as to the suppliant. If one has had the satisfaction of giving things away as I have, and if one has kept to what is right, what need has one to fear death? [64] Even on mature reflection I cannot remember ever having had an impulse to evil—not even in my thoughts. If my path to heaven is therefore clear, why should I feel afraid of death? [65] I have bestowed much money on brahmins, relatives, friends, dependents, on people in distress, and on ascetics who are the ornament of their retreats, giving to each according to his deserts. I did for them whatever they required of me. [66] I have had the satisfaction of founding hundreds of magnificent temples, hospitals, hermitages, assembly halls and watering places. As a result I have no fear of death. So prepare me for your sacrifice or else devour me."

232 Tears of gladness filled Kalmāṣapāda's eyes when he heard

this. His hair bristled, and he came out in goose pimples. The darkness of his evil nature vanished as he looked at the Bodhisattva with profound respect and exclaimed: "Heaven forbid! [67] Should anyone wish to harm someone such as you, a king among kings, may he swallow poison in the full knowledge of its being lethal; may he eat a poisonous snake that has been provoked to anger, or swallow molten iron. May his head split into a hundred pieces, and his heart too! So please tell me those wise sayings. Your words were like a shower of blossom: I am touched to the heart and now am even more interested in hearing them. Besides, [68] now that I have seen my loathsome conduct reflected in the mirror of the Law, perhaps I may have felt a stirring of the conscience and be eager for the Law."

Now the Bodhisattva realized from Kalmāṣapāda's inclination to hear the Law that his mind had been made receptive to it, and he said to him: "If you want to hear about the Law, you should do so in the correct attitude. Now look: [69] give outward expression to your worthy feeling of humility by taking a lower seat. Taste the honey of the holy words in a trance of delight. [70] Let your mind be attentive, calm, pure, and reverent. Then listen devoutly to the Law, as a sick man listens to the words of a doctor."

Kalmāṣapāda immediately spread his shawl over a slab of stone and helped the Bodhisattva up onto this platform, while he himself sat down on the bare ground in front of him. Then, looking intently into his face, he said to the Great Being: "Speak, my master!" And the Bodhisattva spoke. His deep voice carried so that it seemed to fill the forest like the gentle rumbling of a newly formed cloud: [71] "A single chance encounter with a good person establishes something solid and lasting that has no need of constant renewal." "Excellent! excellent!" exclaimed Kalmāṣapāda when he heard this. And, rocking his head and twirling his fingers in approval,[5] he said to the Bodhisattva: "Go on! go on!" So the Bodhisattva quoted the second verse: [72] "Never be far from good people, but practice humility and honor the saintly, for the pollen from those flowers, their virtues, spreads wide and is bound to touch anyone who comes near them." [73] "You noble creature," said Kalmāṣapāda, "how right you were to spend your money in that way, to disregard difficulties, in paying unstinted honor to these wise verses. Go on! go on!" So the Bodhisattva continued: [74] "Royal carriages, inlaid with jewels and gold, grow ugly with age, as do our bodies. But age cannot touch a good man's worth, so constant is the honest man in his love of virtue."[6] "But this is like a shower of nectar," said Kalmāṣapāda. "I feel so refreshed. Go on! go on!" So the Bodhisattva continued: [75] "How far apart are earth and sky, the ocean's near and further shores, the mountain where the sun comes up and the mountain where it sets. But even wider is the gap between the ways of good and bad." Kalmāṣapāda felt his love and respect infused with a feeling of wonder and devotion, and said to the Bodhisattva: [76] "These verses that I have heard from you are lovely. Their meaning shines out all the more for being expressed so elegantly. You have made me feel happy. So, as a reward, I allow you to make four wishes. Choose whatever you want from me."

The Bodhisattva, half surprised, half moved, said: "Who are you to be offering rewards? [77]—you who have no power even over yourself, dominated as you are by your addiction to crime. What sort of favor are you likely to grant someone else when generous behavior is quite alien to your nature? [78] And it could happen that I ask you to grant me a favor that you may not feel inclined to give. No one with any scruples would run such a risk.[7] So you have done enough, quite enough, for me."

Kalmāṣapāda felt slightly ashamed and, bowing his head, said to the Bodhisattva: "My lord, please don't be so wary of me. [79] I will grant your wishes even if it costs me my life. So, my lord king, make your choice confidently, whatever it is you want."

"In that case," said the Bodhisattva, [80] "grant me these four favors, none of them trifling. Swear to be truthful. Avoid doing harm to living things. Release every one of the people you have taken captive. And, hero that you are, do not eat human flesh." [81] "The first three I grant you," said Kalmāṣapāda, "but make your fourth wish something else: don't you understand, I cannot resist human flesh?" "There you are," said the Bodhisattva, "it's happened: did I not say 'Who are you to be granting favors?' Besides, [82] how can you keep your vow to be truthful and to do no harm to living things, if you do not give up eating human flesh, dear king? [83] Didn't you say just now that you would grant my wishes even if it cost you your life? But it turns out not to be so. [84] And how can you be doing no harm to living things while you go on killing people for their flesh? This being the case, of what value are these three favors you have granted?"

[85] "How can I give up the very thing for which I surrendered my royal state, endured hardship in the wild, broke the law, and shattered my reputation?" asked Kalmāṣapāda. "That is precisely why you should give it up," answered the Bodhisattva. [86] "How can you fail to give up such a worthless existence, for which you have forfeited goodness, wealth, happiness, and reputation? [87] Only people who suffer from being mean regret a thing once given. How can you too succumb to such baseness? So enough of this straying along the path of wickedness. You ought to realize who you are. After all, you are the son of Sudāsa. [88] You have the choice of meat from wild animals and tame, as well as of fish from ponds. It is examined by doctors and prepared by skilled cooks. Content yourself with these, but please give up your outrageous habit of eating human flesh. [89] How can you enjoy it here in this lonely forest, deprived of your relatives, your children, and congenial company, far removed from the sound of music-making subdued as the rumble of rain clouds, from the sound of a song in the night, and from all the various pleasures of being king? [90] You should not be the slave of your passions, my lord, but should follow a course that is not at odds with spiritual and material well-being. Single-handed you have defeated kings and their massed armies in the field. Do not now show yourself an utter coward in the matter of subduing your passions. [91] And, my lord king, ought you not to take some thought for the next world too? That is a reason for you not to persist in an evil just because it gives you plea-

sure but rather to turn to something that does no damage to your reputation, the achieving of which gives satisfaction and which you must take like medicine, however disagreeable it may be."

Kalmāṣapāda went up to the Bodhisattva and clasped him by his feet. His eyes were brimming with tears of tender joy, and his throat choked with sobs as he said: [92] "With good reason has your fame spread all over the world, the pollen of your fine qualities and the perfume of your merit pervading everywhere, seeing that no one else but you would take pity on me, an evildoer whose cruel habits have made of me a messenger of Death. [93] You are my master, my teacher, my idol. With bowed head I honor these words of yours. Never again will I eat human flesh, Sutasoma, and I will do just what you tell me. [94] Those princes I seized for my sacrifice are languishing in captivity. Their bright spirits are dimmed, and sorrow weighs heavy on them. Come, let us free them together!"

The Bodhisattva readily agreed and followed him to where the princes were imprisoned. As soon as the prisoners saw Sutasoma they realized they would be set free and were utterly delighted. [95] At the sight of Sutasoma the princes burst into peals of lovely laughter[8] and looked as radiant as masses of white water lilies expanding under the invigorating rays of the moon at the beginning of autumn. The Bodhisattva went up and reassured them, spoke to them kindly, returned their greetings, and then made them take an oath not to do any harm to Kalmāṣapāda. After that he set them free and returned to his kingdom, accompanied by Kalmāṣapāda, with the princes following in his train. There he received them all with appropriate ceremony and reinstated every prince, including Kalmāṣapāda, in his respective kingdom.

So, then—associating with good people, however this may come about, brings lasting joy. Whoever wants to attain such joy should therefore consort with good people.

Ayogṛha—The Prince in the Iron House 32

NOT EVEN THE GLORY OF BEING KING can obstruct one's path to final bliss, once one has felt revulsion for worldly life. One should therefore experience for oneself this feeling of revulsion.

According to tradition, the Lord, when still a Bodhisattva, realized that mankind was prey to endless ills, such as disease, old age, death, and being parted from those one loves and that it was helpless, vulnerable, and without guidance. Spurred on by pity, in his utter goodness of heart, he made up his mind to save the world, by securing whatever advantage, whatever happiness he possibly could for men—even for those who were hostile or unknown to him.

Once he was born into a certain royal family famous both for their decency and their exalted position. These were reflected both in the family's wealth, which increased steadily thanks to their ready affection for their subjects, and in the fact that their proud vassals were completely submissive. The Bodhisattva's very birth was a brilliantly festive occasion, not only for the royal household but for the capital city which shared their joys and sorrows. [1] Brahmins were delighted with the amount of presents they received. Ministers were puffed up with pride in their splendid apparel. The arbors were filled with the mingled strains of various musical instruments, and everywhere people were dancing for joy and behaving recklessly. [2] There was continuous fun and games, singing, and shouting. Excitement mounted as people, delighted with the gifts they received in return for spreading the good news, embraced each other and prayed for the king's happiness. [3] The prison gates were opened, and the prisons were deserted. Splendid flags were hoisted, unfurling color over the squares. The ground was sprinkled with sandalwood powder, flowers, and wine. All in all, the town had about it a delightful air of jubilee. [4] Showers of gold, clothing, ornaments, and other precious objects were pouring out of the houses of the rich as though Fortune herself were set on engulfing the world in imitation of the wild abandon of the Ganges.[1]

Now at that time, whenever a son was born to the king, he died. Supposing that this must be the work of demons, the king had a special nursery made to protect the child. It was all of iron[2] and was curiously encrusted with gold and silver and precious gems. The usual rites for counteracting demons were performed as prescribed in the treatises on demonology and in the Veda. The place was first exorcised by means of the customary auspicious ceremonies, then the boy received the various sacraments from birth onward and was brought up there. The demons were powerless against the Great Being, owing partly to the merit he had acquired through his goodness and partly to the effectiveness of the precautions that had been taken.

In course of time, after he had received all the sacraments, he learned many subjects from teachers outstanding for their knowledge, good birth, and breeding. They had won fame and honor as scholars and cultivated calm, wisdom, and serenity. Day by day his body blossomed with youthful beauty. This, together with his innate love of decency, made him the object of extreme affection, both in his own family and among people in general. [5] People are attracted by a good man and treat him with friendly affection, even though he is no relation or acquaintance of theirs and lives a long way off, simply because of his rare qualities. [6] How else does the autumn moon attract people here on earth when it spreads its beams and fills the sky with dazzling brightness? The Great Being was cosseted with great, almost godlike, luxury, which, thanks to his great merit, was no more than his due. His father began to feel respect as well as affection, looking at him with confidence, all anxiety gone.

One day the time came for the Kaumudī festival,[3] and the

prince was eager to see the beautiful decorations that festooned the city. With his father's permission he climbed into the royal carriage, which was brilliantly decorated with gold, silver, and precious gems. Bright flags and pennants of various colors had been hoisted on it and were flapping in the wind. Its horses were swift but well-schooled and were decked in trappings of gold. The coachman was adroit, dexterous and deft, honest, sober, and steady.[4] His retinue was finely dressed and accoutred with gleaming weapons and armor. Heralded by the delightful sounds of a band, the prince passed through the capital, inspecting the motley crowd of citizens dressed in their best holiday attire. Their eyes were roving in curiosity, and at the sight of him their hearts were transfixed. Eagerly they received him with honor and praise, stretching out their folded hands, bowing before him, and pronouncing blessings. Though it was a sight fit to rejoice the prince's heart, it had the effect of making him recall his former lives—so usual with him was the feeling of revulsion for this earthly existence. [7] "How pathetic is our earthly state," he thought to himself. "It is so horribly transitory. This magnificent Kaumudī festival will soon be just a memory. [8] And yet, though this is the lot of all creatures, how unconcerned people are in their carefree pursuit of happiness, while Death waylays them on every path. [9] Disease, old age, and death—three enemies whose power cannot be resisted—stand ready to strike, and inevitably one must tread the difficult path to the hereafter. How can anyone in his senses have cause for joy? [10] Clouds, with glittering chains of golden light and a roar as of huge oceans, produce waters of a savage fury. They swell up, only to dissolve again. [11] Rivers, with rushing waters that wash away trees that are firmly rooted on their banks, gradually come to look quite meager again, as though they were burned up with sorrow. [12] The violent wind that blows off the peaks of mountains and scatters whole cloud masses, that tosses and whirls the ocean waters, also dies down. [13] With bright leaping flames and glinting sparks, fire consumes deadwood and then goes out. Each season, deep in the forest, some lovely bloom appears and disappears again.

[14] Is there anything joined together that does not end by being parted, any success that is not prone to disaster? That people can be happy when mutability is the lot of all creatures certainly shows a lack of clear-sightedness."

After these thoughts the Noble One could no longer fix his attention on the colorful crowds, delightful though they were as they surged forward to decorate the capital. In revulsion he shut himself off from the high spirits of the festival and presently noticed that he had in fact arrived back at the palace. This only increased his distress. Convinced that his only recourse was the spiritual life, which had nothing to do with sensual pleasures, he made up his mind to embrace it forthwith. At the first opportunity he went to the king and, respectfully joining his hands, begged permission to retire to a hermitage: [15] "I wish to secure my own good by renouncing the world, and it would be a mark of favor were you to grant me permission to do so." [16] At this, the king, who dearly loved his son, trembled and shook, like an elephant pierced by a poisoned arrow or like the deep sea whipped up by the wind, such anguish did he feel for him. [17] Anxious to restrain him, he embraced his son affectionately and, in a tearful voice, said: "My boy, why have you suddenly decided to forsake us in this way? [18] Whose hostile act has made you take this fateful step? It will surely spell his own ruin. Whose family is doomed to weep tears of sorrow? [19] Or perhaps you suspect or have heard that I have done some wrong? Then tell me, so that I may no longer do it—though I am not aware of any such fault in myself."

[20] "How can you who are so ready to show affection possibly be at fault?" said the Bodhisattva. "And who is there capable of making me suffer?" "In that case, why do you wish to forsake us?" asked the king, with tears in his eyes. "Because Death dismays me," answered the Great Being. "Look, my lord—[21] from the very first night that a man lodges in the womb, he steadily advances toward death, every day a little nearer. [22] However well-versed in worldly ways, however powerful, no one escapes old age and death. It is because the

whole world is tyrannized by these two that I wish to retreat to the forest and to live the life of the spirit. [23] Kings in the flush of pride conquer whole armies of frenzied troops, cavalry, chariotry, and elephants, arrayed against them. But they are powerless to conquer that other enemy, Death, though he stands alone. That is why I intend to devote myself to the religious life. [24] Kings can escape their enemies thanks to being protected by huge numbers of exultant troops, cavalry, elephants, and chariotry. But ever since Manu, father of mankind, they have helplessly submitted with all their forces to that enemy of superior might, Death. [25] In battle, raging elephants use their tusks as clubs to batter down the monumental gateways of cities and to crush both men and chariots, as well as other elephants. But those tusks, which can overturn even solid banks of earth, cannot repel the onslaught of Death. [26] In battle, skillful archers pierce the enemy with arrows, even if they are far off, however strongly protected they are by the different kinds of mail and armor. But they never hit that long-standing enemy, Death. [27] Lions can quell the ardor of elephants by sinking the points of their sharp, cutting claws into their frontal lobes. With their roar they can shatter the hearing and the spirits of their enemies. But when they encounter Death, they lie low, robbed of their pride and strength. [28] Kings punish offending enemies in proportion to their crimes. But they tend not to inflict punishment on the enemy whose name is Death, however great his offences. [29] Kings also subdue an offending foe either by friendly persuasion or by other means.[5] But Death is terrible: long habit has hardened it in its pride, and one cannot get the better of it by such things as wheedling words. [30] Snakes bite men with their sharp fangs, which are full of terrible fiery poison fueled by anger. But they make no attempt to bite Death, even though it deserves to be killed for its unremitting ingenuity in contriving harm. [31] However vicious the snakes may be, doctors can neutralize, with spells and antidotes, the poison in the man they have bitten. But Death is an exceptionally venomous snake whose fangs can never be drawn. Neither spells, nor antidotes, nor any other remedy can counteract its poison. [32] With a terrible roar like the thunder of massed clouds, the Suparṇas[6] flap their wings and drain the seas of their water and of the playful shoals of fish within them. Then they seize the serpents who expand their terrible hoods. But they have not the power to assail Death in similar fashion. [33] Tigers, with their greater speed, overtake deer in the forest as they flee in terror, and, pinning them down in playful manner with a single adamantine paw, they proceed to drink their blood. But they cannot behave like that with Death. [34] A deer can escape even from the terrible fangs of a tiger's mouth, but once a man has reached the jaws of Death, with its large fangs—disease, old age, and pain—can his be a happy fate? [35] Demons with horrible, misshapen bodies hold men in a firm grip and suck up their vital forces and strength. But at the first skirmish with Death, their overweening pride is gone. [36] Those who are adept in the magical arts can control demons when they come to make mischief among people engaged in their devotions. This they do with the power acquired from doing penance, with magic spells, and with herbs. But nothing can avert the demon of death. [37] Illusionists can put people into a trance at large gatherings. But Death has some power that prevents even them from duping it. [38] Those who in the past counteracted poison with charms whose strength came from their doing penance, and those excellent doctors, from Dhanvantari[7] onward, who cured mortal ills—all have themselves perished. That is why my mind is bent on the religious life in the forest. [39] Supernatural spirits possess various magic powers which enable them to appear and disappear again, to fly through the air or to land on the ground. But face to face with Death, these powers desert them. [40] The great gods repel the haughty Asuras,[8] and, in turn, the Asuras repel the haughty gods. But even their combined forces, frenzied and brimful of pride, could by no means conquer Death. [41] Now that I have realized how irresistible is the ferocity of Death, our enemy, I cannot take pleasure in life at home. It is not in anger or because I no longer feel affection that I am leaving for the forest; it is because I am set on the religious life."

"But if the threat of Death has, as you say, no remedy, what respite will you get by going to the forest or embracing religion?" asked the king. [42] "Won't Death, the enemy, catch up with you in the forest? Don't hermits who live the religious life die in the forests? Surely the way of life there is possible everywhere? What need is there for you to leave home and live in the forest?"

[43] "Of course Death comes to those who live in the forest as surely as to those who live at home, to the devout and to the wicked alike," said the Bodhisattva. "But the devout have no cause to feel remorse, and the religious life is certainly easier to follow in the forest. Just think, your majesty, [44] the home is a breeding ground of negligence, conceit, lust, greed, and hatred. What opportunity does one get there to practice the spiritual life, which goes counter to all these? [45] Living at home, one is distracted by all sorts of irksome duties. One worries first about how to acquire possessions, then about how to keep them safe. Calamities present or imminent give one no peace of mind. When can one follow the path of serenity? [46] In the forest, however, one sheds all those unpleasant preoccupations, one is spared all the trouble that possessions entail, and one is at ease. Serenity is one's sole preoccupation, pursued in utter contentment. One by one, happiness, virtue, and renown are achieved. [47] Virtue, not riches or power, is a man's safeguard, Virtue, not the amassing of wealth, brings great happiness. Death can only be a source of joy to a virtuous man, for the man who devotes himself to virtue has no fear of an evil fate. [48] Just as good and evil are determined by the different actions associated with them and by distinctive characteristics, so too the reward of wickedness is an evil fate, of conspicuous goodness a happy fate."

With these words the Noble One won over his father, and, after getting his assent, he cast off his royal state as though it were a wisp of straw and went to live in a hermitage. There he cultivated the four stages of trance[9] and the four cardinal

32 · 48 virtues,[10] and, after initiating other men in these, he rose up to the world of Brahma.

So, then—not even the glory of being king can obstruct one's path to final bliss, once one has felt revulsion for worldly life. One should therefore experience for oneself this feeling of revulsion.

The Buffalo

33

One can only show forgiveness if there is someone to be forgiven. That is why good people welcome, as a positive gain, even the man who does them wrong.

According to tradition, the Bodhisattva was once a wild buffalo living in a remote forest. Caked in mud, his body looked like part of a dark cloud walking along. Though as an animal his mental state was so dim that it was difficult for him to recognize what was right, he was by no means idle in the pursuit of good, thanks to his sharp discernment. [1] As though bound by long service, Pity never deserted him. Either his previous actions or his own nature had some influence on his being as he was, [2] which, indeed, is why the Lord spoke of it being impossible to judge the rightness or the rewards of one's actions, since he who was the soul of pity was nevertheless born as an animal and in that state could still recognize what was right. [3] Without one's actions the continuous chain of existences would not occur. Nor can a good action have bad results. So despite his awareness of what was right he must have entered such low states because of some slight traces of previous action.[1]

Now there was a wicked monkey who had noticed that the buffalo invariably displayed a natural benevolence and that he never got angry or irritated but, on the contrary, was always compassionate. Concluding that there was nothing to fear from him, the monkey made a habit of tormenting this buffalo cruelly with every sort of nasty prank. [4] Never is a rascal so utterly impudent as when dealing with the mild and gentle. He turns particularly nasty because he can see no cause to be afraid of them. But should he sense the slightest hint of danger from someone, he grovels with false humility. Faced with such a person, he stifles his insolence. Sometimes, while the Great Being was innocently asleep or drowsily nodding his head, the monkey would suddenly jump on top of him. Another time he would climb up him, as though the buffalo were a tree, and shake him violently. Sometimes he would stand in his way when he was hungry and stop him grazing. At one time he would rub the buffalo's ears with a stick; at another he would climb up on to his head and cover his eyes with his hands just as he was longing to take a plunge into some water. Or else he would mount on his back and then, holding a stick in his hand and riding him by force, play at being Yama.[2] But the Bodhisattva, that Great Being, put up with all these wild pranks of the monkey, without getting upset, irritated, or angry, considering it more as a favor. [5] It is in the nature of the wicked to stray from the path of proper behavior, just as for the good to have to show patience is like receiving a favor—they are so practiced in it.

Now there was a certain sprite who could not bear to see the Great Being insulted like this. Or else he wanted to test his character. So he stood in the way of the buffalo, as the wicked monkey was riding him, and said: "Really, this must stop. Has this wicked monkey bought you? Or have you lost at dice? Or are you perhaps afraid he may do you some injury? Don't you know your own strength, that you are prepared to put up with the indignity of being ridden by him? Surely, my friend, [6] the adamantine tip of your horns, if swung violently, could pierce adamant itself or, like adamant, pierce great mountains. And these hooves of yours, if you kicked out in a rage, would sink into a rockface as into mud. [7] And this body of yours, solid and compact as a rock, achieves perfect beauty by virtue of its strength. Even those who are themselves powerful testify to your strength, which would deter even a lion from approaching you. [8] So seize hold of the monkey and crush him with your hoof or tear out that insolence of his with the tip of your horn. Why put up with the pain and misery this wretch causes you, as though you had no power to stop him? [9] When is a wicked person ever cured by goodness and kindness? Only bitter, scorching, and harsh remedies have any effect in such a case, which is like the spread of some phlegmatic disease."

The Bodhisattva turned to the sprite and spoke gently to him in a way that showed his devotion to patience: [10] "Of course I know he is troublesome, mean, and always bent on mischief. But surely I ought for that very reason to put up with him? [11] When one cannot retaliate against a person because he is stronger than oneself, patience is hardly in question. And in the case of good people, who are never anything but polite and well-behaved, what is there to forgive? [12] Therefore, one should bear with the blunders of someone weaker than oneself, though one is capable of doing otherwise. Better to suffer contempt from him than to show contempt for virtue. [13] Indeed, the best moment for displaying a good character is when one is ill-treated by a weakling. In view of this, why should a man who loves goodness resort to force in such circumstances, since it means only that he loses his patience? [14] Surely it is hard enough to get an opportunity to show patience—that virtue which is always appropriate, depending as it does on others? When someone provides such an opportunity, what reason can there be for being angry with him? [15] When someone behaves without regard to the fact that he is violating his own principles, as if expressly to give me a chance of making good my own faults—suppose I had no patience with him; could anyone be so ungrateful as that?"

"In that case," said the sprite, "you will never escape this torment. [16] Unless you give up being meek and indulgent, you will never repress this unruly scoundrel who has no respect for goodness."

[17] "If happiness is what one wants," said the Bodhisattva, "then inflicting harm on others is not the way either to be happy or to prevent oneself from becoming unhappy. The result will not be to achieve happiness. [18] I persist in patience with the very purpose of rousing his conscience. If he doesn't understand, he will come across those who will not tolerate his behavior, and they will restrain him from his evil ways.

33 · 19 [19] After receiving rough treatment from such people, he will nolonger treat even someone like me in the same way. Once he has realized he is at fault, he will not behave like that again, and that will be a release for me."

The sprite was overwhelmed with feelings of joy, amazement, and respect. "Excellent! excellent!" he exclaimed, rocking his head from side to side and twirling his fingers to show his approval. Then he made some more kind remarks to the Great Being: [20] "How comes it that animals can behave like this and have such an intense respect for goodness? Surely you must be an ascetic from a hermitage who has assumed this shape for some purpose."

After commending the buffalo in this way and flinging the wicked monkey off his back, the sprite taught him a protective charm and thereupon disappeared.

So, then—one can only show forgiveness if there is someone to be forgiven. That is why good people welcome, as a positive gain, even the man who does them wrong.

The Woodpecker

34

EVEN WHEN PROVOKED, A GOOD PERSON cannot turn to evil, it being alien to him.

According to tradition, the Bodhisattva once lived in a forest, as a woodpecker with brightly colored plumage of striking beauty. Although born in that state, he was deeply imbued with compassion and so did not follow the woodpecker's usual diet, which bore the stigma attached to harming living things. [1] Instead he was entirely content with the tender shoots of trees, with the sweet and delicious fragrance of flowers, and with fruits of varying taste, scent, and color. [2] He showed his concern for the good of others by preaching the Law to them when appropriate, by rescuing those in distress as far as he was able, and by preventing those who knew no better from misbehaving. With the Great Being to look after them like this, all the creatures in the forest throve and were happy. It was as though they had a teacher, a kinsman, a doctor, and a king, all in one. [3] Sustained by his great sympathy, he grew in goodness, and that host of creatures, sustained by his protection, also increased their goodness.

One day, as the Great Being roamed through the forest, feeling sympathy for all creatures, he saw in a certain part of the wood a lion, writhing in acute pain, as though he had been hit by a poisoned arrow. His mane was dirty and matted with dust. The Bodhisattva went up to him and, prompted by pity, asked: "What is it, O king of beasts? I can see that you are in a very bad way. [4] Are you suffering from exhaustion after overindulging in feats of pride against elephants or chasing eagerly after deer? Or have you been hit by a hunter's arrow? Or is it some disease? [5] If you can tell me what it is, then do so. Or at least say what can be done about it. What-

34 · 6 ever help I can offer my friends is at your service, if it has power to restore you."

"You good and precious bird, it is not exhaustion that is making me suffer, nor disease, nor a hunter's arrow. It is a splinter of bone that has got caught in the middle of my throat and, like the tip of an arrow, is causing me acute pain. I can neither swallow it down nor cough it up. So this is the moment for a friend to help. If you know how, then make me well again."

The Bodhisattva with his keen intellect thought out a way of extracting the splinter of bone. Taking a stick large enough to prop open the lion's mouth, he told him to open his mouth as wide as he could. The lion did so. The Bodhisattva then duly wedged the stick between the two rows of teeth and went down to the bottom of his throat. With his beak he took hold of the splinter of bone that had stuck crosswise. Loosening it on one side, he grasped it by the other and drew it out. On his way out he let fall the stick that was propping open the lion's mouth. [6] No surgeon, however skillful and practiced, could have extracted that splinter, hard though he tried. But the Bodhisattva managed to do so thanks to his intelligence, which was not something achieved by taking pains but had become an integral part of him in the course of hundreds of existences. [7] Together with the splinter, he removed the pain and misery it caused. He was as happy to have relieved a sufferer as the lion was to have had his suffering relieved. For this is a characteristic of good people: [8] they get more pleasure out of assuring someone else's happiness or averting someone else's misfortune—even though it may be with difficulty—than they do at their own good fortune, however easily come by.

So it was that the Great Being, well pleased at having relieved his distress, said good-bye to the lion, who in turn wished him farewell. Then he went on his way.

Now some time after this the woodpecker was flying around, his brightly colored plumage outspread, without finding any food of the right kind anywhere. As the pangs of hunger began to afflict him, he caught sight of that very same lion feasting on the flesh of a young fawn, not long killed. Its blood, tingeing his mouth, claws, and the tips of his mane, made him look like part of an autumn cloud catching the glow of twilight. [9] Yet, though he had once given help, he could not bring himself to address the lion with anything so disagreeable as a request. Adept though he was, embarrassment imposed a temporary vow of silence on him. [10] Even so, he was forced by need to hover about bashfully within sight of him. But although that scoundrel noticed the woodpecker, he did not invite him over. [11] A seed sown on a rockface, an offering poured on to a heap of cinders that have gone cold—when the moment comes for some return, both are as productive as a favor done to an ungrateful person. And so is the flower on the vidula reed.[1]

The Bodhisattva, thinking he must obviously not have recognized him, went up to the lion with greater boldness and asked him for a share, after first pronouncing a suitable blessing in the manner of a beggar: [12] "May you find it wholesome, O lord of beasts, who earn your livelihood by your prowess! I ask you to treat a beggar kindly—it will ensure you fame and merit." But despite having this kind blessing pronounced on him, the lion, whose habitual cruelty and selfishness made him unused to behaving decently, looked askance at the Bodhisattva and, as though he wanted to burn him up with his bloodshot eyes that were blazing with anger, said: "Stop that. [13] Is it not enough that you are still alive after entering the mouth of the likes of me? I know nothing of a weakling's pity as I devour deer who still twitch with life. [14] Is it to insult me that you come back like this to beg favors? Are you tired of life? Perhaps you want to see what the next world is like?"

This rebuff, expressed so rudely, made the Bodhisattva feel embarrassed, and he immediately flew up into the sky. With the sound of his flapping wings he said to the lion, in effect: "Lock! I am a bird," then flew away.

Now there was a wood sprite who either could not bear that the woodpecker should be so ill-treated or else wanted to discover the extent of his patience. She approached the Great Being and said: "Excellent bird, why do you put up with this ill treatment from that wicked creature whom you once helped, even though you have the power to do otherwise? What is the point in being so indulgent toward that ungrateful beast? [15] Strong as he is, you could blind him if you suddenly swooped down on his face. And you could snatch the meat from between his teeth. So why do you suffer his insolence?"

Now although the Bodhisattva was hurt by being so ill-treated, and although the wood sprite was provoking him, he showed his innate kindness by saying: "Enough. Do not go on like that. This is not the way people like us behave. [16] Good people devote themselves to someone in distress out of pity, not in the hopes of getting something out of it. The other person may or may not realize this, but what is the use of getting angry about it? [17] Anyone who does not acknowledge a favor done is only cheating himself, for no one who wants a return for his favors will help him again. [18] On the other hand, the benefactor, by his restraint, acquires merit and its rewards in the life hereafter—and a fine reputation already in this life. [19] If one does a kindness because it seems the right thing to do, what is there to be regretful about afterward? But if one does it for the sake of getting some return, then it isn't a kindness but a loan. [20] He who decides to harm his neighbor because he is apparently ungrateful for services rendered, first earns a spotless reputation thanks to his good qualities, then behaves just like an elephant.[2] [21] If one's neighbor is too feeble to acknowledge a favor, no more will he attain that grace whose beauty comes from virtue. But that is no reason for an intelligent person to destroy his own lofty reputation. This is what seems right to me in such a case. [22] Anyone who does not behave in a friendly manner even after he has received help from a kind person should be left quietly alone, without anger or recrimination."

The wood sprite was very pleased by the woodpecker's wise words and praised him repeatedly, saying "Excellent! excellent!" and then added these kind words: [23] "Without the trouble of having clothes of bark and matted hair, you are a sage—you are an ascetic who knows the future.[3] It is not merely one's appearance that makes one a saint. In this case the true saint is he who shows goodness." With this observation she commended him and forthwith vanished.

So, then—even when provoked, a good person cannot turn to evil, it being alien to him.

Notes

Abbreviations

BHSD	Franklin Edgerton, Buddhist Hybrid Sanskrit Dictionary
JA	Journal Asiatique
JAOS	Journal of the American Oriental Society
JPTS	Journal of the Pali Text Society
JRAS	Journal of the Royal Asiatic Society of Great Britain and Ireland
MPh	Modern Philology
WZKS(O)	Wiener Zeitschrift für die Kunde Süd (-und Ost) asiens
ZDMG	Zeitschrift der deutschen morgenländischen Gesellschaft

Preface and Introduction

1. The "epilogues" have, however, been omitted. The natural ending of each story is the clinching repetition of the moral stated at the outset. The epilogues point the moral and suggest appropriate occasions for the story to be recited. They are probably by a later hand (cf. Lüders [1926], 53).

2. Beside *āryaśūra* in the colophons of the *Jātakamālā* MSS, there are *bhadantācāryasūra* (*Jātakamālāṭīkā*, fol. 1 v 1); *ācāryasūra* (ibid., fol. 2 r 11) = **ācāryaśūra* (Haribhaṭṭa, *Jātakamālā*, intro. 2 r *slob dpon dpa' bos;* see Hahn [1981], 107, n. 7); and *bhadantaśūra* (Vallabhadeva, *Subhāṣitāvalī* no. 272). The honorifics *ārya* 'noble' (Tibetan *'phags pa*) and *ācārya* 'teacher' (Tibetan *slob dpon*) were interchangeable.

3. See C. E. Godakumbura, *Sinhalese Literature* (Colombo, 1955), 7.

4. Anton Schiefner (tr.), *Tāranātha's Geschichte des Buddhismus in Indien* (St. Petersburg, 1869), chap. 18, p. 92. On the worth of Tāranātha as a source, see J. Naudou, *Les bouddhistes kaśmīriens au moyen âge* (Paris, 1968), 19–22.

5. See Meadows (1986), 18/19; and *Jātakamālāṭīkā,* fol. 55 v 5 ff.

6. See Lüders (1926), 37/8; and cf. the division of the Pali *Cariyāpiṭaka* (a late work derived from jātaka material) into 10 + 10 + 10 + 5.

7. Despite the general resemblances adduced in favor of the identity of the two authors by D. R. Shackleton Bailey, *The Śatapañcāśatka of Mātṛceta* (Cambridge, 1951), 10–12.

8. *Festschrift Böhtlingk* (Stuttgart, 1888), 50/1.

9. = *Philologica Indica* (Göttingen, 1940), 73–77.

10. See Bunyiu Nanjio, *Catalogue of the Chinese Tripiṭaka* (Oxford, 1883), 301, 372; Lin Li-kouang, *L'Aide-Mémoire de la Vraie Loi* (Saddharmasmṛtyupasthānasūtra) (Paris, 1949), 102, 105, 310, 313.

11. J. Takakusu (ed.), *A Record of the Buddhist Religion as Practised in India and the Malay Archipelago A.D. 671–695)* (Oxford, 1896), 162/3.

12. See Hahn (1981).

13. See F. W. Thomas in *Album Kern* (Leiden, 1903), 405 f.

14. See Lüders (1941).

15. See Michael Hahn, *Zentralasiatische Studien* 16 (1983), 309–320, for different renderings of this title.

16. See Michael Hahn, *ZDMG,* suppl. 5 (1983), 284. Tāranātha (A. Schiefner [tr.], *Tāranātha's Geschichte des Buddhismus in Indien* [St. Petersburg, 1869], 181) records that Śūra was praised by Dharmakīrti as a master of meter.

17. The Sanskrit *Jātakamālāṭīkā* (fol. 1 v 7) expressly uses the word *campū* to describe the *Jātakamālā,* referring to Daṇḍin (late seventh century A.D.?) as authority. See his *Kāvyādarśa* 1. 31.

18. See Schlingloff (1971), 60, nn. 9 and 10; and (1987), 96 f.

19. See Lüders (1926), 47. Some of the *Kalpanāmaṇḍitikā* fragments were from the same manuscript, found at Toyoq, which contained the *Jātakamālā* fragments.

20. See Hahn (1977). For a sketch of the development of Buddhist narrative literature, see Hahn (1985), introd. 10–16.

21. Commentary to Daṇḍin's *Kāvyādarśa* 1.50, quoting *Jm.* 8.41.

22. Chap. 10.22 = Stchoupak/Renou (tr.), (Paris, 1946), 161.

23. As pointed out by Meadows (1986), 11, in her acute analysis of the dominant themes of the *Jātakamālā.*

24. See bibliography entries for Hultzsch, Krom, Lüders, Oldenburg, Schlingloff, and van Erp.

Prologue

1. The allusion is to earlier versions of these stories; see Introduction, p. xiv.

1 · *The Tigress*

There is no parallel in Pali, but cf. *Suvarṇabhāsottamasūtra* 18 (ed. Nobel, 206.10 ff.); *Divyāvadāna* 32 (ed. Cowell and Neil, 477 ff.); Kṣemendra, *Avadānakalpalatā* 51.32 ff. (*Avadānakalpalatā* 51.45/6 = *Divyāvadāna* 479.1–8), 95.15–18; I. J. Schmidt, *'dzaṅs-blun oder Der Weise und der Thor* (St. Petersburg, 1843), 1:19 ff., 2:22 ff.; T. Watters, *On Yuan Chwang's Travels in India* (Royal Asiatic Society Oriental Translation Fund, vol. 14, 1904), 1:253/4; L. Feer, Le Bodhisattva et la famille des tigres, *JA* (1899), 272 ff.; Chavannes, no. 4; Schlingloff (1987), 145.

1. *The three jewels:* the Buddha, his teaching (*dharma*), and the community of monks (*saṃgha*), referred to at the end of the Prologue.

2. *Supreme vow:* to become a Buddha. There is a reference here to the first three of the ways a Bodhisattva attracts people to himself and to virtue (*saṃgrahavastu*).

3. *Eighteen branches of knowledge:* four Vedas, six Vedāṅgas, Purāṇas, Mīmāṃsā, Nyāya, Dharma, and four Upavedas.

4. *Śakra:* 'the powerful', originally an epithet (and synonym) of Indra, lord of the gods. In Buddhist texts the name Śakra replaces Indra. Here the god is referred to by another epithet, *sahasrākṣa* 'thousand-eyed' as at 5.11 *sahasranetra.*

5. *The Law:* Dharma—'the way things are' and so 'what is right', 'religion', 'duty', and, in the specialized Buddhist sense, 'the Buddha's teaching', 'the Law'.

6. *The cardinal virtues:* love (*maitrī*), compassion (*karuṇā*), sympathetic joy (*muditā*), and disinterestedness (*upekṣā*). Cf. tale 7.39.

7. *Māra:* god of love and sensual pleasure (and death), the Bodhisattva's main adversary, corresponding in some ways to Kāma in the Hindu tradition.

8. *The Better Way:* or 'the best vehicle' (*yānavara*), i.e., the Mahāyāna, as opposed to the Hīnayāna and Pratyekabuddhayāna—the three 'vehicles' to salvation. See Introduction, p. xviii.

9. *The whole hierarchy of beings:* gods, heavenly spirits (*gandharva*), earthly spirits (*yakṣa*), and snake spirits of the underworld (*nāga*).

2 · *Śibi*

Cf. Pali jātaka no. 499 (ed. Fausbøll, 4:401–412).

1. *The Śibis:* a people living near the confluence of the Jhelum and Chenab in the Panjab. As often, the king is called by the name of his country.

2. *The three pursuits of life:* in the ideology of ancient India, the three pursuits of life (*trivarga, puruṣārtha*) were formulated as moral

goodness (*dharma*), social and material advancement (*artha*), and sensual pleasure (*kāma*). See also tales 4.6, 9.18, 10.5, 13.37, 20.11, 70, 23.4+,71, 28.41, and 31.38,40+.

3. The underlying idea, common throughout the ancient world, is that the king is bound to the land he rules as husband to wife. See tale 3.18.

4. *Sumeru, Meru:* a mythical mountain, at the center of the Universe (*axis mundi*). See also tales 8.11, 41, 61, and 9.91+.

5. Details in Pali version (ed. Fausbøll, 4.407).

6. The allusion is to *satyādhiṣṭhāna* 'taking a stand on truth' in verses 36/7 (=verse 22 in the Pali version). Known as *saccakiriyā* 'the practice of truth' in Pali, it is based on the belief that truth has power to affect things in the material world as well as in the spiritual. The statement of truth is something between an oath and a magical charm. See also tales 14.30/31, 15.8, and 16.7, and, further tale 9, n. 5, on libation. Further details may be found in Burlingame, *JRAS* (1917): 429 f.; Norman Brown, *Review of Religion* 5 (1940), 36–45; Lüders, *ZDMG* 98 (1944), 1–14, and *Varuṇa* (Göttingen, 1959) 2:487–496; Dillon, *MPh* 44:137, for Celtic parallels; Tawney/Penzer, 3:179; Weiler in *Indological Studies in Honour of W. Norman Brown* (1962), 238 f.; Wayman in *Emeneau Ṣaṣṭipūrti Volume* (Poona, 1968), 365–369.

3 · *The Dumpling*

Cf. Pali jātaka no. 415 (ed. Fausbøll, 3:406–414); *Divyāvadāna* 7 (ed. Cowell and Neil, p. 88); Somadeva, *Kathāsaritsāgara* 27.79–105 (Tawney/Penzer, 3:7–8).

1. *Kośala:* the modern district of Oudh in Uttar Pradesh.

2. The moon is particularly bright in autumn when the skies are clear. Cf. tales 7.2, 8.11, 12.21, and 31.95 and see tale 22.17+ for a description of autumn. Also see tale 13, no. 2, on the Kaumudī festival.

3. See tale 2, no. 3.

4. *Dust . . . a good gift:* cf. *Divyāvadāna* 26 Pāṃsupradāna (ed. Cowell and Neil, p. 366); *Saddharmapuṇḍarīkasūtra* 2.81.

4 · *The Merchant*

Cf. Pali jātaka no. 40 (ed. Fausbøll, 1:231–234).

1. *Pratyekabuddha:* one who has attained enlightenment but lives by himself and does not teach others.

2. While begging alms, the monk should lower his gaze and pay no attention to the people around him. Cf. Aśvaghoṣa, *Buddhacarita* 10.13.

3. *Mahāraurava:* a hot hell. See L. Feer, *JA* (1892), 8ᵉ série, 20:

185 ff.; É. Lamotte, *Le Traité de la Grande Vertu de Sagesse de Nāgārjuna,* (Louvain, 1949), 2:959–960.

4. See tale 2, n. 2.

5. Cf. the pit of fire transformed into a lotus pond in 'Aśvaghoṣa, *Sūtrālaṃkāra*' (tr. É. Huber [Paris, 1908], 376).

5 · *Aviṣahya the Merchant*

Cf. Pali jātaka no. 340 (ed. Fausbøll, 3:128–132).

1. *Kubera:* god of wealth and lord of the earth spirits (*yakṣa*).

2. Kings, thieves, fire, water, and unfriendly kinsmen are the five enemies (*ari*) of wealth. See also tales 3.21, 21.1+, and 31.32; Aśvaghoṣa, *Saundarananda* 1.40, '*Sūtrālaṃkāra*' (tr. É. Huber [Paris, 1908]), 60.

6 · *The Hare*

Cf. Pali jātaka no. 316 (ed. Fausbøll, 3:51–56); Chavannes, nos. 21, 139; and see Schlingloff (1987), chap. 12.

1. *Fast day* (*poṣadha,* also *upoṣadha*): the days preceding the four quarters of the moon on which laymen were expected to follow eight rules of abstinence (*śikṣāpada*). On the half-month days, monks gathered to hear the Teaching. Cf. tale 3.3+.

2. Because it subordinates moral and spiritual to material interests, worldly wisdom (*nīti*), as taught in Kauṭilya's *Arthaśāstra,* is consistently condemned, or at least is shown to be superficial, in the *Jātakamālā.* Cf. tales 8.14, 9.10, 19.27, 20.13, 22.94, 23.20+ (also 23.50+, 51), 27.17+, and 31.52+, 54. See E. H. Johnston, *JRAS* (1929): 81–84; Carol Meadows, *Ārya-Śūra's Compendium of the Perfections* (Indica et Tibetica 8 [Bonn, 1986]), 9 ff.

3. This verse, based on the fourth verse of the Pali Sasajātaka (or on a common source), is also to be found in *Avadānaśataka* 37 (ed. Speyer, 210.1/2), from which Śūra may have borrowed it (pace Alsdorf, *WZKSO* 5 [1961], 3/4).

4. For the association of the hare with the moon (and with fire), in India and elsewhere, see John Layard, *The Lady of the Hare* (London, 1944); George Ewart Evans and David Thomson, *The Leaping Hare* (London, 1972), esp. chaps. 10, 11.

7 · *Agastya*

Cf. Pali jātaka no. 480 (ed. Fausbøll, 4:236–242).

1. See tale 4, n. 1.

2. See tale 1, n. 6.

8 · *Maitrībala*

There is no parallel in Pali, but cf. R. Gnoli (ed.), *The Gilgit Manuscript of the Saṅghabhedavastu* (Rome, 1978), 2:20/1, and see Schlingloff (1972), 61, n. 16 and (1987), chap. 14 and pp. 148/9.

1. See tale 5, n. 1.
2. See tale 2, n. 4.
3. Śrī or Lakṣmī, goddess of Fortune, is conventionally pictured as seated on a lotus and holding lotuses in her hands (hence her epithet Padmā).
4. See tale 5, n. 1.
5. See tale 1, n. 4.
6. These are the five moral commandments (*pañcaśīla*) incumbent upon a layman.

9 · *Viśvaṃtara*

Cf. Pali jātaka no. 547 (ed. Fausbøll, 6:479–596); Chavannes, no. 500; and see Cone/Gombrich, *The Perfect Generosity of Prince Vessantara* (Oxford, 1977), xxxv ff.; Schlingloff (1987), 146/7, 154, n. 29.

1. See tale 2, n. 1.
2. A prince's education comprised four branches of knowledge (*vidyā-catuṣṭaya*): philosophy (*ānvīkṣikī*), the three Vedas (*trayī*), economics (*vārttā*), and politics (*daṇḍanīti*), according to *Arthaśāstra* 1.2 (ed. Shama Sastri [Mysore, 1919], 6).
3. The streams of ichor trickling down the elephant's face are tacitly compared with the streams of colored minerals that trickle down the slopes of the Himalaya.
4. *Kailāsa:* the holy mountain in the Himalaya, north of Lake Mānasa (see tale 22, n. 1)—the abode of Śiva and Kubera—huge and snow white like the luck-bringing elephant (*bhadramṛga*). Cf. verse 5+, where the elephant is compared to a peak in the Himalaya.
5. *Libation to ratify a gift.* To take one's oath on water, either by pouring it or by having a pot full of water (*pūrṇapātra*) beside one, seems to have been a common Indo-European inheritance. The pouring of water to ratify any solemn transference of property is common in the Indian tradition (see Lüders, *Varuṇa* (Göttingen, 1959), 2:32/3; Lamotte, *Le Traité de la Grande Vertu de Sagesse de Nāgārjuna,* [Louvain, 1949], 2:679, 685; Cowell [ed], *Jātakas,* Index Volume [Cambridge, 1913], 17 s.v. *Gift*). For Greece, see Hesiod, *Theogony,* 784 ff., and for Iran, see Avestan Yašt 5 (*Arədvī Sūra*), 76–78. The underlying belief is close to that of *satyādhiṣṭhāna/saccakiriyā* (see tale 2, n. 6): see Lüders, *Varuṇa* (Göttingen, 1959), 2:15–17, who suggests (ibid., 36) that the connexion with water may have been—in India, as in Greece—originally that one swore by the Styx, the waters of death,

which would bring about one's ruin if one swore false. Note also how Varuṇa, god of waters, is also god of the oath. Cf tale 9.93.

6. See tale 2, n. 2.

7. *Viśvakarman:* the architect in the heavenly counterpart to earthly society.

8. See tale 9, n. 5.

9. See tale 1, n. 7.

10 · The Sacrifice

Cf. the similar but not identical Pali jātaka no. 50 (ed. Fausbøll, 1:259–261).

1. Drought (*anāvṛṣṭi*) was commonly considered as being due to some fault in the king of the country afflicted. See, e.g., *Rāmāyaṇa* 1.8.12. As mentioned in tale 2, n. 3, the king was thought to be wedded to the Earth—to the territory he ruled. Prosperity and fertility of man, beast, and soil depended on the just rule of the king. See J. Gonda, *Ancient Indian Kingship from the Religious Point of View* (Leiden, 1966), 10; Myles Dillon, *Celts and Aryans* (Simla, 1975), 102, 130/1, for wider connexions. Cf. also tale 23, n. 8.

2. See tale 2, no. 2.

3. As he would if he were about to undertake a ritual sacrifice.

4. *Mūrdhnaś chattranibhasya keśaracanāśobhā* perhaps echoing *keśaśriyaṃ chattranibhasya mūrdhnaḥ* (Aśvaghoṣa, *Saundarananda* 5.51). Cf. the stock epithet of the newborn child: *chattrākāraśiras* (*Divyāvadāna* [ed. Cowell and Neil], 2.26, 58.3, 99.18, 330.19, 441.8, 523.18) and *chattrākāraśīrṣa* (ibid., 26.3). Also cf. *chattrākāraśiras* (*Avadānaśataka* 1:121.1, 135.6, 197.10, 219.4, 2:27.11), *chattrākṛtiśīrṣa* (*Mahā-bhārata* 12 [Śāntiparvan], 322.10), and, in expanded form, *saṃpūrṇāmalacandramaṇḍalasamachattrorubhāsvacchirāḥ* (*Divyāvadāna* 588.22). The comparison of the head with a parasol is to emphasize its perfect roundness at birth. Cf. *paripūrṇottamāṅga* 'with fully developed head' (*Lalitavistara* [ed. Lefmann, 1.107.11]), one of the eighty *anuvyañjana* or secondary characteristics of a *mahāpuruṣa*. An intriguing parallel (or borrowing?) is to be found in the Pahlavi *Dēnkard* (ed. Madan, 603.19, 604.13), where the infant Zarduxšt (Zoroaster) is described as 'round-headed' (*gird-vaγdan*). See also the suggestive article by E. W. Burlingame, *The Buddhist-Zoroastrian Legend of the Seven Marvels*, in *Festschrift Bloomfield* (1920), 105 ff., showing the correspondence between the birth legends of Zoroaster and the Buddha. Note also 'Ārya-Śūra', *Pāramitāsamāsa* 4.21, *chattrābham uṣṇīṣalalāmaśīrṣam* 'a parasol-like head marked with the *uṣṇīṣa*', where *uṣṇīṣa* 'turban' is brought into conjunction with *chattra* 'parasol', both auspicious symbols of kingship. The epithet *uṣṇīṣa-śīrṣa* (Pali *uṇhīsa-sīsa*), one of the thirty-two *lakṣaṇa* or primary characteristics of the

mahāpuruṣa, lit. 'with turbanned head' (i.e., which looks turbanned because large and well rounded) caused problems of iconography. At first the Buddha was depicted with a twisted knot of hair (*kaparda*) on top of his head, but this was later reinterpreted as a peculiar protuberance on his skull—an apology for a turban.

5. i.e., by being shaved off. Rules for ritual observance (*dīkṣā*) are given in *Śatapathabrāhmaṇa* 3.1.1 ff. The *dīkṣita* must fast and shave off his beard (*Śatapathabrāhmaṇa* 3.1.2). See J. Gonda, *Change and Continuity in Indian Religion* (The Hague, 1965), 315 ff.

11 · Śakra

Cf. Pali jātaka no. 31 (ed. Fausbøll, 1:198–206) and see Schlingloff (1973) and (1987), ch. 10.

1. The battle between gods and titans, the central theme of Hindu mythology, is here used as the background to a Buddhist parable. See also tale 25, n. 1.

2. *Garuḍa* (also called *suparṇa*): mythical birds, part eagle and part human, the arch-enemies of the snake spirits (*nāga*). For the widespread antithesis of eagle and snake in world mythology, see R. Wittkower, *Journal of the Warburg Institute* 2 (1939), 293–325. The *garuḍa* is associated with the *śālmali* tree (as the eagle with the world tree Yggdrasil in Norse tradition?). Cf. tale 32, n. 6

12 · The Brahmin

Cf. Pali jātaka no. 305 (ed. Fausbøll, 3:18–20).

13 · Unmādayantī

Cf. Pali jātaka no. 527 (ed. Fausbøll, 5:209–227) and Somadeva, *Kathāsaritsāgara* 15.63 f., 33.62 f., and 91.3 f. (=Tawney/Penzer, *The Ocean of Story,* vol. 2 [1924], 6–8, vol. 3 [1927], 241–244).

1. Treatises on physiognomy (*sāmudrika*) correlated the minutest details of the external anatomy, male and female, with character traits and personal destiny. There were also manuals that dealt specifically with marks that were (in)auspicious and with times that were (un)favorable for marriage (*vivāha*).

2. *Kaumudī festival:* the great autumnal moonlight festival, celebrated at full moon in the month of Kārttika (October-November). Kaumudī "moonlight" is the personified wife of the moon.

3. *And I am not immortal:* i.e., still subject to the round of birth and death, influenced by one's good and bad deeds (*karma*).

4. See tale 2, n. 2.

5. *Bṛhaspati:* the priest in the heavenly counterpart to earthly society, who is also thought of as the god of wisdom.

14 · *Supāraga*

Cf. Pali jātaka no. 463 (ed. Fausbøll, 4:136–143).

1. Reading with best manuscripts: *āharaṇāpasaraṇakuśalatvād*. Cf. Pali *Suttanipāta* commentary (*Paramatthajotikā*) 2.330.24 *tassā nāvāya āharaṇāpasāraṇādi-upāyajānanena maggapaṭipādanena upāyaññū.*

2. *Supāraga:* Sanskritization, influenced by fanciful etymology (*tasya paramasiddhayātratvāt*), of Pali *Suppāraka* = Sanskrit *Śūrpāraka*. See Edgerton, *BHSD*, 600a; É. Lamotte, *Le Traité de la Grande Vertu de Sagesse de Nāgārjuna* (Louvain, 1944) 1:343, n. 1.

3. *Bharukaccha:* the modern Broach on the Gulf of Cambay, between Bombay and Ahmedabad.

4. *Suvarṇabhūmi:* the Golden Khersonese, Malay Peninsula. For details, see Paul Wheatley, *The Golden Khersonese* (Kuala Lumpur, 1961).

5. *Fish:* possibly sharks—or dolphins. Semantically one may compare, beside *kṣura* 'razor', Old Indian *vāśī* 'razor' and Avestan *vāsī*, Pahlavi *wās* 'sea monster'.

6. The gloss to *pattanadvitayād* (Kern, 90, l. 19) in the Sanskrit ṭīkā (fol. 63 v 4/5) is *suvarṇabhūmipattanadvayaṃ laṅkāśobhaḥ kaṭahadvīpaṃ ca.* Laṅkāśobha = Langkasuka, Kaṭahadvīpa (more correctly Kaṭāha-) = Kĕdah, the two main ports of Suvarṇabhūmi. But the two ports in question are perhaps the port of departure, Bharukaccha/Supāraga, and the port of destination in Suvarṇabhūmi.

7. *Kṣuramālī*, lit. 'whose crests are (like) razors'.

8. *Dadhimālī*, lit. 'whose crests are (like) curds'.

9. *Agnimālī*, lit. 'whose crests are (like) fire'.

10. *Kuśamālī*, lit. 'whose crests are (like) kuśa grass'.

11. *Nalamālī*, lit. 'whose crests are (like) reeds'.

12. *The Mare's Mouth* (*vaḍabā-mukha*): an abyss in the ocean, leading to the lower regions, from which issues the submarine fire. For the association of the mare with the idea of a submarine fire, see W. D. O'Flaherty, *JRAS* (1971): 15 ff., and *Women, Androgynes and Other Mythical Beasts* (Chicago, 1980), chap. 7.

13. The twelve Ādityas, eleven Rudras, and eight Vasus, together with Heaven and Earth, make up the stock number of thirty-three gods. The Maruts (storm gods) form another group.

14. *Devī:* the Great Goddess.

15. See tale 2, n. 6.

15 · *The Lord of the Fish*

Cf. Pali jātaka no. 75 (ed. Fausbøll, 1:329–332).

1. See tale 1, n. 2.

2. See tale 2, n. 6.

3. *Parjanya:* the rain god.

16 · *The Young Quail*

Cf. Pali jātaka no. 35 (ed. Fausbøll, 1:212–215), *Mahābhārata* 1.220+, = *Śārṅgakopākhyāna;* Chavannes, no. 371; and see Schlingloff (1987), 143/4.

1. Verses 2 and 3, "quoted from the canon of the Sthaviras" according to the scribal annotation, correspond, though not exactly, with *Dhammapada* verses 244 and 245. According to Sylvain Lévi (*JA* [1912], 10e série, 20:288 ff.), the two verses quoted by Śūra come from a non-extant recension or are a rehandling of the verses as we know them. The introductory and concluding lines (= Kern, 98, lines 19 and 24 [not translated here]) are presumably annotations by a scribe who recognized their provenance. According to Lüders (1926), 49, n. 1, the two verses are a quotation which possibly was first interpolated at a later date.

2. See tale 2, n. 6.

17 · *The Jar Full of Spirits*

Cf. Pali jātaka no. 512 (ed. Fausbøll, 5:11–20); and see Schlingloff (1987), 148.

1. See tale 5, n. 1.

2. *Vṛṣṇi and Andhaka:* a mythological allusion (less frequently indulged in by Śūra than by Aśvaghoṣa). Vṛṣṇi and Andhaka were two brothers belonging to the Yādava branch of the Candravaṃśa. See Aśvaghoṣa, *Buddhacarita* 11.31; Lüders, *Philologica Indica* (Göttingen, 1940), 84, n. 3.

18 · *The Man without an Heir*

There is no parallel in the Pali jātaka collection.

1. The family friend's concern is explicable in terms of the traditional theory of the four stages (*āśrama*) of a brahmin's life: student (*brahmacārin*), householder (*gṛhastha*), hermit (*vānaprastha*), and finally homeless wanderer (*sannyāsin*). This ideal itself represents an attempt to reconcile the conflicting claims of the world and the spirit. The importance of having a son was that only male descendants could make the necessary ritual offerings (*śrāddha*) to the dead.

19 · *The Lotus Stalks*

Cf. Pali jātaka no. 488 (ed. Fausbøll, 4:304–314). See Rosa Klein-Terrada, *Der Diebstahl der Lotusfasern* (Freiburger Beiträge zur Indologie, Bd. 15, 1980) for parallels, though scarcely an advance on the earlier articles by J. Charpentier (*ZDMG* 64 [1910], 73) and K. Geldner (*ZDMG* 65 [1911], 306/7). See also Schlingloff (1987), 147/8.

1. *Subsidiary Vedas* (*upaveda*): medicine (*āyurveda*), skill in arms (*dhanurveda*), music (*gāndharvaveda*), and applied arts (*śilpaśāstra*) are appended to the four Vedas, Ṛg-, Yajur-, Sāma-, and Atharva-, respectively. Cf. tale 1, n. 3.

2. It will be noticed, here and elsewhere (e.g., tales 13.6, 25.1, and 30.4), that a verse sometimes repeats what has been said already in the prose—a characteristic of the Pali version also—as though to summarize or clinch the point of the prose.

3. *Kacaṅgalā:* a town near Benares. According to the Pali commentary, it was hard to find building materials there.

4. i.e., the monkey should belong to a snake charmer.

5. Here follows an interpolation in which the characters of the story are identified with disciples and followers of the Buddha in a previous existence. The same verses and names (with slight variants) occur at the end of the Pali version of this story, but the identification (*samodhānam*) of persons in the past (*atītavatthu*) with those in the present (*paccuppannavatthu*) is usual at the end of Pali jātakas.

20 · *The Royal Treasurer*

Cf. Pali jātaka no. 171 (ed. Fausbøll, 2:63–65).

21 · *Bodhi*

Cf. Pali jātaka no. 443 (ed. Fausbøll, 4:22–27).

1. See tale 5, n. 2.

2. In Sanskrit poetry the sheldrake and shelduck (*cakravāka*, *-vākī*) are the type of faithful attachment between husband and wife. Faithfulness in danger, as illustrated in the next jātaka, appears to be a general characteristic of geese and ducks (see Schlingloff, *ZDMG* 127 [1977], 369 f.).

3. See tale 1, n. 5.

22 · *The King of the Geese*

Cf. Pali jātakas nos. 502, 533, and esp. 534 (ed. Fausbøll, 4:423–430, 5:337–354, 354–382); Somadeva, *Kathāsaritsāgara* 3.26–35 (in brief), 114.17 f. (at greater length). Also see Schlingloff, *ZDMG* 127 (1977), 371, n. 6, and (1987), chap. 13.

1. *Lake Mānasa:* Sven Hedin, *Trans-Himalaya* (1909), 2:111, described this holy lake (the modern Manasarowar in Southwest Tibet) as follows: "The oval lake, somewhat narrower in the south than in the north, and with a diameter of about 15½ miles, lies like an enormous turquoise embedded between two of the finest and most famous mountain giants of the world, the Kailas in the north and Gurla Mandatta in

the south, and between huge ranges, above which the two mountains uplift their crowns of bright white eternal snow."

2. *'Eager to fly north'*: this is a literary convention (*kavisamaya*) noted by Viśvanātha, *Sāhityadarpaṇa* 7.23. The geese actually migrate earlier.

3. *Rāhu:* the demon who is said to try to swallow sun and moon and thereby cause eclipses (see Tawney/Penzer, 2:81 ff.).

4. The form in which the Bodhisattva preaches the *rājadharma* in verses 66–70 recalls, in miniature, such stock passages in the epic as *Rāmāyaṇa* 2.94, the so-called *kaccit* chapter.

5. See tale 1, n. 4.

23 · *Bodhi the Wandering Ascetic*

Cf. Pali jātaka no. 528 (ed. Fausbøll, 5:227–246).

1. See tale 2, n. 2.

2. *Triple staff* (*tridaṇḍa*): a staff made of three sticks, which could also be used as a tripod for cooking.

3. *The four stages of trance and the five kinds of transcendent knowledge:* see Kern, *Manual of Indian Buddhism,* 56, 60; Edgerton, *BHSD* 50b s.v. *abhijñā,* 287a s.v. *dhyāna.*

4. For the false doctrines, see E. H. Johnston, *JRAS* (1931): 567; Aśvaghoṣa, *Buddhacarita* 9.58, 62.

5. *'Causes for denying causality'*: the 'point' rests on the Sanskrit word *hetu,* which means 'cause' and 'reason'.

6. *Śliṣṭair* in the Sanskrit is quite possibly itself a *śleṣa* (double entendre) meaning both "close" and "ambiguous, equivocal", i.e., "founded on ambiguities". The Bodhisattva's argument does rather depend on ambiguities in the Sanskrit, which cannot be exactly reproduced in English.

7. See tale 6, n. 2.

8. Expression of the widespread belief that a king's moral behavior is intimately linked with the prosperity of the land—and here (as in tale 11.29), more especially, with the healing properties of plants. Cf. *Buddhacarita,* 2.8, and see tale 10, n. 1.

24 · *The Great Ape*

Cf. Pali jātaka no. 516 (ed. Fausbøll, 5:67–74); Chavannes, no. 47.

25 · *The Ibex*

Cf. Pali jātaka no. 483 (ed. Fausbøll, 4:267–275).

1. The war between gods and titans was fought beside the ocean. See tale 11, n. 1.

2. *'Like a carved leogryph'* (*toraṇa-vyālakavad*): an architectural simile—the rearing ibex is compared to a 'lion bracket'. See J. -Ph. Vogel, The Vyālaka in Indian Art, in *Orientalia Neerlandica* (Leiden, 1948), 298 f.

26 · *The Antelope*

Cf. Pali jātaka no. 482 (ed. Fausbøll, 4:255–263); Chavannes, no. 58. See also Schlingloff (1987), 253.

1. It was customary for kings to be awoken by the sound of music. Cf. tale 31.89 (possibly), and *Rāmāyaṇa* 2.65; Māgha, *Śiśupālavadha* 11.1, 10.

2. The Deer's Head (*mṛgaśiras*) corresponds to Orion's Head.

3. *'Three Ways'*: by thoughts, by words, and by deeds.

27 · *The King of the Monkeys*

Cf. Pali jātaka no. 407 (ed. Fausbøll, 3:369–375); Chavannes, no. 56. See also Schlingloff (1987), 250/1.

1. Wordplay on *rasa* = (1) 'taste, flavor,'—and hence (2) 'aesthetic emotion'.

28 · *Kṣāntivādin*

Cf. Pali jātaka no. 313 (ed. Fausbøll, 3:39–43): *The Gilgit Manuscript of the Saṅghabhedavastu* (ed. R. Gnoli [Rome, 1978]), 2:4 ff.; Somadeva, *Kathāsaritsāgara,* 28.29 f. See A. Attenhofer, Parallelen zum Kṣāntivādijātaka (*Festschrift Kuhn,* München, 1916), 353–356; Schlingloff (1987), 219–221.

1. Known from other sources as Kali, Kalabha (Pali Kalābu).

2. A stock image in Sanskrit poetry is that of the peacocks' excitement at the approach of the monsoon.

3. The underlying idea is that spiritual energy (*tejas*) acquired by practicing physical austerities can affect things on the physical plane (as can the power inherent in truth, on which see tale 2, n. 6).

29 · *The Inhabitant of Highest Heaven*

Cf. Pali jātaka no. 544 (ed. Fausbøll, 6:219–255).

1. *Kāmadhātu:* the sphere of the senses, the lowest of the spheres into which the Buddhist universe is divided (see É. Lamotte, *Histoire du Bouddhisme Indien* [Louvain, 1958], 34/5).

2. *Videha:* a kingdom north of the Ganges and east of the Gandak (the modern Tirhut division), with Mithilā as its capital.

3. *Yama:* lord of the underworld.

4. *Saṃghāta:* a hot hell where people are crushed by two colliding mountains. See L. Feer, *JA* (1892), 8e série, 20:192/3, comparing the Symplegades of Greek myth; É. Lamotte, *Le Traité de la Grande Vertu de Sagesse de Nāgārjuna* (Louvain, 1949), 2.958 (and, on the hells generally, 955 ff.).

5. *Vaitaraṇī:* '(the river) without a ford'—the river of the underworld. See Feer, *art. cit.*, 205/6, comparing the Styx of Greek myth; Lamotte, *op. cit.* 2:962.

6. The two hellhounds (dark and light, hence *śabala* 'brindled') belong already to the Indo-European conception of hell. See Maurice Bloomfield, *Cerberus, the dog of Hades* (London, 1905); B. Schlerath, Der Hund bei den Indogermanen, *Paideuma* 6 (1954), 25–40.

30 · The Elephant

There is no parallel in the Pali jātaka collection. Cf: Kṣemendra, *Avadānakalpalatā* 96.9–15. See also Schlingloff (1987), 149/50.

1. A solemn vow (*praṇidhi, praṇidhāna*) in which the speaker declares his (usually religious) wish and claims its fulfillment on the grounds of his own worthy acts or motives. Cf. tales 1.30–32 and 8.53–55.

2. *Garuḍa:* a mythical being, half-bird half-man, prototype of the *garuḍas* (see tale 11, n. 2).

3. See tale 1, n. 7.

4. The Guardians of the World (*lokapāla*), stationed at the four points of the compass, are mounted on elephants (*diṅnāga*).

5. The white elephant, as already noted in the story of Viśvaṃtara, was considered especially lucky.

31 · Sutasoma

Cf. Pali jātaka no. 537 (ed. Fausbøll, 5:456–511); *Bhadrakalpāvadāna,* 34 (S. Oldenburg, *JRAS* [1893]: 333/4, and *Buddhist Legends* [St. Petersburg, 1894], 83–85); Chavannes, no. 41. See also Schlingloff (1975) and (1987), chap. 9; K. Watanabe, The Story of Kalmāṣapāda and its Evolution in Indian Literaturue, *JPTS* 6 (1909), 236–310; J. Ensink, Mitrasaha, Sudāsa's Son, with the Spotted Feet, in *Pratidānam,* (Festschrift Kuiper, 1968), 573–584, and The Man-Eater Converted, in *ṚTAM, Journal of the Akhila Bhāratīya Sanskrit Parishad* 2–6 (1970–75): pt. 2, 33 ff.

1. *Sutasoma:* 'one who has extracted the soma juice', but also *suta* 'son' and *soma* 'moon'.

2. *Subsidiary Vedas* (*upaveda*), see tale 19, n. 1; *ancillary sciences* (*vedāṅga*): (1) phonetics (*śikṣā*), (2) meter (*chandas*), (3) grammar

(*vyākaraṇa*), (4) exegesis (*nirukta*), (5) astronomy (*jyotiṣa*), and (6) ritual (*kalpa*). Cf. tale 1, no. 3.

3. See tale 5, n. 1.

4. See tale 2, n. 2.

5. *'Rocking his head and twirling his fingers'*: a typically Indian gesture of approval, with a pedigree of two millenia. Cf. tales 30.25, 31.35, and 33.19+.

6. Adapted from—or a variant of—*Dhammapada* 151.

7. If Kalmāṣapāda breaks his promise to grant the four wishes, he will suffer for it, and Sutasoma will be the cause.

8. In Sanskrit poetry, laughter suggests dazzling whiteness (cf. 'a dazzling smile'), as noted by Viśvanātha, *Sāhityadarpaṇa* 7.23. By extension the root *has-* 'laugh' is found in words expressing dazzling brightness, e.g., tale 32.6.

32 · *Ayogṛha*

Cf. Pali jātaka no. 510 (ed. Fausbøll, 4:491–499).

1. Bhagīratha, by his prayers, induced the heavenly river Ganges to flow down to earth, so as to purify the ashes of the sixty thousand sons of King Sagara. Ganges, annoyed at being diverted from the sky, threatened to inundate the whole world, but Śiva broke the river's fall by letting it stream on to his head and thus averted catastrophe.

2. For the use of iron to scare away evil spirits, in India and elsewhere, see Tawney/Penzer 2:166 ff.

3. See tale 13, n. 2.

4. Cf. Aśvaghoṣa, *Buddhacarita* 3.8

5. The four means of getting the better of an enemy are conciliation (*sāman*), bribery (*dāna*), sowing dissension (*bheda*), and armed force (*daṇḍa*), according to *Arthaśāstra,* 2.10 (ed. Shama Sastri [Mysore, 1919], 74).

6. *Suparṇas* (or *garuḍas,* see tale 11, n. 2): mythical birds, human-headed eagles, arch-enemies of the snake spirits (*nāga*) who live beneath the ocean.

7. *Dhanvantari:* the physician of the gods, supposed author of the Āyurveda and founder of Indian medicine.

8. *Asuras:* demons, primordial antagonists of the gods (see tale 11, n. 1).

9. See tale 23, n. 3.

10. See tale 1, n. 6.

33 · *The Buffalo*

Cf. Pali jātaka no. 278 (ed. Fausbøll, 2:385–388); Chavannes, no. 432. See also Schlingloff (1987), 144/5.

1. A rather belated (and feeble) explanation of how such a paragon as the Bodhisattva could be born as an animal. The adaptation of animal fables to serve as Buddhist parables precludes too close a scrutiny of the workings of *karma*.

2. Yama, as lord of the underworld, held the rod of punishment (*daṇḍa*). The buffalo was his symbolic mount.

34 · *The Woodpecker*

Cf. Pali jātaka no. 308 (ed. Fausbøll, 3:25–27); Chavannes, no. 51.

1. The flower of the *vidula* reed cannot be used as an offering to the gods. Cf. *Mahābhārata,* 13.105.8 *vidulasyeva tat puṣpaṃ moghaṃ janayituḥ smṛtam.*

2. An allusion to the elephant's habit of first spraying itself with water, then rolling in the dust.

3. *An ascetic who knows the future:* no special meaning intended—only the jingle of the Sanskrit words *viditāyatir yatiḥ.*

Bibliography

Bryner, Edna. 1956. *Thirteen Tibetan Tankas* [illustrating the Jātakamālā], Colorado: The Falcon's Wing Press.

Chavannes, Édouard. 1910–35. *Cinq Cents Contes et Apologues extraits du Tripiṭaka chinois et traduits en français*. 4 vols. Paris: Ernest Leroux.

Cone, Margaret, and Richard F. Gombrich. 1977. *The Perfect Generosity of Prince Vessantara*. Oxford: Clarendon Press.

Cowell, E. B., et al. (tr.). 1895–1907. *The Jātaka, or Stories of the Buddha's Former Births*. 6 vols. Cambridge: Cambridge University Press.

Fausbøll, V. (ed.). 1877–97. *The Jātaka together with Its Commentary*. 7 vols. London: Trübner.

Hahn, Michael. 1977. *Haribhaṭṭa and Gopadatta: Two Authors in the Succession of Āryaśūra—on the Rediscovery of Parts of their Jātakamālās* (Studia Philologica Buddhica occasional paper ser., no. 1). Tokyo: The Reiyukai Library.

———. 1981. Das Datum des Haribhaṭṭa. In *Studien zum Jainismus und Buddhismus: Gedenkschrift für Ludwig Alsdorf*, Klaus Bruhn and Albrecht Wetzler, eds., 107–120. Wiesbaden: Franz Steiner.

———. (ed.). 1982. *Die Subhāṣitaratnakaraṇḍakakathā* (Nachrichten der Akademie der Wissenschaften in Göttingen, 1. Philologisch-historische Klasse, no. 9). Göttingen: Vandenhoeck & Ruprecht.

———. (ed.). 1985. *Der Grosse Legendenkranz (Mahajjātakamālā)* (Asiatische Forschungen 88). Wiesbaden: Harrassowitz.

Hultzsch, E. 1912. Jātakas at Bharaut. *JRAS* (1912): 399 ff.

Kern, Hendrik, 1891. *The Jātaka-mālā: Stories of Buddha's Former Incarnations, Otherwise Entitled Bodhisattva-avadāna-mālā, by Ārya-çūra*. Critically edited in the original Sanskrit (Harvard Oriental Ser., vol. 1). Cambridge, MA: Harvard University Press (repr. 1914, 1943).

Khoroche, Peter. 1985. Jātakamālāṭīkā. *South Asian Studies* (Journal of the Society for South Asian Studies, British Academy, London) 1:63–66.

———. 1987. *Towards a New Edition of Ārya-Śūra's Jātakamālā* (Indica et Tibetica 12). Bonn: Indica et Tibetica Verlag.

Krom, N. J. 1927. *Barabudur—Archaeological Description* (English version), vol. 1, chap. 5. The Hague: Martinus Nijhoff.

Lamotte, É. (tr.). 1944–80. *Le Traité de la Grande Vertu de Sagesse de Nāgārjuna (Mahāprajñāpāramitāśāstra)* 5 vols. Louvain: Institut Orientaliste.

Lüders, Heinrich. 1902. Ārya-Śūra's Jātakamālā und die Fresken von Ajaṇṭā. *Nachrichten von der Königlichen Gesellschaft der Wissenschaften zu Göttingen, Philologisch-historische Klasse* (1902): 758–762. (English version by James Burgess in *The Indian Antiquary* 32 (1903): 326–329.) Reprinted in Heinrich Lüders, *Philologica Indica* (1940), 73–77, Göttingen: Vandenhoeck & Ruprecht.

———. 1926. *Bruchstücke der Kalpanāmaṇḍitikā des Kumāralāta* (Kleinere Sankrit-Texte 2). Leipzig: Brockhaus.

———. 1941. *Bhārhut und die Buddhistische Literatur* (Abhandlungen für die Kunde des Morgenlandes, 26, 3). Leipzig: Brockhaus.

Meadows, Carol. 1986. *Ārya-Śūra's Compendium of the Perfections: Text, Translation and Analysis of the Pāramitāsamāsa* (Indica et Tibetica 8). Bonn: Indica et Tibetica Verlag.

Oldenburg, S. F. 1893. On the Buddhist Jātakas. *JRAS* (1893): 301–356.

———. 1894. *Buddhist Legends: Bhadrakalpāvadāna and Jātakamālā* (in Russian). St. Petersburg: Imperial Academy of Sciences.

———. 1897. Notes on Buddhist Art. *JAOS* 18 (1897): 183–201.

Schlingloff, Dieter. 1971. Das Śaśajātaka. *WZKS* 15 (1971): 57–67.

———. 1972. Jātakamālā-Darstellungen in Ajantā. *WZKS* 16 (1972): 55–65.

———. 1973. A Battle-Painting in Ajantā. In *Indologen-Tagung 1971*, Herbert Härtel and Volker Moeller, eds., 196–203. Wiesbaden: Franz Steiner.

———. 1975. Die Erzählung von Sutasoma und Saudāsa in der Buddhistischen Kunst. *Altorientalische Forschungen* 2:93–117. Berlin: Akademie Verlag.

———. 1977a. Die Jātaka-Darstellungen in Höhle 16 von Ajantā. In *Beiträge zur Indienforschung, Ernst Waldschmidt zum 80 Geburtstag gewidmet*, 451–478. Berlin: Museum für Indische Kunst.

———. 1977b. Zwei Anatiden-Geschichten im alten Indien. *ZDMG* 127 (1977): 369–397.

———. 1981. The Mahābodhijātaka in Bhārhut. In *Ludwik Sternbach Felicitation Volume*, 745–749. Lucknow: Akhila Bhāratīya Sanskrit Parishad.

———. 1987. *Studies in the Ajantā Paintings: Identifications and Interpretations*. Delhi: Ajanta Publications.

Speyer, J. S. 1895. *The Jātakamālā: Garland of Birth-Stories of Ārya-śūra* (Sacred Books of the Buddhists, vol. 1). London: Henry Frowde.

Tawney, C. H., and N. M. Penzer. (tr.). 1924–28. *The Ocean of Story* (Somadeva's *Kathāsaritsāgara*). 10 vols. London: privately printed.

Thomas, F. W. 1903. The Works of Ārya Śūra, Triratnadāsa and Dhārmikasubhūti. In *Album Kern,* 405 ff. Leiden: E. J. Brill.

Van Erp, Th. 1943. De Geschiedenis van het Ruru-hert in de Reliëfs van Barabudur en van Bharhut. *Maandblad voor Beeldende Kunsten,* twintigste jaargang, no. 11 en 12 (November-December 1943): 199–208.